From Havana to Hollywood

SUNY series, Afro-Latinx Futures
―――――――――
Vanessa K. Valdés, editor

From Havana to Hollywood

Slave Resistance in the Cinematic Imaginary

PHILIP KAISARY

Cover Credit: Elio Rodriguez Valdes, "Gone with the Macho," Las Perlas de tu boca, silkscreen on paper, 27.5" × 19.5", edition of 8. 1995. Elio Rodriguez and 532 Gallery Thomas Jaeckel, New York City, 532gallery.com. ©

Published by State University of New York Press, Albany

© 2024 State University of New York

All rights reserved

Printed in the United States of America

No part of this book may be used or reproduced in any manner whatsoever without written permission. No part of this book may be stored in a retrieval system or transmitted in any form or by any means including electronic, electrostatic, magnetic tape, mechanical, photocopying, recording, or otherwise without the prior permission in writing of the publisher.

Links to third-party websites are provided as a convenience and for informational purposes only. They do not constitute an endorsement or an approval of any of the products, services, or opinions of the organization, companies, or individuals. SUNY Press bears no responsibility for the accuracy, legality, or content of a URL, the external website, or for that of subsequent websites.

For information, contact State University of New York Press, Albany, NY
www.sunypress.edu

Library of Congress Cataloging-in-Publication Data

Name: Kaisary, Philip, author.
Title: From Havana to Hollywood : slave resistance in the cinematic imaginary / Philip Kaisary.
Description: Albany : State University of New York Press, [2024] | Series: SUNY series, SUNY series, Afro-Latinx Futures | Includes bibliographical references and index.
Identifiers: ISBN 9781438498492 (hardcover : alk. paper) | ISBN 9781438498508 (ebook)
Further information is available at the Library of Congress.

In memory of Benita Parry, 1931–2020

Contents

List of Illustrations	ix
Acknowledgments	xiii
Introduction: Havana, Hollywood, and the Politics of Slave Resistance in the Cinematic Imaginary	1
Chapter 1 "Our First Cry of Freedom": From Revolution to Liberation in Gillo Pontecorvo's *Burn!*	35
Chapter 2 "Cinema Must Be Revolutionary in Itself": Afro-Cuban Resistance, the Haitian Revolution, and Black Comedy in Tomás Gutiérrez Alea's *La última cena*	73
Chapter 3 Sergio Giral's "*Negrometrajes*": Subverting Sentimental Abolitionism and Reconstructing the History of Slavery	107
Chapter 4 The Slave Narrative in Hollywood: Steve McQueen's Adaptation of Solomon Northup's *Twelve Years a Slave*	149
Conclusion	175
Notes	177
Bibliography	211
Index	231

Illustrations

I.1	Elio Rodriguez Valdes, "Gone with the Macho," *Las Perlas de tu boca*.	17
1.1	Marlon Brando as Sir William Walker attired with a lavender scarf, *Burn!*	37
1.2	Evaristo Márquez as José Dolores striking a pose that evokes the iconography of Toussaint Louverture, *Burn!*	38
1.3	Revolutionaries in waiting, *Burn!*	45
1.4	Carnival and Black cultural life in Queimada, *Burn!*	46
1.5	General Dolores and the army of the people, *Burn!*	57
1.6	Pontecorvo's cinematographic portraiture: child in the adoring crowd, *Burn!*	58
1.7	Dolores captured, *Burn!*	61
1.8	Jacob Lawrence, "Toussaint Captured," *The Life of Toussaint L'Ouverture, No. 17* (1938), Aaron Douglas Collection, Amistad Research Center, Tulane University, New Orleans.	62
1.9	Jacob Lawrence, "General Toussaint L'Ouverture," *The Life of Toussaint L'Ouverture, No. 20* (1938), Aaron Douglas Collection, Amistad Research Center, Tulane University, New Orleans.	63
1.10	*Jacobin* magazine logo.	63
1.11	Anne-Louis Girodet, *Portrait of Citizen Belley* (1797), Châteaux de Versailles et de Trianon, Versailles.	64

x | Illustrations

1.12	Kimathi Donkor, *Toussaint L'Ouverture at Bedourete* (2004), Collection of the artist.	64
1.13	Dolores at his desk, *Burn!*	65
1.14	Henri Cartier-Bresson, *Martin Luther King. Atlanta* (1961), Foundation Henri Cartier-Bresson.	65
1.15	Walker's incomprehension and loss of power, *Burn!*	69
2.1	The Count's grotesque apostolic parody, *La última cena*.	80
2.2	Carl Fischer, "Muhammad Ali as Saint Sebastian." Photograph 1967 (photographed), ca. 2004 (printed). Victoria and Albert Museum, London.	84
2.3	Don Manuel in the slave hut, *La última cena*.	87
2.4	Alea's cinematic portraiture that evokes Velázquez, *La última cena*.	91
2.5	Diego Velázquez, "Portrait of Juan de Pareja," c. 1650.	92
2.6	Portrait of Sebastián, *La última cena*.	92
2.7	The Count kisses his slaves' feet, *La última cena*.	94
2.8	The Count's Last Supper, *La última cena*.	96
2.9	The Count and Sebastián at the supper table, *La última cena*.	99
2.10	Sebastián: free, *La última cena*.	103
3.1	The eponymous Francisco, *El otro Francisco*.	113
3.2	Portrait shot of Dorotea, *El otro Francisco*.	117
3.3	Crispin, played by Samuel Claxton, *El otro Francisco*.	123
3.4	Rebels burning the cane fields, *El otro Francisco*.	129
3.5	An enslaved woman's act of resistance, *Rancheador*.	132
3.6	Mataperro, framegrab, *Rancheador*.	134
3.7	Morales and his family, *Rancheador*.	136
3.8	Mataperro: triumphant Black liberty, *Rancheador*.	139

3.9	Mataperro in *el monte*, *Rancheador*.	139
3.10	Fromesto's scream, *Maluala*.	144
3.11	Edvard Munch, *The Scream* (1893).	145
4.1 & 4.2	Steve McQueen, *Caribs' Leap*, super 8mm color film video and sound installation, two screens (2002).	153–54
4.3	Steve McQueen, *Western Deep*, super 8mm color film video and sound installation (2002).	154
4.4 & 4.5	Steve McQueen, *Gravesend*, 35mm color film, transferred to HD digital format, video and sound installation (2007).	155
4.6	The Northups shopping in a highly glamorized Saratoga Springs, *12 Years a Slave*.	160
4.7	Sunlight and flora on the bayou, *12 Years a Slave*.	166
4.8	Caterpillar and cotton plant, *12 Years a Slave*.	168

Acknowledgments

Midway through the research and writing of this book, my dear friend and mentor Benita Parry passed away. My debt to Benita is so great that thanks expressed in a formal acknowledgment feel wholly inadequate. More than anyone else, it was Benita who encouraged me to develop my research and writing on the cinematic representation of slavery into a book. The example of Benita's life and scholarship has shaped the way I think, research, and write, and how I choose to live my life. Writing this book has allowed me to engage in imaginary conversation with Benita, and if the final product is worthy of association with her, then I know I can justifiably consider this project a success.

More than twenty years ago, Marcus Wood inspired with his wit, bravura style, and enthusiasm a young graduate student who had come to Sussex University to undertake a master's in postcolonial studies. Marcus became a fast friend and his influence on me—intellectual and personal—has been profound. For inspiring conversations on Brighton beach, in subterranean London bars, in galleries, and over numerous coffees, I will always be grateful. Alyssa Goldstein Sepinwall, a fellow traveler in the world of research into the representation of slavery on-screen, has been supportive and has generously offered suggestions and advice. Along the way, Alyssa has become a friend and a terrific intellectual jousting partner for whom I am thankful.

Vanessa Valdés has championed my work for some eight years now, and my friendship with her feels like a wondrous and unexpected gift. Her boundless generosity and her intelligence, savvy, and positive spirit make collaborating with her a pure pleasure. Her steadfast support has been indispensable to this project. Meanwhile at SUNY Press, I could not have wished for a more collegial and encouraging editor than Rebecca

Colesworthy. I am truly grateful for her expertise and enthusiastic support of this project from the outset. Other members of the SUNY Press dream team to whom I am particularly indebted include Julia Cosacchi, Aimee Harrison, and Ryan Morris, and I thank them for their invaluable support and guidance. Thanks also to Alexandra Hoff for her copyeditor's eagle eyes and expertise.

The seed of the idea that would eventually become this book was planted during my residence at Vanderbilt University's Robert Penn Warren Center for the Humanities and School of Law as a Fulbright Visiting Scholar in 2015–2016. I am grateful to the US–UK Fulbright Commission, whose support gave me vital time and space, and to the Vanderbilt community, which welcomed me with open arms. For their intellectual companionship and their extraordinary support, kindness, and hospitality, I am indebted to Daniel Sharfstein, Colin Dayan, Vera Kutzinksi, Paul Kramer, Celso Castilho, Richard Blackett, Jane Landers, Catherine Molineux, Bob Barsky, David Wasserstein, Mona Frederick, and Joy Ramirez. I must also thank Paula Covington, Vanderbilt's Latin American Studies librarian extraordinaire as well as the librarians in Vanderbilt's audio-visual resources department.

In 2016, I left Nashville for Ottawa, Canada, to take up my current post at Carleton University, whereupon I deprioritized my research on slavery and film while I pursued other projects. However, my "slavery on screen" project, as I was then calling it, refused to wait patiently on the back burner. Instead, it snuck into my teaching and research that sought to contest the marginality of the Haitian Revolution in human-rights theory and historiography. In grappling with the question of how human rights might yet be radicalized, I found Gillo Pontecorvo's *Burn!* (which I discuss in this book's first chapter) to be a terrifically useful film *to think with*. So, by the end of 2019, this project had forced its way back onto the front burner of my attention, although in truth it had never really left. However, only a few months after I had belatedly resolved to give this project the attention and priority it deserved, the pandemic struck, and the world went virtual. The years 2020 through 2022 were testing times and only slow progress was made. However, the award of a Social Sciences and Humanities Research Council (SSHRC) Insight Development Grant and the honor of receiving a Research Achievement Award from Carleton University provided invaluable support and momentum that helped carry me through. In addition, the award of a Research Engagement Grant in 2021 and a Research Completion Grant in 2023 from Carleton University's

Faculty of Public Affairs, as well as the award of the 2023–2025 Ruth and Mark Phillips Professorship in Cultural Mediations by Carleton's Institute for Comparative Studies in Literature, Art, and Culture, all helped me to get this project over the finish line. However, research dollars alone are insufficient to bring a project such as this to completion. It takes a village, as they say. In that respect, I cannot say enough about my colleagues at Carleton—past and present—who have been supportive, kind, and (not least!) fun to work with. I am especially indebted to Stacy Douglas, Paul Keen, Ummni Khan, Umut Özsu, Sarah Brouillette, Sukeshi Kamra, Pascal Gin, Amy Bartholomew, Vincent Kazmierski, Doris Buss, Zeina Bou-Zeid, Ania Zbyszewska, Mike Christensen, Ratna Rueban Balasubramaniam, Dale Spencer, Sarah Casteel Phillips, Christine Duff, Laura Horak, Aubrey Anable, Aboubakar Sanogo, Audra Diptée, Christiane Wilke, Sheryl Hamilton, Ron Saunders, Peter Swan, André Plourde, and Kamari Clarke.

I have long known the indispensability of a good librarian, and at Carleton I have had the good fortune of working with three of the best: Julie Lavigne, Patty Paquette, and Alana Skwarok. Their heroics in obtaining via interlibrary loan and other sources hard-to-find films and various materials from across the globe was nothing less than extraordinary. My doctoral graduate students, Cait Jones, Andrea McKenzie-Howell, and Steve Suntres, have inspired me with the quality of their own work, and for their intellectual camaraderie I am grateful. I should also like to thank Cait for her research assistance that helped me to shepherd this project into and through the production stages. Aaron O'Quinn and Cecily Dawson also provided research assistance for which I am grateful. I would like to thank Gabrielle Etcheverry for her transcriptions of the original Spanish and for her assistance with translation in chapter 2.

Adjusting to life in Ottawa and Canada was made easy by the warmth and kindness of many different people and groups. I am especially indebted to Michael Hawes, the president and CEO of Fulbright Canada, and Chad Gaffield of the University of Ottawa's Department of History. Their wise counsel and support gave me confidence and helped me to feel at home in my adopted city. My friends and former colleagues at my old stomping ground of Warwick University will always be central to my thinking, and I will always be grateful to them for their kindness, nurturing support, and intellectual companionship. My Warwick lit-crit comrades—Nick Lawrence, Neil Lazarus, Pablo Mukherjee, Stephen Shapiro, and Rashmi Varma—know well that you can take the boy out of the gang, but you can't take the gang out of the boy. Sharae Deckard is a bigger influence on me than she realizes. I daresay that Jim Graham is also unaware of how indebted I am to him for his positive example. And I cannot acknowledge the Warwick gang without mention of Benita Parry once again, who was so central to everything that we did and that we continue to do. In my intellectual journey, there will always be Benita.

I tried out many of the ideas in this book in my teaching and at various conferences, workshops, and seminars too numerous to list here. I would like to thank my past and present students, fellow panelists, and interlocutors at all these events over the years. My thanks also to David Alderson, Denis Bourque, Honor Brabazon, Timothy Brennan, Jerry Carlson, Nathan Dize, Rachel Douglas, Michael Drexler, Charles Forsdick, Julia Gaffield, Christian Høgsbjerg, Jon Holyoak, Sarah Kalhok Bourque, Kevin Mallory, Natalie Marie Léger, Auritro Majumder, Phil Marshall, Christopher Maurer, Mariana Past, Zuzana Pick, Paul Raffield, Maki Salmon, Charles de Segundo, Craig de Veer, Illan rua Wall, Charles Walton, Andrew Williams, and Alice Zhou. I also thank the anonymous readers for their careful consideration of an earlier version of this manuscript; their incisive reports made important and illuminating suggestions.

My partner, Tara, and our children, Georgia and Oscar, have provided infinite love, companionship, and support for which I am grateful beyond words. Tara, Georgia, and Oscar have also tolerated with good humor and sympathy many a dinnertime in which they listened to me talking about films they have not (yet) seen. Their patience, kindness, and indulgence deserve special mention. As ever, my brother, Peter, has been steady as a rock and a source of support. In the summer of 2022, as I was nearing a complete first draft of the manuscript that would become this book, my father sustained a life-changing, tragic accident. There have been some truly difficult days since. For their unconditional love and support, I thank my parents, Amir and Karen, who will always be in my heart. I hope this book will bring some small measure of joy into their lives.

Thanks are due to the following publications, in which earlier drafts of limited sections of this book have appeared. In all cases, the previously published material has been substantially reworked. *MELUS: Multi-Ethnic Literature of the United States* 42, no. 2 (2017); *PALARA: Publication of the Afro-Latin/American Research Association*, no. 23 (2019); Vanessa K. Valdés (ed.), *Racialized Visions: Haiti and the Hispanic Caribbean* (SUNY University Press, 2020).

P. J. K., Ottawa, Canada,
Unceded Algonquin Territory, December 2023

Introduction

Havana, Hollywood, and the Politics of Slave Resistance in the Cinematic Imaginary

Reflecting on his involvement the previous year in a failed film project about American race relations, in 1933 Langston Hughes wrote: "O, Movies. Temperaments. Artists. Ambitions. Scenarios. Directors, producers, advisers, actors, censors, changes, revisions, conferences. It's a complicated art—the cinema. I'm glad I write poems."[1] Hughes was right, of course, about the fraught nature of moviemaking in general, but even he could not have known how, years later, his words would appear prophetic, impeccably summing up the entire troubled endeavour of making films about Black history.[2] This book concentrates on one element of this historically problematic relationship between filmmaking and race: the presence or absence of Black resistance to slavery in the cinematic imaginary. By means of the examination of a corpus of cinematic feature films produced in either Havana or Hollywood, I argue that with only some very rare exceptions the representation of Black agency in Hollywood has always been, and very much remains, taboo. Contrastingly, I argue that Cuban cinema should be recognized for its foregrounding of Black agency. I then show how the impact of this foregrounding we encounter only rarely in Hollywood films but frequently in Cuban cinema challenges the ways in which slavery has been fundamentally *misremembered* and *misunderstood* in North America and Europe. Finally, I argue that the widespread absence of representation of Black agency in Hollywood slavery films should be understood in systemic terms and as an instance of a longstanding aversion to the recognition of historical Black achievement.

The task of responding to the principal problem that arises from this racialized representational imbalance in the history of cinema provides this study with its impetus. It is an inescapable fact that Hollywood slavery films have established a popular historiography of slavery for a global audience and have therefore played a major role in the generation of public knowledge and opinion about slavery and its inheritance. However, from the earliest days of cinema, Hollywood has promoted, at best, a very partial view of slavery. Moreover, the prevailing attitudes about slavery that Hollywood's reductionism has helped to shape have become hegemonic; or, to put it in Raymond Williams's terms, Hollywood slavery films have played a role in the transmission and incorporation of a transnational dominant and effective culture in which Black subjectivity, Black points of view, Black voices and stories, and Black historical achievement are all routinely marginalized or overlooked.³ Of course, a highly acclaimed Hollywood movie about a major historical slave insurrection does exist, but its setting is not in the Americas but in Ancient Rome and its heroic slave protagonist is not of African descent but is a Roman gladiator played by Kirk Douglas. While Stanley Kubrik's acclaimed 1960 film adaptation of Howard Fast's *Spartacus* novel is widely regarded as an iconic celebration of humankind's eternal struggle for freedom, both its actuality and its enduring cultural impact make the extreme rarity of Hollywood films telling the story of a "Black Spartacus" all the more striking.⁴ As we know from the rich historiographical bibliography on slave resistance in the Atlantic world, from W. E. B. Du Bois's *The Suppression of the African Slave Trade*; to C. L. R. James's *A History of Negro Revolt* and his classic account of the Haitian Revolution, *The Black Jacobins*; to Eugene Genovese's *Roll, Jordan, Roll*, this lack is not for want of historical source material.⁵ As James Walvin succinctly puts it, "the history of black slavery in the Americas can be interpreted in terms of the slaves' persistent efforts to resist their bondage."⁶ Yet the ideas presented in this rich vein of historical inquiry have rarely registered within Hollywood. Moreover, while Hollywood's imperviousness to historically documented Black resistance to slavery is easy to demonstrate, the pressing need for critical redress is not widely appreciated. The extent of the problem is perhaps best demonstrated by the fact that a flurry of Hollywood slavery films released in the twenty-first century that on the surface appear to present progressive, anti-racist points of view have in fact all variously silenced, disavowed, or diminished Black agency, and yet for the most part this erasure has not been considered problematic nor even noted in the first place.⁷ Michael Apted's *Amazing Grace* (2006), Steven Spielberg's *Lincoln* (2012), and Steve McQueen's *12 Years a Slave* (2013), among others, all serve as examples of films that have effaced the historically documented worldmaking actions of enslaved populations of African descent. *Amazing Grace,* which is a biopic of the abolitionist leader William Wilberforce, even goes so far as to make its subject the inspiration for the Haitian Revolution, thereby, as Charles Forsdick has observed, contributing to a "wider denial of the agency of enslaved people."[8] It appears that the failure to recognize Black agency as a historical force that has brought about progressive social transformation is so ingrained that much of the time it is a problem that flies under the radar. Consequently, contemporary debates over slavery, race, and racism are taking place in a public and cultural sphere that has been shaped in part by a cinematic tradition that has always served to perpetuate potent fantasies and misunderstandings about slavery that have long since been debunked by historians. Moreover, such debates are not without significant material consequences. Consider, for example, the fact that as Kenneth Mohammed notes, *reparations* "seems a dirty word whenever Caribbean leaders utter it," even though in 2021 the United Nations formally called for reparations "as one element of accountability and redress" that are required to end discrimination, violence, and systemic racism against people of African descent.[9]

In response to this problem, this study considers a corpus of cinematic feature-length films produced in either Havana or Hollywood between 1969 and 2013 that challenge, and in one case exemplifies, the longstanding cultural tradition of eliding Black resistance to slavery. The examples drawn from Havana comprise *La última cena* (*The Last Supper*) of 1976 by Cuba's most feted filmmaker, Tomás Gutiérrez Alea, and a trilogy of films by one of Cuba's most underappreciated filmmakers, Sergio Giral—*El otro Francisco* (*The Other Francisco*) of 1974, *Rancheador* (*The Slave Hunter*) of 1976, and *Maluala* of 1979. These four Cuban films make Black resistance to slavery their explicit theme, and consequently each one represents a challenge to the discourses of apprehending slavery and abolition that predominate in North America and Europe. The two examples drawn from Hollywood are binary opposites when it comes to the representation of Black agency: one makes it a focal point, whereas the other closes its eyes to it. Gillo Pontecorvo's *Burn!* from 1969 is that rare and radical bird—a film that strived to break free of the constraints imposed by its genesis in a Hollywood studio environment to communicate a stunning and radical message of Black insurrection as a liberatory historical force and a praxis of what Massimiliano Tomba terms "insurgent universalism."[10] Additionally, not only does *Burn!* make Black resistance to slavery and neocolonial oppression central to its narrative and ideological thrust, but it also takes on other tenacious myths intimately connected to slavery, including the myth that British abolitionism was fundamentally driven by the motives of philanthropism, moral virtue, and humanitarian sentiment. This myth is roundly debunked in *Burn!*, which instead identifies British abolitionism's strategic function as a tactic for the realization of greater profits and imperialist hegemony. On the other hand, the second Hollywood film considered in these pages, Steve McQueen's 2013 triple Oscar-winner *12 Years a Slave*, systematically omits the accounts and references to Black resistance that are present in the source material on which the film was based: Solomon Northup's slave narrative of 1853, *Twelve Years a Slave*. Furthermore, as the analysis will show, the effacement of Black agency we encounter in *12 Years a Slave* functions as a crucial element of the film's disablement of the critique of slavery as a social structure.

Therefore, this project considers, in a comparative framework, a corpus of slavery films produced in either Havana or Hollywood that challenge or exemplify the longstanding cultural pattern of silencing or disavowing Black resistance. I consider whether the films under examination offer perspectives that might disrupt racialized social orders as well as whether and how they reveal, critique, or fall victim to a plethora of tenacious, vital, and resilient myths that impede the development of informed discussions about slavery and its legacies. One of the striking features of this corpus of films is that except for McQueen's *12 Years a Slave*, all the films considered in these pages are, to a greater or lesser extent, neglected films despite their considerable merits. *Burn!* boasts one of the greatest performances by one of Hollywood's greatest actors, Marlon Brando, yet cinephiles rightly lament its status as an "overlooked gem."[11] Tomás Gutiérrez Alea's films are regarded as jewels of what is now referred to as "world cinema" (on which more later), and Sergio Giral's trilogy has been recognized for its striking originality. Yet Cuban cinema has a history of being viewed tardily and unevenly, especially in North America.[12] For political, economic, and ideological reasons, all have fallen into varying degrees of "neglect and secondariness," to borrow Edward Said's turn of phrase. Therefore, following Said's argument for a *worldly* approach to comparative cultural criticism, this study sets its sights on restoring these unjustly neglected cultural works to "their place in the global setting" such that we can better understand their forms and values and so that they might shape the discourses informing struggles for racial and social justice today.[13]

Some detailed consideration of Said's argument for *worldliness* as a critical-ethical imperative is warranted since it provides this book's argument with a crucial component of its modus operandi. As Neil Lazarus has noted, *worldliness* is very much a keyword when it comes to Said's work, and consequently readers of Said encounter it throughout his corpus.[14] For example, in his 1983 monograph *The World, the Text, and the Critic*, Said wrote of the urgent need for literature to be studied in "worldly" and "historical . . . but no less theoretically self-conscious" ways.[15] In *The World, the Text, and the Critic* the reader will also encounter Said writing in admiration of "Lukács' ideas about theory" as being "completely committed to worldliness and change."[16] A decade later, in 1993's *Culture and Imperialism*, the term *worldliness* first appears early in the book's introduction as part of the argument for reading works with attention to "their complex affiliations with their real setting."[17] And in one of *Culture and Imperialism*'s most celebrated passages, the now canonical counter-reading of Jane Austen's *Mansfield Park*, Said again mobilizes *worldliness* as an interpretative tool that enables the identification of the novel's global perspective and its entanglement in empire and slavery despite the sparse explicit references in the novel to the Bertram family's slave plantation in Antigua.[18] One further striking example from *Culture and Imperialism* that casts light on the importance Said attached to the term comes when we read his lament for the loss of a critical appreciation for culture's "rich worldliness."[19] This loss, Said contended, arose from a "hypertrophy of vision" that he attributed not only to academic specialization, relentless commodification, and the rise of identity politics, but also to the historical period of post–Cold War American ascendency that unleashed a heady mixture of "patriotism, relative solipsism, social authority, unchecked aggressiveness, and defensiveness toward others."[20] However, the clearest definition that Said provided in his writings of worldliness as a *critical project* is to be found in his 1991 essay "The Politics of Knowledge."[21]

"The Politics of Knowledge," Said's biographer Timothy Brennan writes, should be understood as one of Said's boldest statements on the culture wars in which academia had become immersed, and its argument makes the Fanonian point that "affirming the existence of a nonwhite 'other' is not itself an argument and certainly not a progressive one."[22] Turning to the essay itself, consider the following lines: "[T]o be an independent postcolonial Arab, or black, or Indonesian is not a program, nor a process, nor a vision. It is no more than a convenient starting point from which the real work, the hard work, might begin."[23] The impetus for the essay was provided by Said's experience in a hostile Q and A following his presentation of a draft of the introduction to *Culture and Imperialism* at a historical studies seminar on the theme of imperialism, hosted by Rutgers University in the fall of 1990. In the seminar's Q and A session, Said was assailed for not having mentioned "living non-European non-males" in his draft or presentation.[24] Said's eloquent response struck a passionate tone of intellectual urgency, and it made the point that a great deal of his work was concerned precisely with "just the kind of omission" with which he had been charged and that *Culture and Imperialism* would indeed include a focus on the works of non-Europeans. However, it also made the point—and this is the crux of the argument—that "it does not finally matter *who* wrote what, but rather *how* a work is written and *how* it is read."[25] That is to say, as Brennan puts it in his gloss of Said's essay, "it is perfectly imaginable, in other words, that anticolonial sentiments can be expressed by reading Yeats or Shelley critically."[26] For Said, the goal of the "great revisionary" projects of feminism, subaltern studies, Black studies, and anti-imperial resistance had never been the mere substitution of "one center for another."[27] On the contrary, "it was always a matter of opening and participating in a central strand of intellectual and cultural effort and of showing what had always been, though indiscernibly, a part of it, like the work of women, or of blacks and servants—but which had been either denied or derogated."[28]

The goal of "The Politics of Knowledge" was thus nothing less than the rescuing of the politics of an integrationist, emancipatory, universalist humanism from the rising tide of a "flat-minded" politics of identity and separatism that Said admonished as "an impoverishing politics of knowledge based only upon the assertion and reassertion of identity, an ultimately uninteresting alternation of presence and absence."[29] The point he was trying to make, Said wrote, could be "summed up in the useful notion of worldliness," an instructive concept that brings into vision the project of a comparative cultural criticism demanding to think seriously about the relationship between cultural works and the world, an intellectual project that for Said we simply cannot do without:

> By linking works to each other we bring them out of the neglect and secondariness to which for all kinds of political and ideological reasons they had previously been condemned. . . . *Worldliness* is therefore the restoration to such works and interpretations of their place in the global setting,

a restoration that can only be accomplished by an appreciation not of some tiny, defensively constituted corner of the world, but of the large, many-windowed house of human culture as a whole.[30]

Worldliness in this sense provides one of the political and theoretical foundations of this book's argument and the rationale for its corpus. Aiming to retrieve neglected representations of Black resistance to slavery and Black historical achievement and to bring them into scholarly discussion and the broader public sphere of knowledge, I maintain that a critical understanding of the slavery films of Gillo Pontecorvo, Tomás Gutiérrez Alea, and Sergio Giral should not remain in the domain of the area specialist but rather should be brought out of "the neglect and secondariness" to which they have been consigned and into conversation with more widely appreciated and commented upon films in a great contest over forms, values, and the telling of history. I also proceed from the conviction that a necessary companion to the work of retrieval and recuperation that a project of worldliness entails is the critical reconsideration of works that have been lavished with critical praise—and so do not require "recuperation" or "bringing out of neglect"—in order that we can rethink their situation, ideology, and politics, as well as their acquiring of hallowed or canonical status. This then, I suggest, is an appropriate theoretical rationale for approaching McQueen's *12 Years A Slave*, a film that has been considered an instant classic, and for doing so comparatively in relation to films that have been unjustly neglected.

One of this book's primary critical tasks is thus a *recuperative* one that aims to restore films addressing slavery by Gillo Pontecorvo, Tomás Gutiérrez Alea, and Sergio Giral to "their place in the global setting" and to consider them as contributions to a radical and alternative anticolonial filmmaking tradition that developed for the most part in the Third World, as it was then called, from the late 1960s onward. The broad brushstrokes of the history of this radical filmmaking tradition reveal that its fortunes dovetailed with the fate of the politics of "revolution." Third World political cinema, or "Third Cinema" as it was dubbed in contradistinction to First (commercial) and Second (art or auteur) cinema, met with a hostile environment for its reception in the West almost from its inception.[31] As Neil Lazarus has put it, globally the 1970s were marked by "the reassertion of imperial dominance," and after 1975 "the prevailing political sentiment in the West turned sharply against anticolonial nationalist insurgency and revolutionary anti-imperialism."[32] Furthermore, conditions in the West for the reception of the project of a Third Cinema were made more unfavourable still as the world transitioned from the post–World War II era of embedded liberalism to the post-1979 era of disembedded neoliberalism.[33] And certainly after the collapse of historical communism in 1989, the category of Third Cinema came increasingly to be regarded as outmoded, the cinema of a chimeric political vision that had lost its lustre. As such, Third Cinema went the way of both "nation" and "socialism," which David Scott, breathing the air of postrevolutionary defeat, has argued can no longer inspire "visionary horizons of new beginnings any of us can look toward as though they were fresh thresholds of aspiration and achievement to be fought for and progressively arrived at."[34] Further, symptomatic of Third Cinema's declining fortunes has been the remarketing and repackaging of some of its most acclaimed films under the banner of a politically defanged "world cinema."[35]

This demise of Third World political cinema was mapped against the rising tide of neoliberalism by Fredric Jameson, who, in a 1992 essay based on one of his spring 1990 lectures at the British Film Institute, remarked that:

> Third-World cinema itself is rarely today defended as a space in which models for alternate cinema are to be sought. Indeed the very term Third World seems to have become an embarrassment in a period in which the realities of the economic have seemed to supplant the possibilities of collective struggle, in which human agency and politics seem to have been dissolved by the global corporate institutions we call late capitalism. The promise of alternate forms in the cinema of that now distant period we call the 60s (but which covered the 70s as well, in chronological retrospect), included the promise of alternate ways of life, alternate collective and communal structures, that were expected to emerge from a variety of struggles against economic, military, and cultural imperialism (and in some cases, those of China, Cuba, and Vietnam, for example, this promise overlapped with the Second-World project of the constructions of socialism) . . . the autarchy of the socialist countries and the cultural and social possibilities of Third-World or post-colonial areas have seemed to evaporate under the dreary requirements of modernization and the balanced

budget (or the Debt). Third-World "culture" however, in the narrow sense, has been gratefully absorbed by the international entertainment industry, and has seemed to furnish vibrant but politically acceptable images of social pluralism for the late capitalist big city.[36]

In response to the historically specific situation of living in the faint afterglow of the project of Third World political cinema, Jameson argued that "we need to invent some new questions to ask of Third-World cinema [and] of the Third World generally, as the last surviving social space from which alternatives to corporate capitalist daily life and social relations are to be sought."[37] Thus, following Jameson, I seek in this project to pose some new questions of films that we can align with or juxtapose against the project of Third World political cinema and that provoke discussion vis-à-vis the representation of Black resistance to slavery: How does the corpus of films under consideration here challenge the dominant modes of remembering slavery and abolition? And how might the emancipatory visions they present rebuke the bleakness of our contemporary political imaginary, which, since the disappointments of the 1960s, has gripped so much work undertaken in the academy in the humanities and social sciences?[38] Part of the critical and *worldly* task undertaken in this book, then, is the recovery of examples of alternate cinematic practices that aspired to speak of alternate politics, alternate ways of life, and alternate communal structures, and to do so not as part of an antiquarian project, but as part of a project aiming to reveal the historical and contingent (and therefore changeable) truth of our present reality. This project thus strives to rebuke the critique that attachment to universal, emancipatory political programs are in our times anachronistic and to embrace and "to take pleasure in the possibility of change in all things."[39] So, far from their perception as naïve, utopian, misguided, or outmoded, the political aspirations of Third Cinema are treated here as a resource to draw on in the attempt to conceive of radical futures and radical alternatives to the hegemony of global capitalism.

This emphasis on and valuation of Cuban and Third Cinema distinguishes this study from existing scholarship on slavery and film that has been a field of considerable activity for some years now and especially since the turn of the twenty-first century. *Toms, Coons, Mulattoes, Mammies, and Bucks* by Donald Bogle, an eminent African American film and television historian, constitutes a useful starting point for a synoptic overview of this field of scholarship. First published in 1973 and now into an updated and expanded fifth edition that appeared in 2016, Bogle's book is a landmark study that documents the deplorably restricted and stereotyped range of roles that have been available to Black actors throughout the history of American film. However, this is only the starting point for Bogle's thesis, which advances the argument that "the essence of black film history" is to be found in how Black actors have subverted these stereotypes.[40] Following in Bogle's footsteps came two pioneering book-length studies whose focus is specifically on the representation of slavery and slave revolt on screen: Natalie Zemon Davis's *Slaves on Screen: Film and Historical Vision* and Alyssa Goldstein Sepinwall's *Slave Revolt on Screen: The Haitian Revolution in Film and Video Games*.[41] Davis's *Slaves on Screen* is notable for its attention to the ways in which the historical slavery film could function as a "thought experiment," and it seeks to measure the potential of "fiction films" for "telling about the past in a meaningful and accurate way."[42] While Davis's book considers two of the films that I consider in these pages (*Burn!* and *La última cena*), it does not consider the ways in which the Haitian Revolution haunts, informs, and structures these works. Nor, despite its inclusion of Alea's *La última cena*, does it offer consideration of whether and why Cuban and Third Cinema has done a better job of representing slavery than has Hollywood.

Sepinwall's *Slave Revolt on Screen* provides an overview of the Haitian Revolution's cultural currency in film and video games and offers welcome analysis of Haitian cinematic perspectives as well as foreign views of the revolution. Sepinwall also analyzes North American, European, and French Caribbean video games about the revolution, noting that the market reach of video games is now greater than that of independent film.[43] Sepinwall also discusses *Burn!* but dismisses it as a "benevolent banalization"—a claim I investigate in these pages and argue does not hold up to scrutiny.[44] In addition, on the basis of her analysis of Alea's *La última cena* and a French-Cuban adaptation of Alejo Carpentier's 1962 novel *El siglo de las luces* (*Explosion in a Cathedral*), Sepinwall considers that Cuban cinema has downplayed the agency of enslaved people.[45] This view is diametrically opposed to the argument I elaborate in these pages. The originality of the argument I pursue here is also made apparent by attending to the underlying structural and theoretical differences that divide Sepinwall's approach from my own. Whereas Sepinwall maps her analysis onto a Haitian/non-Haitian binary (and argues that non-Haitian visions of the Haitian Revolution and slave revolt in general have overall been unsatisfactory), my reading of Cuban and Third Cinema (in opposition to Hollywood productions) suggests that a dialectics of core and periphery provides a more compelling explanatory schema for interpreting cinematic production engaged with the subject of Black resistance to slavery (and, by implication, cultural production in the era of capitalist modernity more generally).[46]

One further comment is warranted to elaborate the theoretical approach I have employed in this study. My approach has drawn—implicitly, if not explicitly—on Said's twin concepts of *"strategic location"* and *"strategic formation"* as outlined in *Orientalism*. While "strategic location" is, Said explains, "a way of describing the author's position in a text," "strategic formation" is "a way of analyzing the relationship between texts and the way in which groups of texts, even textual genres, acquire mass density, and referential power among themselves and thereafter in the culture at large."[47] This methodology has the advantage of drawing attention to how representational forms are constituted by, and constitutive of, reality. Attention to this relationship between representational forms and the world logically asserts the integration of representations into reality, revealing that representations are indeed part of reality and not just its rendering. While in *Orientalism* this method enabled Said to reveal how "the field of Oriental studies had managed to create a fantastical projection about Arabs and Islam" that satisfied and aligned with the expectations and biases of its Western audience, the method is generative also for the purposes of this present study.[48] Hence, *From Havana to Hollywood: Slave Resistance in the Cinematic Imaginary* takes as its starting point the "fantastical projections" about enslaved Black people in the Americas that we can identify in Hollywood films from its earliest days to the present. Like the Orientalist tradition that Said indicted, this filmic cultural tradition both cultivated and satisfied the prejudices of its intended audience. This filmic tradition, the general contours of which will be sketched in brief in this introduction's next section, gave license to a host of racist or racialized themes, tropes, and characterizations, including, inter alia: the erasure of Black agency, the construction of racist character archetypes, and the representation of Black culture en masse as crude and primitive. Against the hegemony of these representations that have acquired a "density" and "referential power among themselves and . . . in the culture at large," *From Havana to Hollywood* considers a corpus of films that sought to contest the stories about Black enslaved peoples that had been and were continuing to be told in Hollywood.

Black Agency Gone Missing: Slavery on Screen in Hollywood

While this introduction is not the place for a comprehensive survey of the history of the representation of slavery on screen in Hollywood, a thematic sketch of the general contours, predominant characteristics, and trajectory of Hollywood slavery films over the years is necessary since it provides the background against which the chapters to follow should be read. Therefore, the sketch that follows provides, in the Althusserian tradition of symptomatic reading, a critical summary that notes selected tropes, themes, and patterns but also silences, gaps, and contradictions. By this strategy, the ideological history of slavery on screen in Hollywood is sketched as a problem to which, in different ways, the films by Pontecorvo, Alea, Giral, and McQueen studied here should be considered responses or interventions.

Film historians widely consider the Lumiere brothers' 1895 film *La Sortie des ouvriers de l'usine Lumière* ("Workers Leaving the Lumière Factory") to be the world's first motion picture. The world's first slavery film was not far behind: on August 3, 1903, a film adaptation of Harriet Beecher Stowe's 1852 novel *Uncle Tom's Cabin* premiered at Hubert's Museum and Theatre, a New York City dime museum and nickelodeon, making it the earliest American feature film.[49] The fourteen-minute film (which was considered full-length at the time) was made by Edwin S. Porter for Thomas Edison's film company, and it was one of at least nine film adaptations of *Uncle Tom's Cabin* made in the silent-movie era of 1903 to 1927. The history of slavery on screen in Hollywood had begun in earnest: no other story was filmed as often in the silent era as was *Uncle Tom's Cabin*, and to this day it remains probably the most-filmed American novel.[50] While the 1903 Edison-Porter adaptation is notable for various technical filmmaking accomplishments including the use of intertitles, of more significance is the cultural-ideological template it established for future slavery films. Far from following in the footsteps of the antislavery movement to which Stowe's novel was a sacred text, Stephen Railton has observed that the Edison-Porter adaptation offers an essentially "eulogistic account of slavery" in which Stowe's protest novel is transformed into a minstrel show complete with happy, dancing slaves.[51] So, while the representation of slavery on screen is nearly as old as cinema itself, the filmography of slavery, as Brenda Stevenson has noted, "began with all of the ugly, stereotyped characterizations and storylines one would expect of the racial nadir of the early twentieth century."[52]

"The racial nadir of the early twentieth century" found its most complete filmic expression in D. W. Griffiths's notorious 1915 film *The Birth of a Nation*, a three-hour long film adaptation of *The Clansman*, a novel and stage play authored by the white supremacist Thomas Dixon Jr.[53] It is not an exaggeration to state that *The Birth of a Nation* brought about a revolution in American filmmaking. The astounding novelty of *The Birth of a Nation* at the time, as well as the unprecedented enormity of its impact and success, is hard to fathom more than 100 years later. It was the first film of its kind in any number of respects and a pseudohistorical epic Civil War drama of extraordinary—and chilling—ambition. On February 18, 1915, *The Birth of a Nation* became the first film to be screened in the White House; President Woodrow Wilson, a college acquaintance of Dixon's, was among the many millions duped by the film's delusions, and on viewing the film he remarked, "It is like writing history with lightning, and my only regret is that it is all so terribly true."[54] *The Birth of a Nation* was also the first film to be projected for the justices of the US Supreme Court and the members of the United States Congress. It became the first cinematic blockbuster and the most profitable film of its time, and perhaps of all time once profits are adjusted for inflation. Melvyn Stokes estimates that it may have been seen by more than 200,000,000 viewers worldwide.[55] It was also, as Stevenson notes, "voted by more than two hundred movie critics as the most important contribution to the first fifty years of cinema," and as recently as the 1970s eminent critics continued to praise *The Birth of the Nation* as perhaps the most important film of all time.[56] It was however grotesquely racist: it lauded the Ku Klux Klan while ridiculing, insulting, and humiliating southern freed Blacks. Committed to separatism—the coda recommends the deportation of all African Americans—and producing a genuinely "impoverishing politics of knowledge," the film's transparent racism was clear to those committed to racial justice. The NAACP and America's Black community at large voiced their disapproval, but their protests met with little success.[57]

Of course, *The Birth of a Nation* did not singlehandedly construct the discourse of disparaging and belittling Black people, Black history, and Black culture, though it clearly contributed to the popularity and endurance of racist sentiments. *The Birth of a Nation* should be situated in a genealogy of deep-seated racism stretching back centuries. At the time of the film's release, longstanding arguments for racial hierarchies, including Aryanism, Anglo-Saxonism, and Social Darwinism, had been invigorated by the popularity of eugenics and scientific racism, which were at the time leading movements in medicine, politics, and public discourse in Europe and North America. Only after 1942, when information about Nazi Germany's Holocaust death camps became public knowledge, would the pseudoscience of eugenics be disgraced. Further, the reactionary myth of the "Lost Cause," which had grown rapidly in popularity throughout the 1890s—the decade to which we can trace the genesis of cinema—also played a critical role in the success of *The Birth of a Nation* that should not be underestimated. The Lost Cause, as the legal scholar Michel Paradis has remarked, should be understood as a revisionist history in which the Confederacy's motivation to fight a treasonous war to defend slavery is recast as the embodiment of the true vision of the Founding Fathers of the United States.[58] But, as the scholars Connelly and Bellows have observed, the Lost Cause is more nebulous than any ordinary revisionist history. Its "spirit," they write, "has slipped blithely through the time and space of generations of southerners."[59] From its inception, Lost Cause mythology tapped into an appetite for romanticizing the antebellum "Old South." According to Lost Cause sentiments, the slaveholding Confederacy was "a glorious organic civilization" that the avaricious, industrial "Yankee North" had attempted to destroy.[60] The mythological Old South was thus projected as a rural idyll in which a distinctive Southern culture—noble, chivalrous, and pious—had flourished as a genteel way of life. This way of thinking enabled the South to portray itself as the Civil War's victimized, tragic hero and the virtuous counterpoint to the wicked North. The aftermath of the South's defeat on the battlefield—with its attendant ruins and devastation, psychological trauma, and a public discourse flooded with self-pity and sorrow—provided fertile ground for this sentimental and romantic mythology to take root. At its heart lay white supremacy, but, ever shifting and malleable like all the best mythologies, the Lost Cause held that the South had fought for liberty and freedom and that slavery was incidental rather than fundamental to the outbreak of the Civil War. While proponents of Lost Cause ideology have differed on the question of precisely how slavery should be remembered, one of its essential, scandalous tenets was that slavery in the antebellum South had been a paternalistic institution and that the enslaved themselves had been generally contented with their lot. The success of Lost Cause mythology can be measured by the fact that by dint of "sheer sentimentalism, political argument, and by recurrent celebrations and rituals," Lost Cause values became an "integral part of national reconciliation" in the postbellum United States.[61] Lost Cause acolytes could be found in the North as well as the South and even as far away as in Britain. There, the Southern States had always enjoyed a degree of political sympathy for various reasons, including the historical dependence of the British cotton industry on the production of raw cotton by enslaved labor in the antebellum American South. Cultural reasons should also not be underestimated, not least Southern culture's aping of British aristocratic manners and values.[62] The wide transmission of Lost Cause mythology was effected in print—consider, for example, the popularity of Southern plantation genre writing that was published in mass-circulation magazines for a mainly Northern readership, and of course in film.[63] While *The Birth of a Nation* should be recognized as the filmic apotheosis of Lost Cause mythology and an exemplar of widely held racist views of the early twentieth century, it should be noted that Lost Cause values are inscribed throughout the history of Hollywood film, explicitly so up to the era of Civil Rights and implicitly thereafter. Crucially for this book's argument, within the discourse of the Lost Cause, Black resistance to slavery was unthinkable other than as the actions of a savage, dangerous, and ungrateful race.

Extraordinarily successful but also deeply controversial, one of the legacies of *The Birth of a Nation* was that for the most part Hollywood turned its back on slavery as a subject for feature films until the late 1920s. "The baleful influence" of *The Birth of a Nation*, Melvyn Stokes has argued, resulted in the narrowing of "the range of Black characters shown in American films in general and its influence led to the movie industry itself banning the showing of miscegenation on screen."[64] However, *The Birth of a Nation*'s defense of the antebellum Lost Cause and its scandalous racism was contested by Oscar Micheaux's *Within Our Gates* of 1920, which is thought to be the oldest-surviving film by an African American director. Micheaux had "read avidly" the widespread and intensely negative response to *The Birth of a Nation* in the Black press, which called "for a champion to counter the slander of Griffith and Hollywood."[65] Rising to the challenge, Micheaux's *Within Our Gates* depicts diverse forms of Black agency in the Jim Crow South, shows the reality of Dixieland racism, and generally throws Griffith's "phobic white supremacism" and "Manichean historicism" back in his face.[66]

The arrival of sound films in 1927 opened new worlds of cinematic possibility, including the incorporation of what was thought to be "Black" music. Further, the Great Depression of 1929, which extended throughout the 1930s, generated conditions that encouraged a renewed and powerful nostalgia for the Old South: "Hard times and high industrial unemployment made the supposed stability and seemingly timeless rural way of life in the antebellum South appear especially appealing. To those suffering economic instability or threatened by unemployment in cities, the romantic myth of the Old South was a highly seductive one."[67]

Consequently, Hollywood's "Golden Age," the beginnings of which we can date to the mid-1930s, saw the emergence of two popular new genres: the plantation musical and the plantation melodrama. These films, Stevenson writes, characterized enslaved people as "happy, devoted, passive black simpletons."[68] Without doubt, the most popular and influential film of the plantation genres was Victor Fleming's 1939 *Gone with the Wind*, which remains the highest-grossing film of all time at the global box office.[69] Based on Margaret Mitchell's Pulitzer Prize–winning and bestselling novel of the same title, *Gone with the Wind* won eight Oscars, one of which was awarded to Hattie McDaniel in the category of best supporting actress for her performance as the Black house servant "Mammy." McDaniel thereby became the first African American to win an Oscar. Moreover, in the opinion of Donald Bogle, by the sheer "force of her own personality" McDaniel's Mammy "became free of the greatest burden that slavery—on screen and off—inflicted on blacks: a sense of innate inferiority."[70] However, Bogle's positive assessment of the significance of McDaniel's performance should be countered with Stevenson's view that "the Mammy character was consistent with stereotypical depictions of black female house slaves" and her observation that it erased "the reality of the physical, emotional, and sexual abuse of domestic slaves."[71] As we will see, Sergio Giral's trilogy in particular will contest this hackneyed mode of representing enslaved Black women who were forced to labor in domestic settings. *Gone with the Wind* also relegated its Black characters in general into the background. The picture's undisputed stars were Vivien Leigh and Clark Gable, who played the lovers Scarlett O'Hara and Rhett Butler who were immortalized in the film's movie poster, which became arguably the most iconic image of Hollywood's "Golden Age." The poster's enduring iconicity is attested to by the wide set of parodies it generated, including its humorous and subversive reworking by the Cuban artist Elio Rodriguez Valdes[72] (cover and fig. I.1). Rodriguez Valdes's fictitious movie poster of 1995, "Gone with the Macho," cunningly draws attention

Figure I.1 Elio Rodriguez Valdes, "Gone with the Macho," Las Perlas de tu boca, silkscreen on paper, 27.5″ × 19.5″, edition of 8. 1995. © Elio Rodriguez and 532 Gallery, Thomas Jaeckel, New York City.

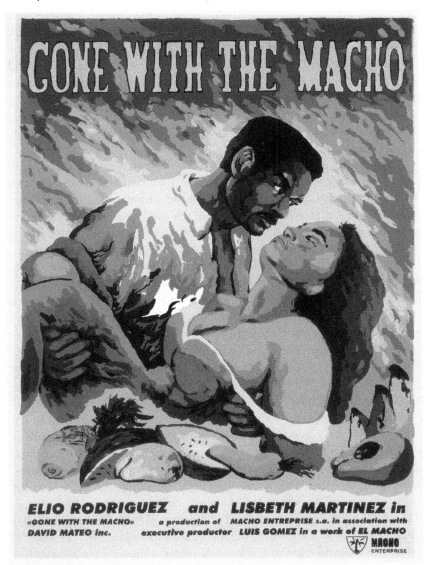

to the routine marginalization of Black characters in the era of "Golden Age" cinema in general and in *Gone with Wind* in particular. Additionally, via the poster's title, the Black male figure's intense and desiring gaze—as well as the tropical, phallic fruit—"Gone with the Macho" parodies and confronts the "all too common stereotype of the virile, sexy, powerful black male."[73] Thus, notwithstanding the qualified breakthrough represented by McDaniel's success, *Gone with the Wind* must ultimately be understood as a romantic memorial to the Lost Cause and as a canonical example of Hollywood's anxieties about race in the early to mid-twentieth century. Rendering Black resistance *illogical* and *unthinkable*, *Gone with the Wind* played a remarkable role in the embedding of a conservative mythologization of slavery.[74]

After 1945, mainstream American films began to emerge that offered a more nuanced representation of slavery than had the earlier films of the plantation musical and the plantation melodrama genres.[75] There was something of a shift away from some of the stock stereotypical character types such as the "Jezebel," the "Mammy," and the "Uncle Tom," and with the advent of the Civil Rights Movement, American television documentaries addressing the history of the abolitionist movement began to appear.[76] One highly unusual slavery film that appeared in this period is *Lydia Bailey*, a 1952 swashbuckler directed by the Romanian Jean Negulesco and released by 20th Century Fox. Somewhat extraordinarily, *Lydia Bailey* presents a sympathetic view of the Haitian Revolution—an event Hollywood has not touched with a bargepole since. *Lydia Bailey*'s plot centers on an idealistic white American lawyer, Albion Hamlin—an unexpected personification of worldliness and change and a fictional representation of the falsity of "the supremely stubborn thesis that everyone is principally and irreducibly a member of some race or category."[77] Hamlin becomes entangled in the events of the Revolution while visiting Haiti to secure the signature of a white American heiress, the eponymous Lydia Bailey, on various legal documents. Hamlin and Bailey soon fall in love and Hamlin enthusiastically sides with the rebel slaves, strikingly declaring that he "would kill every white man" he "could lay his hands on" if he were to find himself in the same position as the enslaved population of Saint Domingue. Bailey initially sides with the French, but she is soon persuaded by her lover to switch her allegiance to the Black rebels who are shown exerting a degree of military and political agency unusual for both 1952 and a Hollywood production. The French are represented unambiguously as villainous, and

Toussaint Louverture (played by Ken Renard) is depicted in a positive light. Also extremely unusually, Haitian culture is not presented as demonic. In her analysis, Alyssa Goldstein Sepinwall has noted that the film's depiction of a vodou ceremony "appeared not as one of pig-blood drinking, but of deeply spiritual singing and dancing." While this still "reflected a 1940s tourist view of Vodou dance, it is still remarkable that the filmmakers did not imagine the religion in an entirely savage way."[78] However, although the film's overall atypical sympathy for the revolution should be stressed, it should also be noted that at various junctures the film portrays Haitian Blacks as irrational and hysterical, it equates Blackness with a highly charged sexuality, and it represents the land of Haiti itself as exotic and a place of eerie primal power. At the box office, the film was a failure: 20th Century Fox let it "quietly fall into obscurity" and it rapidly became "an obscure memory" in both the Unites States and Haiti.[79]

In 1969—the year of the release of Gillo Pontecorvo's *Burn!*, which is the subject of analysis in this book's first chapter—another American film that depicted Black resistance to slavery would materialize: Herbert Biberman's *Slaves*.[80] Biberman was a Communist and a member of the "Hollywood Ten," the group who in 1947 had been called before an investigative committee of the United States House of Representatives (the House Un-American Activities Committee). The Hollywood Ten refused, on First Amendment grounds, to answer the committee's question: "Are, you now, or have you ever been, a member of the Communist party?" For their refusal, all ten members of the group were found in contempt of Congress, jailed, and barred from working in Hollywood. Produced outside the major Hollywood studios more than twenty years after his release from jail, Biberman's *Slaves* completely upended the view of slavery as a benevolent institution and of the enslaved themselves as passive and contented. Instead, Biberman's *Slaves* depicted slavery as an exploitative and abusive system and portrayed its rebellious Black slave protagonist in heroic terms. Also significantly, *Slaves* treated white plantation women empathetically, linking their subjugation to "the control planters exerted over enslaved people."[81] However, like the film's representation of Black agency, its sensitive depiction of the situation of white plantation women is unfortunately anomalous; regrettably, it set no precedent and did not lead to similar examples. Instead, as the chapter on Steve McQueen's *12 Years a Slave* will demonstrate, the trope of the wicked plantation mistress has become hegemonic.[82]

Why, then, did *Slaves* fail to usher in a whole-scale transformation in the representation of slavery on the big screen? The answer is uncomplicated: "*Slaves* failed completely at the box office." As Melvyn Stokes explained:

> Its only audience of reasonable size was African American residents of big cities. As long as films covering slavery did so within the context of the nostalgia for the Old South, it was possible to make films that appealed to the dominant white audience in the United States. When Old South films were no longer produced—in large part because of the shift in racial attitudes as a result of the growing effectiveness of the civil rights movement in the late 1950s and 1960s—it was harder and harder to see how slavery could be featured in a commercially successful film.[83]

Therefore, after the commercial failure of Biberman's *Slaves*, film producers recognized that a different strategy would be required to solve the conundrum of how to make a slavery film with mass appeal in the second half of the twentieth century. The longstanding tradition of plantation pornography appeared to offer one potential solution. As Marcus Wood's work has demonstrated, plantation pornography has become a huge international business, and its roots can be traced to at least the eighteenth century.[84] *Mandingo*, a 1975 slavery film directed by Richard Fleischer based on Kyle Ostoot's 1957 bestselling soft-core pornographic novel, is the most well-known and significant filmic example of the genre.[85] Set on a "slave-breeding" plantation in Alabama and starring world heavyweight champion boxer Ken Norton, *Mandingo* combined erotic themes and violence while drawing on elements of the "blaxploitation" genre. Ghastly, exploitative, and prurient, *Mandingo* nevertheless did undercut earlier representations of slavery as benign by focusing on practices including the sexual violence of forced reproduction, sexual cruelty, domination, and exploitation, thereby revealing their endemic relationship to slavery and offering a memorable indictment of the antebellum South's white male enslaving class. Significantly, *Mandingo* also depicts Black resistance in the form of a failed slave revolt. On its release, the film met with near-universal hostility from critics. White critics tended to consider it immoral and obscene, while Black critics tended to consider the film "a racist insult fabricated by an uncaring and money-hungry white entertainment establishment."⁸⁶ However, there is considerable evidence that the film was popular with Black audiences who were largely persuaded by "the film's portrayal of sexual exploitation as a constituent element of the American slave system" and considered that *Mandingo* "spoke the truth about interracial sexual history."⁸⁷ In the years since its release, a number of academic reassessments have appeared, most notably an essay by Robin Wood in which he made the now-notorious claim that *Mandingo* is "the greatest Hollywood film about race."⁸⁸ The film was a box-office success, spawned the (less commercially successful) sequel *Drum*, and has remained perennially in print.⁸⁹

In contrast to *Mandingo*'s complexities and contentious inheritance, the politics and impact of *Roots*, an eight-part TV miniseries adapted from Alex Haley's Pulitzer Prize–winning novel that was aired in prime time on a major US television network in January 1977, are somewhat easier to trace. *Roots* was a breakthrough moment in the history of slavery on American screens: the total US audience was around 130 to 140 million viewers, and it was critically praised and lauded with prizes and awards including a Golden Globe and nine Emmys. A fictionalized account of Haley's maternal family genealogy that he traced to the Gambia in the 1750s, *Roots* strove to present slavery in a manner that challenged its earlier representation as benign. Thus, "it showed the experience of the Middle Passage . . . , a shipboard slave rebellion, and the sexual exploitation of enslaved women."⁹⁰ Moreover, *Roots* also sought to rehabilitate African identity as a carrier of positive qualities and strove to tell its story from the perspective of its Black characters who "exhibited humanity, cultural pride, talent, intelligence, and a desire for freedom."⁹¹ However, in the process of adapting Haley's novel for the small screen, the producers "made a range of compromises to make *Roots* palatable to a mainly white television audience."⁹² These included the creation of a great many new white characters and the manufacturing of a platitudinous and paradoxical message of interracial harmony.⁹³ More problematic still was the presentation of what Marshall Berman accurately described as an "extravagantly idealized" version of a "familial and ethnic past" in which "all ancestors are beautiful, noble and heroic" and "all pain and hate and trouble spring from groups of oppressors 'outside.' " For Berman, the resultant production consequently lacked "the depth to transform empathy into real understanding," and *Roots* thereby failed to contribute to the generation of "a modern ethnic awareness."⁹⁴ However, *Roots* made an undeniable cultural impact, and its impressive audience figures suggested that a major Hollywood movie about slavery might be commercially viable after all. It took until the 1990s before a Hollywood studio was prepared to test the waters.

If anyone could crack the 1990s mass market with a slavery film made for the multiplex, then surely it would be Hollywood's director of blockbusters par excellence: Steven Spielberg. Riding high after the success of *Schindler's List*, Spielberg (in)famously stated that his aspiration was to do "for the American experience of slavery what *Schindler's List* [had done] for the Holocaust."[95] Spielberg's aspiration would remain unfulfilled. Unlike *Schindler's List*, Spielberg's 1997 slavery film, *Amistad*, was a box-office disappointment.[96] Despite the marketing power of the Spielberg name and DreamWorks's deep pockets, the US returns barely covered the production costs.[97] *Amistad* is at its core a misleading legal drama. It tells the story of the February 1839 slave insurrection aboard the *Amistad* and ends triumphantly with the US Supreme Court's 1841 decision that the rebels' enslavement had been illegal and that they were thus free under American law.[98] While the film suggests that the Supreme Court decided the rebels' case on the basis of broad principles of liberty and justice, the rebels were in fact held to be free on a technicality. Several points are worthy of emphasis. First, it is notable that *Amistad* celebrated African, not African American, agency but even so displays only a superficial curiosity about African culture. Second, it is noteworthy that Spielberg's representation of Cinque, the exceptionally beautiful and eloquent African leader of the rebellion, is of a piece with his appropriation by mid-nineteenth century abolitionists who discovered that he could be "easily absorbed into extant tropes for the representation of the African prince."[99] And third, and I suggest most significantly, despite the catalyst for the film's narrative being a slave-ship rebellion, the American legal system emerges as the film's true hero. The coherence of this position is of course dependent on legal historical ignorance. Not only does *Amistad* misrepresent the case that is the film's subject, but its suggestion that the nineteenth-century US Supreme Court was in any way a reliable moral compass on questions of race cannot be squared with the court's history. *Dred Scott* in 1856 (which held that African Americans, whether free or enslaved, were not United States citizens and that enslaved persons were legal property and consequently rightless) and *Plessy v. Ferguson* in 1896 (which upheld the "separate but equal" doctrine of racial segregation)— both cases that were heard *after* the *Amistad* case—serve to demonstrate the delusions of imbuing the nineteenth-century Supreme Court with a progressive racial politics.[100] However, as we will see, Spielberg's *Amistad* did set a precedent for the celebration of liberal law—and an obsession with abolition—in the slavery films that would appear in the first two decades of the twenty-first century.

We have established that the representation in positive terms of Black resistance to slavery is a rarity in the history of Hollywood. However, the representation of the abolition of slavery is most certainly not. In the years since the bicentenary of the British 1807 Abolition of the Slave Trade Act and the sesquicentennials of the American Civil War of 1861–1865, the 1863 Emancipation Proclamation, and the 1865 Thirteenth Amendment to the US Constitution, there has been an upsurge in cinematic attention to the history of abolition. Strikingly, these "abolition films" offer no new perspectives of their own. Instead, they recycle in various ways "the terribly convincing and very joyful lies" that emerged in nineteenth-century cultural materials generated by the legal abolition of slavery in Britain and North America.[101] One especially debilitating fiction within this celebratory discourse of abolitionism has been the idea that abolition was a "gift" codified in law that was generously given by whites to Blacks. In this discourse, law is configured as the receptacle and guarantor of freedom, and Black resistance to slavery is typically marginalized or written out altogether. By this strategy, the history of slavery is transfigured into a platform for the celebration of *white* moral indignation and courageous political leadership via attention to a quasi-canonized set of white patriarchs conceived of as glorious, philanthropic, moral crusaders. In the British and American contexts, the key figures are Thomas Clarkson, William Wilberforce, William Lloyd Garrison, and Abraham Lincoln. White female abolitionists—consider, inter alia, Mary Wollstonecraft, Sarah and Angelina Grimké, and Maria Chapman—are generally excluded from this hallowed canon. Curiously, moreover, within a multiplicity of visual materials celebrating abolition they are typically replaced by "a variety of female abstract personifications—Justice, Liberty, Britannia, Columbia, Brasilia."[102] Black abolitionists, male and female—consider, inter alia, Olaudah Equiano, Frederick Douglas, Harriet Tubman, Frances Harper, and Sojourner Truth—are typically banished altogether. Evidence that this partial and delusional mode of remembering slavery and abolition remains hegemonic in Britain and North America can be found in the abolition films of recent years. Take, for example, the previously mentioned 2006 film *Amazing Grace*, which was made to extol the 1807 Slave Trade Act and glorify Wilberforce.[103] Rather as Spielberg's *Amistad* had celebrated the American legal system and the US Supreme Court in defiance of overwhelming historical evidence, *Amazing Grace* transfigures the 1807 Act into a secular-holy text, a high-water mark of humanitarian ethics when in reality it was no such thing. On this point, Marcus Wood's analytic précis of the act's language, which he dubs "grim" and "nit-picking," is instructive: "Its main concerns have nothing to do with the rights of emancipated blacks. The text is really concerned to define the manner in which the black body can continue to be exploited . . . The act is at no point celebratory about the arrival of liberty; indeed the words *freedom* and *liberty* are not mentioned."[104]

What the 1807 Act actually did is little understood. Among its primary concerns was the dismantling of the complex insurance business the slave trade had required and the regulating of the new state-sanctioned slave bounty-hunter industry the act inaugurated. British slave patrol ships would now scour the high seas for contraband slaves for profit. Each captured slave had a value in "head money" and came with a cut for the king. Once in British possession, enslaved men were enlisted into the British army or navy and dispatched to fight in Britain's imperial wars. The act explicitly denied pension rights to these coerced soldiers and sailors. It also entrapped captured slave women and children in a fourteen-year debt-bondage arrangement. But, of course, attention to what the act actually said and did is hardly conducive to the making of a feel-good movie. Snubbing Black voices, excising Black suffering and agency, and making countless errors of historical fact, *Amazing Grace* was nevertheless a critical and popular success in both the UK and the US.

Steven Spielberg's *Lincoln* biopic of 2012, which presents Lincoln as a Christlike redeemer of the American nation, suffers from comparable problems as *Amazing Grace*.[105] As fetishistic in its focus on the Thirteenth Amendment as *Amazing Grace* was on the 1807 Act, *Lincoln* has no enslaved characters and manages not to show a single enslaved person other than in photographs. Black revolutionary agency is consequently invisibilized in this triumphalist "great white man history" par excellence that in its eagerness to construct a domineering national mythology of liberal sympathy manages to displace both a worldly perspective and the project of reintegration. Steve McQueen's *12 Years a Slave* of 2013 will not be considered here since it is the subject of detailed analysis later, but at this juncture it should be noted that in common with *Amistad*, *Amazing Grace*, and *Lincoln*, *12 Years a Slave* fetishizes law, omits Black resistance, and gives its audience a heartthrob of an (entirely unbelievable) abolitionist in the form of Brad Pitt who plays the minor but critical character of

Samuel Bass, the tender-hearted Canadian who helps Solomon Northup secure his freedom and return to his family and home in New York state.

Quentin Tarantino's 2012 *Django Unchained*, a stylized revenge thriller that revives the archetype of the "Black cowboy," does not belong to the genre of the "abolition movie"; instead, its lineage can be traced to the plantation genre film. Like the plantation films that were released in Hollywood's "Golden Age," *Django Unchained* features a "Southern belle" who proudly defends the values of the Old South. It also revives the "Uncle Tom" stereotype but with an excessiveness that is inimitably characteristic of Tarantino. As Peter Bradshaw put it, "To make liberals everywhere uneasy, Tarantino and [Samuel L.] Jackson make Stephen the biggest, nastiest 'Uncle Tom' ever: utterly loyal to his white master, and severe in his management of the below-stairs race in the Big House."[106] For some of its critics, *Django Unchained* also evoked the plantation films of Hollywood's "Golden Age," as they considered it a fundamentally fictive and fraudulent appropriation of slavery offering only "an illusory sense of redemption for two fictional former slaves": Django, played by the effortlessly cool Jamie Foxx, and Broomhilda, Django's beautiful wife played by Kerry Washington.[107] Other critics could not look past the film's graphic and relentless depictions of extraordinarily brutal violence, insisting that Tarantino simply cannot have it both ways: "preposterous entertainment" such as *Django*, they argued, cannot at the same time be "taken seriously as a rewarding study of American slavery."[108]

By the time Nate Parker's controversial *The Birth of a Nation* movie premiered at the January 2016 Sundance Film Festival, there was a greater, but still deeply limited, appreciation in the North American public sphere of how race continued to function as a vector of ongoing discrimination and injustice. The fatal shooting in February 2012 of the Black American teenager Trayvon Martin, and the subsequent acquittal in July 2013 of his killer, George Zimmerman, prompted widespread condemnation. It also resulted in the founding of the Black Lives Matter movement, a collective committed to the eradication of white supremacy and to the protection of Black lives from both state and vigilante violence. Black Lives Matter quickly established an international reach and momentum while also provoking a predictable conservative countermovement that mobilized in 2014 under the slogan "All Lives Matter." Then, in July 2014, African American Eric Garner was killed in New York City by a white police officer who had placed him in a restraint while arresting him. No charges were ever brought against the arresting officer, and video footage of Garner's killing, which had been captured on a mobile phone, circulated widely, provoking condemnation and outrage among those committed to racial justice and equality. The following month, August 2014, saw the fatal shooting by a white police officer of another Black American teenager, Michael Brown, in Ferguson, Missouri. Then, in June 2015, twenty-one-year-old white supremacist Dylann Roof murdered nine African American men and women who were attending a bible-study group at the Emanuel African Methodist Episcopal Church in Charleston, South Carolina. These high-profile racial atrocities prompted attention to the embeddedness of racial injustice throughout American society, and some commentators sought structural and historical explanation. As Ta-Nehisi Coates put it in an influential 2014 article titled "The Case for Reparations," published in *The Atlantic*: "Two hundred fifty years of slavery. Ninety years of Jim Crow. Sixty years of separate but equal. Thirty-five years of racist housing policy. Until we reckon with our compounding moral debts, America will never be whole."[109]

Also in the mid-2010s, Hollywood was proving itself a place of institutionalized racism (in case there was any doubt). In both 2015 and 2016 there were no Oscar nominees of color. Such was the context for Nate Parker's *The Birth of a Nation*, a movie by a Black actor making his directorial debut based on the Nat Turner slave rebellion of August 1831. Explicitly seeking to supplant Griffiths's *The Birth of a Nation* of 1915, Parker had high hopes for the political impact his film might have.[110] Appearing as it did in the post-Ferguson Black Lives Matter cultural-political moment, Parker's hope appeared timely. However, though adored at Sundance, by the time the movie was officially released the reviews had turned lukewarm at best.[111] The consensus among both academic and popular critics was that the film failed to realize the enormous filmic potential of the Nat Turner rebellion.[112] Regrettably, Parker's *The Birth of a Nation* was a box-office disaster.

Parker's *The Birth of a Nation*, for all its weaknesses, remains an important film simply for the fact that it was the first attempt to give cinematic form to the most famous slave revolt on American soil. However, the lack of attention from within Hollywood to the most spectacular instance of Black revolution in the Americas, the Haitian Revolution, is striking—*Lydia Bailey* notwithstanding. Indeed, Hollywood's aversion to the filmic potential of the extraordinary historical events that took place in the French colony of Saint Domingue between 1791 and 1804 has become notorious. Over the years, a number of high-profile film projects centered on the Haitian Revolution have been attempted but have failed. The diverse and illustrious list of filmmakers, actors, and artists who have attempted a film about the Haitian Revolution includes Sergei Eisenstein, Richard Wright, and Danny Glover.[113] The hostility and paranoia exhibited in Hollywood toward the Haitian Revolution was treated as a source of satire by the comedian, actor, and filmmaker Chris Rock in his independently produced film of 2014, *Top Five*, which has been the subject of analysis by Alyssa Goldstein Sepinwall.[114] Rock's *Top Five* tells the story of the fictional Black actor and director André Allen who decides to make a film about the Haitian Revolution. Comic and incisive social satire ensues: "Allen enthusiastically tells others about the significance of [the Haitian Revolution] and he urges them to see his film. However, *Top Five*'s white characters have never heard of the Haitian Revolution, and they are hostile to a film about slave revolt, because it chronicles Black violence against whites. Allen's film within a film becomes a catastrophic flop."[115] *Top Five* thus pointed out, with sharpness and wit, the barriers that exist within the United States to the making of a film about the Haitian Revolution and, more broadly, Hollywood's "near-total disinterest in portraying Black revolutionaries sympathetically."[116] Instead, Haiti's filmic representational history in Hollywood bears witness to its excessive imperialist denigration. Colorful takes on Haitian "voodoo," zombies, and a derogatory general emphasis on "black magic" and witchcraft have for long predominated in films impinging on Haiti's revolutionary history. Consider, for example, Victor Halperin's 1932 film *White Zombie*, the first feature-length zombie movie, which was based on William Seabrook's 1929 novel *The Magic Island*, as well as more recent productions such as *The Serpent and the Rainbow*, Wes Craven's sensationalist adaptation of Wade Davis's anthropological work.[117]

Although Hollywood's enduring hostility to the subject of Black resistance to slavery should by now be clear, Kasi Lemmons's Harriet Tubman biopic of 2019 constitutes an example that breaks with some of the dominant themes and tropes we have identified, including the construction of abolition as a white gift and the near-total dismissal of Black female political agency.[118] *Harriet* communicates the drama of Tubman's self-emancipation and foregrounds her self-reliance as well as her willingness to place herself in danger as a principled and daring "conductor" on the Underground Railroad. Significantly, the film also ruptures Hollywood's established character archetypes for Black women by portraying Tubman's transformation into "Moses the Slave Stealer" and an armed, disciplined, and capable leader. However, the film is not without its shortcomings, and on examination their ideological pattern can be discerned. *Harriet* is silent on reactionary politics north of the Mason–Dixon line in the years leading up to the Civil War (the whys and wherefores of the passage of the Fugitive Slave Act of 1850—a critical moment in the film—go unexplored and unexplained). Moreover, the film also fails to identify the universalism at the core of Tubman's emancipatory project. Some comparable criticisms are also pertinent to *12 Years a Slave* and will be elaborated in the discussion to come. Nevertheless, the existence of a Tubman biopic at all should be considered a landmark in the history of Hollywood. The film took some twenty-five years to reach the screen: the script, which was first drafted in the early 1990s by Gregory Allen Howard, one of the most successful African American screenwriters to have worked in Hollywood, was snubbed for more than twenty years.[119] Howard credits the commercial and critical success of *12 Years a Slave* as the pivotal event that generated the context in which a movie about Harriet Tubman finally became realizable. However, the legacy of *12 Years a Slave* is double-edged: while it helped open the doors to *Harriet*, it also apparently made viable a production as ill-considered as *The Underground Railroad*, a 2021 television miniseries produced by Amazon Studios.[120] As the critic Joanne Laurier has noted, the series (which has otherwise received high critical praise) is unconstrained by actual history, and the alternative history of slavery it serves up is evidence of the profoundly problematic place at which mainstream representations of slavery on screen have arrived after more than 120 years.[121]

While the ideas and evidence presented in the historiographical tradition that established the actuality of Black agency throughout the history of Atlantic slavery have registered only rarely within Hollywood, it must be acknowledged that they have long inflected the work of independent filmmakers as well as filmmakers working in other settings. Films centered on Black agency and slave resistance do exist, but they are often hard-to-find, low-budget affairs, and/or they are made far from the metropolitan centers of imperialist domination. Consider, for example, the works of two canonical independent American filmmakers: John Sayles and Charles Burnett. Sayles's *The Brother from Another Planet* (1984) is superficially a droll, shaggy-dog tale set in 1980s Harlem. However, it interweaves science fiction with sociological analysis to reveal itself as a meditation on contemporary American life, which it finds to be segregated and profoundly alienated. This socially degraded life, the film implies, must be thought in relation to the insidious inheritance of American slavery. The film's protagonist is the titular "Brother," a three-toed, mute, humanoid alien with a variety of unusual powers who passes for a Black human man. Throughout the movie, he is tracked by two mysterious white men attired in black suits, one of whom is played by Sayles. These men, who are both threatening and absurd, have been described by the critic David Shumway as "interplanetary bounty hunters" and their aura is ominously Kafkaesque.[122] The Brother's wanted status, his longing for freedom, and the prejudice and repression he encounters combine to mark him out as a science-fictional fugitive slave. However, the Brother is not the only character on a quest for freedom. One of the film's many comic sequences involves two middle-aged white males from Indiana who have traveled to New York City to attend a university conference on "self-actualization." Lost in more ways than one, they stumble into an African American bar in Harlem, the regulars of which have taken the Brother in to provide him with support and a place of refuge. The two tourists awkwardly attempt to engage the Brother in conversation, but, being mute, he of course says nothing. Sayles thereby sets up a memorably parodic indictment of white American paranoia and the vastness of America's race- and class-based divisions. That the tourists are unaware of the Brother's alien identity imbues the exchange with a dramatic irony that enhances the satirical effect. However, the film does offer a positive, as well as a critical, vision. Black agency takes both individual and communal forms, and meaningful victories are won. The Brother is methodical and ultimately successful in his pursuit of a drug baron after his discovery of a young Black woman who has died of a heroin overdose. Additionally, while Harlem is in a state of decay, the multiracial staff of Harlem's welfare office—a state agency—provide empowering and needed assistance. Also significant is the film's depiction of the Black community taking united action in the Brother's defense when the mysterious men in black finally catch up to their alien. Furthermore, in the film's denouement, the men in black become the hunted—not the hunters—when other alien fugitives from slavery arrive to assist the Brother. In *The Brother from Another Planet*, individual action, a caring community, a progressive state, and group solidarity all have a role to play in the securing of liberty and the possibility of a better future.

Differing markedly from the extravagant science-fictional satire of *Brother from Another Planet* are *Nightjohn* (1996) and *Nat Turner: A Troublesome Property* (2003), two films by Charles Burnett whom the critic Jonathan Rosenbaum has considered America's "most gifted and important black filmmaker."[123] *Nightjohn* is a slavery movie intended for family audiences, while *Nat Turner: A Troublesome Property* is a documentary film that offers a thoughtful overview of Turner and the endless disagreement generated by his rebellion. *Nightjohn* was originally made for television and is an adaptation of a successful young adult novella, *Sarny* by Gary Paulsen. Such was *Nightjohn*'s positive critical reception that the critic James Naremore reports that Disney, who had coproduced the film with Hallmark, "offered to give away free VHS copies as a public service, but rescinded the offer when the demand became too great."[124] *Nightjohn* tells the story of a twelve-year old enslaved girl named Sarny and the transformational impact on her life of her friendship with the eponymous Nightjohn, a fugitive from slavery who teaches her to read and write. Notwithstanding the limitations imposed by its format, modest budget, and rushed filming schedule, *Nightjohn* conveys the systemic terror of slavery and even affords its audience some insight into slavery's function in the political economy of the antebellum American South. The inherently liberatory and subversive power of literacy is conveyed with clarity and economy, and the film is to a remarkable extent unblemished by the characteristics that would mark it out as a "typical Disney product."[125]

Burnett's *Nat Turner* documentary is another kind of film entirely, and it is particularly strong when it comes to demonstrating that the battle over the meaning of Nat Turner has always been an intensely ideological struggle that has produced polarizing and incompatible points of view. Burnett employs a variety of documentary techniques—dramatic reenactment, "talking-head" interviews, and archival images—to demonstrate that Turner exists as an endlessly mutable and mysterious cultural icon who lends himself to both sympathetic recuperation and demonization. The striking achievement of Burnett's documentary, however, is the way it resists a descent into endless relativism. The scarcity of reliable historical information we have about Turner's life will ensure that he remains a "troublesome" subject, but Burnett nevertheless makes clear that Turner's desire for freedom was explicable and ethical.

Another low-budget and little-known film that considers Black agency in the context of slavery is the French, Senegalese, and Martinican coproduction *Le passage du milieu*, directed by Guy Deslauriers and scripted by Claude Chonville and Patrick Chamoiseau. Completed in 1999 and released in France in 2001, an English-language adaptation titled *The Middle Passage* appeared shortly thereafter. The English-language version, which boasts a narration written by the renowned African American crime fiction novelist Walter Mosley, eventually made its way onto DVD format in 2003. *The Middle Passage* is an experimental docufiction film that posits the slave ship as a locus of unimaginable horror and suffering but also as an incubator of a new, Creole identity. The film, the critic Sophie Saint-Just has observed, is "deliberately crafted as a non-pleasurable didactic experience."[126] Deslauriers's film thus evokes the view of the English Romantic–period radical writer William Hazlitt, who wrote of the Middle Passage that it "involuntarily staggers and appals the mind" and that it was "a mass of evil so monstrous and unwarranted" that it cannot "be endured, even in thought."[127] The film's depiction of Black agency centers on the way in which the slave ship served to bring together African peoples of disparate origins who nevertheless consequently formed social bonds and who would over time collectively develop what Paul Gilroy described as a "Black Atlantic counterculture of modernity."[128]

The 1993 production *Sankofa*, which was directed by the Ethiopian filmmaker Haile Gerima, also constitutes an attempt to represent Black resistance to slavery on the big screen. *Sankofa* tells the story of a Black American fashion model named Mona who is transported back in time to the Lafayette plantation in the antebellum South, where she is transformed into an enslaved domestic worker named Shola whose capacity for defiance grows throughout the film.[129] Consider also the trilogy of slavery films by the celebrated Brazilian filmmaker Carlos Diegues: *Ganga Zumba* (1963), *Xica da Silva* (1976), and *Quilombo* (1984). While the trilogy undeniably charts Diegues's retreat from a radical, oppositional politics to a celebratory cultural politics, they remain significant as attempts to recuperate the theme of Afro-Brazilian self-liberation within national Brazilian discourse. The first film of the trilogy, *Ganga Zumba*, invites a reading from the perspective of a Fanonian Marxist-Leninism. As Robert Stam puts it, it is "an ode to black liberation" inspired by the legend of Palmares, the largest and most enduring community of fugitives from slavery in the Americas, and the heroic Ganga Zumba and Zumbi dos Palmares, the two most-celebrated leaders of Palmares. The enormously popular *Xica da Silva* of 1976, on the other hand, draws together comedy and tragedy under a carnivalesque theme.[130] This filmic version of the story of "the slave who became queen" is an attempt to revitalize the legend of

Xica da Silva as an anti-imperialist nationalist heroine. However, for all its ostensible anti-racism and its presentation of female Black agency, its depiction of its lead character falls foul of exoticizing sexism and racism. Finally, *Quilombo*, a culturalist utopian appropriation of the Palmares legend, fuses the subject matter of *Ganga Zumba* with *Xica*'s carnivalesque theme. It also adds its own distinctive elements including a theatrical and fantastical mise-en-scène and spectacular visuals that anticipate elements of an Afro-Futurist aesthetic. *Quilombo* also provides mesmeric and heroic portraits of Ganga Zumba, Zumbi, and the often-neglected figure of Dandara, Zumbi's wife who is presented as an inspirational revolutionary warrior and a key citizen of Palmares. However, unlike the earlier *Ganga Zumba*, *Quilombo* eschews revolutionary politics. Instead, released in 1984 in the final days of Brazil's military dictatorship, *Quilombo* eagerly anticipates a multiracial, democratic Brazil for which Palmares is posited as an antecedent model. Yet, for all its visual charisma, its sense of humor, and its proud celebration of Afro-Brazilian resistance, *Quilombo* is silent on the dilemma of how its class-free, multiracial utopian vision might be made to fit within a capitalist society.

Thus, a project examining representations of slave resistance on screen must be alert not only to "rogue" or atypical examples that have emerged within Hollywood, but also to examples produced by independent filmmakers and in the national cinematic traditions of the former "Third World."[131] *From Havana to Hollywood: Slave Resistance in the Cinematic Imaginary* thus considers films either representing or eliding slave resistance produced in either Havana or Hollywood. The locations of Havana and Hollywood are vividly contrasting contexts, and this contrast undergirds the book's comparative frame that is attentive to differences arising from the production of commercial cinema in the context of a market economy and the production of cinema in the context of socialist, revolutionary Cuba. The first chapter addresses Gillo Pontecrovo's *Burn!*, which I maintain is very much a "renegade" Hollywood production that bears the imprint of its independently minded director and that narrates a story of anti-slavery, anticolonial, and anti-imperial resistance in a manner that forces comparison with the Haitian Revolution.[132] Filmed on a set location in Colombia and starring Marlon Brando alongside Afro-Colombian, British, and American nonprofessional actors, I argue that *Burn!* bridges "mass" and "elite" culture and should be recognized as a film that fuses the traditions of "First," "Second," and "Third" cinema. Chapters two and three argue that we can identify a radical restoration of Black agency in the works of two giants of Cuban cinema: Tomás Gutiérrez Alea and Sergio Giral. I argue that the corpus of Cuban films examined here, all produced in the 1970s—*La última cena* by Alea and *El otro Francisco, Rancheador,* and *Malualua* by Giral—are searing, innovative, aesthetically accomplished, and politically engaged films that offer perspectives that effectively reveal the limitations of Hollywood slavery films.[133] Finally, chapter four offers a detailed reading Steve McQueen's *12 Years a Slave* and argues that, notwithstanding the film's progressive aspirations, it inadvertently gives new life to sentimental ways of apprehending the history of slavery.[134] Comparing McQueen's adaptation to Solomon Northup's original text, I identify systemic patterns of omission and addition that blunt the film's effectiveness as a vehicle for a progressive racial politics. I draw out the situation and ideological thrust of each of the works under examination, considering how each film reconfigures, or fails to register, the history of Black resistance to slavery via differing aesthetic strategies and innovations. I elaborate the existence of a radical, alternative filmic tradition and place the perspectives of marginalized filmmakers in dialogue with those of filmmakers whose works have achieved positions of cultural dominance. This study critically examines a corpus of films that have reckoned with slavery's inheritance and considers their productive capacities and limitations. Implicit throughout is the question: How might the medium of film contribute to a renewal of emancipatory politics today?

Chapter 1

"Our First Cry of Freedom"

From Revolution to Liberation in Gillo Pontecorvo's *Burn!*

JOSÉ DOLORES: Freedom is something you take for yourself.

—*Burn!* screenplay[1]

In his 1988 essay "The Quest for Gillo Pontecorvo," Edward Said offered his opinion that he considered Gillo Pontecorvo's *The Battle of Algiers* (1966) and *Burn!* (1969) to be "the two greatest political films ever made."[2] Given the seminal status of *The Battle of Algiers* in cinematic history, it is a safe assumption that at least one half of Said's assessment will not have raised many eyebrows. *The Battle of Algiers*, a stunning neorealist reenactment of events that took place in the years 1954–1957 in the capital city of Algiers during the Algerian war of independence, is widely and justly regarded as one of the greatest anticolonial films of all time. Pontecorvo had already, and unexpectedly, achieved international recognition with his previous feature film, the Holocaust drama *Kapò* (1960), but the impact of *The Battle of Algiers* was on a different scale altogether. Shot in a grainy black and white to impart the visual aesthetics of newsreel footage, *The Battle of Algiers* is a devastating condemnation of French direct colonial rule in Algeria.[3] Banned in France until 1970 and not screened in Paris until October 1971, it was however lavished with praise, prizes, and awards, and it remains a widely watched and commented-on film that "shows little sign of aging."[4]

Burn!, on the other hand—Said's high praise notwithstanding—has never commanded quite the same cultural currency as its more celebrated predecessor, and its place in film history is much more equivocal. *Burn!* narrates a story of slave resistance and revolution on a fictionalized Caribbean island called "Quiemada" that at the outset of the film is a Portuguese slave colony. The plot centers on the awakening of a revolutionary consciousness among the enslaved population and the rivalry of imperialist nations in the capitalist world-system. It is the late 1830s and Britain wishes to foment a slave revolution to destabilize the colony, oust the Portuguese, and install the local white bourgeoisie as the leaders of a nominally independent state. By this strategy, the British intend to break up the Portuguese sugar monopoly that was a result of the colonial mercantile system that granted colonizing powers exclusive access to the produce of their own colonies. As a consequence, this would enable the British Royal Sugar Company to enter into and subsequently dominate the lucrative business of buying and selling Queimada's sugar on the global marketplace. Abolitionist Britain's embrace of "free labor" and "free trade," then, it is revealed, is driven not by white philanthropic humanitarianism, but by the desire for profits and imperialist hegemony. The means by which the British intend to achieve their objective is by striking up an alliance with the colony's discontented bourgeois settler class and manipulating Black resistance against the Portuguese for their own purpose. A rebel maroon named Santiago has been identified as a threat to the Portuguese, and a British agent is dispatched to Queimada to foment and orchestrate the resistance. However, the British plan is foiled before it could even begin: Santiago has been caught and he and his men executed. With Santiago dead, and the enslaved population apparently cowed and fearful, Britain's aspirations for imperialist domination in Queimada appear to have been thwarted. However, all this changes when—by chance—the British agent encounters a Black porter whom he identifies as possessing all the necessary attributes to lead a revolution. The enslaved population rises up, the Portuguese governor is assassinated, and the local bourgeoisie are installed as nominal leaders of an independent Queimada. The British appear to have gotten their way: Queimada's sugar and profits are theirs while the formerly enslaved population, having been outmaneuvered by both the British and the puppet Quiemadan government, are freed from slavery but denied political power and forced to return to the plantations as low-paid laborers.

Ten years pass but, refusing to be manipulated endlessly, the oppressed Black population rises up once again in defiance of their subjugation.

The British, having instigated Black insurrection on the island ten years previously, now send in their army to wage a total war of genocidal and environmental destruction to put down the new Black revolution and to capture the very same revolutionary leader they had cultivated. However, despite burning much of the island to cinders—including entire villages that had provided support to the rebel guerillas—and carrying out massacres and atrocities, *Burn!* shows that Black resistance will reemerge and that a yearning for liberation endures through all. *Burn!* thus recalls the words of Toussaint Louverture, the heroic leader of the Haitian Revolution: in Queimada, as in revolutionary Saint Domingue, Black freedom "will spring up again by the roots for they are numerous and deep."[5] The film thus communicates a powerful condemnation of colonial and neocolonial interference and insists upon the cause of liberation as an ethical imperative for the dispossessed.

The viewer is drawn into this explicitly political and intricate plot primarily via the film's two thoroughly compelling lead characters. On the one hand, there is Sir William Walker, a charming but Machiavellian English agent employed first by the British Admiralty and later by the British Royal Sugar Company. Walker—fascinating, intelligent, and seductive—is played with charismatic aplomb by Marlon Brando, sumptuously attired in "billowing scarves, pale, chic linens, [and] riding boots"[6] (fig. 1.1). On the other hand, there is José Dolores, a Black porter who

Figure 1.1. Marlon Brando as Sir William Walker attired with a lavender scarf, *Burn! Source:* Gillo Pontecorvo, dir., *Quemada* (*Burn!*) (Produzioni Europee Associati, 1969).

becomes a revolutionary leader and the film's transcendent hero, who is played with remarkable presence and magnetism by the Afro-Colombian nonprofessional actor Evaristo Márquez, memorably described by one critic as having the appearance of "a mahogany saint"[7] (fig. 1.2).

Much of the film's dramatic energy and appeal derives from the on-screen relationship between these two lead characters, one an imperialist mercenary and the other a Black revolutionary leader of profound moral fortitude and conviction who becomes a Fanonian hero. Throughout the film, their relationship is variously configured as one of master-pupil, father-son, friends, rivals, and, finally, enemies. Neither man will survive the narrative, but by the film's end, Dolores's victory over Walker is without doubt. Dolores dies a martyr, hanged by the British, his example and the ideals for which he gave his life animating the continuing struggle. Walker, on the other hand, is slain by an unnamed rebel who is projected as a successor to Dolores. As Dolores had been, Walker's killer is a Black porter. This heavy symbolism transmits the lesson that the French General Charles Leclerc had belatedly learned in the course of the Haitian Revolution but which the British in Queimada had not yet fully appreciated: the counterrevolution requires more than the elimination of a solitary leader

Figure 1.2. Evaristo Márquez as José Dolores striking a pose that evokes the iconography of Toussaint Louverture, *Burn! Source:* Gillo Pontecorvo, dir., *Quemada (Burn!)* (Produzioni Europee Associati, 1969).

since there are many thousands of rebel leaders in waiting.[8] As Walker collapses—in broad daylight on a rubble-strewn and bustling street beside the docked ship he was about to board—Ennio Morricone's marvelous musical motif "Osanna" begins to play, a triumphant paean to resistance that begins with a chorus of voices that recalls the ululation of the women in the Casbah in *The Battle of Algiers*. This musical accompaniment makes clear that the deeper significance of the scene is not in Walker's death itself but in its depiction of the rebirth of resistance. Yet, uncertainty remains: Does Walker's death signify confidence in a revolutionary future or is a new cycle of violence about to begin?[9] In *Burn!*, the realization of liberation appears as endlessly deferred, a process rather than a point of arrival. Augmenting the emotional power of the death scene is the fact that Walker hears his killer's voice before he sees his face and he mistakes the voice for that of Dolores. This mistake affords Walker the fleeting fantasy that somehow his former friend cheated death and avoided his fate of execution. However, Walker's joy is short lived, as the rebel dispatches him with a single knife blow to the abdomen. Walker dies disillusioned and distraught, mourning Dolores, cognizant of the appalling horrors for which he is responsible, and painfully aware that for all his brilliance, his was a life wasted fighting on the wrong side of history.

The analysis that follows in this chapter will argue for a sympathetic rereading of *Burn!* as a landmark example of a radical approach to the challenges of rendering "slavery on screen." *Burn!* foregrounds Black agency and contends that expansionist, modern, capitalist imperialism is the deep causal explanation for the suffering of the oppressed and that, therefore, neither abolition nor formal independence are necessarily guarantors of liberation. Instead, in narrating what Natalie Zemon Davis has described as "a fictional parable of linked historical transitions from slave regime to free labor; from old imperial colony to independent nation dominated by foreign capital," *Burn!* formidably demands nothing less than a revolutionary challenge to the hegemonic global imperialist order.[10] Nevertheless, *Burn!* finds reasons for belief that progressive social transformation may be possible in historical incidences of Black resistance from across the Americas that are evoked throughout. Further, as with the examples we will consider in the chapters to come on later slavery films by Tomás Gutiérrez Alea and Sergio Giral, and in contrast to Steve McQueen's *12 Year's A Slave*, *Burn!* constitutes a rebuke to any attempt to configure slavery in antiquarian or feudalistic terms. Instead, as a corollary to its critique of capitalist imperialism, *Burn!* shows the formative role slavery played in the creation of the modern self and the modern world. In a manner that recalls Eric Williams's argument in *Capitalism and Slavery*, *Burn!* shows that slavery rose and fell in correlation to the demands and desires of the economies of the imperialist powers, and that slavery was supplanted by neocolonial systems of labor exploitation.[11] However, the horizon of self-liberation—a principle of hope that sustains resistance as a politics of principle—retains its powerful magnetism for the dispossessed throughout. While other sympathetic scholarly readings of *Burn!* are not hard to find, even a cursory examination of the scholarly literature generated by Pontecorvo's *Burn!* reveals a striking lack of consensus.[12] Therefore, this chapter provides a critical sketch of the contrary scholarly responses to *Burn!* in order to situate my own argument for a new and sympathetic rereading. The chapter proceeds upon a critical examination of *Burn!* that first considers its bridging of "mass" and "elite" culture, a consideration that takes inspiration from Fredric Jameson's virtuoso and now-canonical reading of Joseph Conrad's *Lord Jim* and *Nostromo* in *The Political Unconscious*.[13] Then, the circumstances of *Burn*'s genesis within Hollywood will be considered in juxtaposition to Pontecorvo's singular artistic and political vision; this reveals a film marked by a confluence of the characteristics of "First," "Second," and "Third" Cinema.[14] Finally, the film's Césairean and Fanonian critique is elaborated in relation to the anti-imperialist politics of Third Cinema. The argument throughout seeks to provide a layered and nuanced critical construction of Pontecorvo's *Burn!* that reveals a radical avowal of revolution and resistance and an affirmation of Black agency in history, even while it promises no certainty of conclusive victory.

Burn!'s Critical Reception:
A Radical Masterpiece or a "Benevolent Banalization"?[15]

Given *Burn*'s compelling narrative of extraordinary scope, depth, and complexity—it exceeds *The Battle of Algiers* on all three of these measures—it is a matter of considerable disappointment that *Burn!* did not meet with greater popular and critical success. While a 2004 cinematic rerelease of a restored print of the uncut Italian version of the film did attract renewed critical attention—positive and negative—the critic Carlo Celli has noted that on its initial release *Burn!* "received a cool public and critical reception" and that it arguably remains Pontecorvo's "most undervalued film."[16] Celli's view echoes Joan Mellen's assertion made in 1972 that "Gillo Pontecorvo's *Burn!* must surely be one of the most underrated films of recent years."[17] Some explanation for the film's underwhelming reception is to be found in the circumstances of its release. *Burn!* was released—or, as the critic Pauline Kael put it, was "dumped"—without fanfare, advance screenings, or publicity by a fearful United Artists who wished to distance themselves from the film's incendiary politics.[18] Nevertheless, some critics and audiences—particularly, but not exclusively, those outside the core capitalist countries—were, from the outset, enthusiastic.[19] For example, its attention to matters of slave resistance, revolution, and imperialism ensured that it made a profound impact on many Third World filmmakers (as had *The Battle of Algiers* before it), while film critics in various locations within Europe's southern periphery—Italy, Spain, and Turkey—were notably more enthusiastic than critics elsewhere.[20] And in North America and Britain, *Burn!* still plays fairly regularly on the art-house movie-theater circuits where its cult sensibility is admired by film enthusiasts who have long regarded it as an "overlooked gem."[21] Cinephiles have also long appreciated the film for Marlon Brando's "finely ambiguous" performance, which Brando himself considered as comprising "the best acting" of his entire career.[22] As a result, *Burn!* has always been in circulation in various formats—videocassette, DVD, and now online. However, scholarly critique has always been deeply divided over *Burn!*, along lines of disagreement that are easy to discern.

For some critics, *Burn*'s artistry, scope, ambition, and revolutionary message make it a movie to celebrate. For Charles Forsdick and Christian Høgsbjerg, for example, *Burn!* is "the film that has so far come closest to recognizing the revolutionary spirit of the enslaved men, women and children who made the Haitian Revolution" and constitutes "a glorious fusion of Black Power, anti-Vietnam war sentiment, and hardened anti-imperialist politics."[23] For Natalie Zemon Davis, *Burn*'s "beauty and complexity" carries it "beyond narrow didacticism."[24] These positive assessments echo a much-earlier defense of the film from its early critics by Joan Mellen: "Not since Eisenstein has a film so explicitly and with such artistry sounded a paen to the glory and moral necessity of revolution."[25]

Comparison with *The Battle of Algiers* also makes clear the scale of *Burn*'s achievement: while *The Battle of Algiers* focuses exclusively on colonial rule and anticolonial struggle, *Burn!* offers a more expansive analysis. While *The Battle of Algiers* homes in, with stunning clarity, on the historical moment of anticolonial struggle and decolonization in

Algeria in the years 1954–1957, *Burn!* directs our attention to an earlier history: that of the nominal conquest of independence and the abolition of slavery in the nineteenth-century Caribbean. Thus, the two films address distinct historical phases and geographical places of anticolonial and anti-imperialist struggle and conclude at different points in their historical trajectories. *The Battle of Algiers* concludes with the triumphant moment of the achievement of independence and so consequently does not address questions of neocolonialism. In *Burn!*, on the other hand, the moment of independence is not the source material for the film's climactic ending, which is more equivocal even as it affirms the inevitability of resistance to imperial domination. In *Burn!*, Queimada achieves independence midway through the film, and the first act of the new provisional government of the republic of Queimada (a government of and for the planter class and international capital) is to proclaim the abolition of slavery, but these matters of independence and abolition are in this case demonstrated to be merely the orchestrated precursors to indirect imperialist economic penetration and control. *Burn!* thus transposes into cinematic form Fanon's thesis that "the apotheosis of independence becomes the curse of independence."[26] The narrowness of Dolores's political options when attempting to negotiate a new political settlement with Quiemada's provisional government is revealed without equivocation. When the British envoy asks him pointedly, "What if Queimada were not to sell any more sugar? How would these people live?" Dolores has no answer. The point is then underscored by Walker:

> WALKER: "Who'll govern your island, José? Who'll run your industries? Who'll handle your commerce? Who'll cure the sick? Teach in your schools? . . . Civilization is not a simple matter José. You cannot learn its secrets overnight. Today civilization belongs to the white man, and you must learn to use it. Without it you cannot go forward."

Seeing no way out of the neocolonial trap, Dolores agrees to dissolve the rebel army and orders his men to return to the plantations. As such, the critic Mike Wayne has noted that *Burn!* "foregrounds precisely what is missing from *The Battle of Algiers*: economics, profits, the bourgeoisie, political maneuvering by western powers and the growth in political consciousness of the exploited."[27] *Burn!* thus registers what Fredric Jameson calls the "special case" of the history of Latin America's penetration by capital: the overthrowing of European colonialism throughout Latin America in the early nineteenth century, which opened up the continent's newly independent nations to neocolonial and imperialist manipulation at an earlier historical moment than occurred in Africa and Asia.[28] As a result, although both films have powerful contemporary twenty-first-century resonances—consider Palestine, Afghanistan, Iraq, and Haiti, to name only the most obvious examples—it is *Burn!*, not *The Battle of Algiers*, that wrestles with the question of how to oppose ongoing oppression resulting from the matrix of global imperialist capitalism that is our contemporary world order. Consider, for example, the fact that after the completion of the first phase of Walker's work in Queimada, his next assignment is in "Indo-China," mention of which is indicative of the global reach of nineteenth-century British capital and an oblique reference to the contemporary Vietnam War. This identification of capital's power to adapt continuously its mode of exploitation and to move with ease across the globe illustrates that independence should not be mistaken for liberation and compels us to reconsider the triumphant ending of *The Battle of Algiers*.

However, other prominent and more recent critics have been quick to find fault with the film. These criticisms have variously—and I will suggest, erroneously—maintained that *Burn!* undermines the historic actuality of the agency of enslaved Blacks, represents mixed-race women in a manner that revivifies the colonial tropical temptress trope, and treats Africans in exoticizing terms while making heroes of its bourgeois European characters. Both the historian Brenda Stevenson and the legal scholar Alan Stone, for example, claim that the film represents slaves as being incapable of resistance other than as part of a white organized conspiracy: "slave revolutionaries have to be duped into revolting" (Stevenson), and "there is a patronizing psychological assumption in *Queimada* that did not appear in *The Battle of Algiers*" (Stone).[29]

These assertions arise from the film's depiction of Walker's manipulation of Dolores, which, it is alleged, troubles the film's assertion of Black agency while the plotline evokes conspiracy theories as to the origins of the Haitian Revolution that serve to deny the political and interventionist capabilities of enslaved Blacks. While this chapter's argument as a whole constitutes a rebuttal of these assertions and the elaboration of a contrary reading, a specific response is nevertheless warranted. First, it should be noted that while initially successful, Walker's manipulation of Dolores is ultimately a failure. Second, it should also be noted that from beginning to end, *Burn!* directs our attention to the resistance of the dispossessed to their exploitation—from the sixteenth century to the twentieth century—and places it at the very centre of the history of empire. Black resistance on Queimada is shown to have preceded Walker's arrival and continues to exist after Walker's death. Resistance has fundamentally shaped the island's past and present, and it will continue to shape its future. Nor is Amerindian resistance overlooked: in the opening scene, Walker is informed that the island's name recalls the long history of Indigenous resistance that could only be quashed by a military strategy of genocidal, total destruction—the burning of the entire island in the sixteenth century. This foreshadows the utter destruction the British will wreak upon Queimada by the film's end: Walker will direct a brutal anti-guerilla war against Dolores and his rebels, with entire villages torched and their inhabitants massacred. Walker's scorched-earth strategy alludes to the use of napalm by the American military in Vietnam, while his anti-guerilla war recalls 1960s guerilla movements in Latin America and their repression by the United States, including the murder of Che Guevara in La Higuera, Vallegrande, Bolivia, on October 9, 1967. As such, the film's living anti-imperialist politics are clearly signaled and resistance to another empire in another century evoked. The effect is the production of a filmic constellation of anti-imperial resistance that criss-crosses the globe from the Atlantic world to southeast Asia, encompassing the British, Portuguese, and American empires, traversing a singular history of modernity from the sixteenth to the twentieth centuries.

Further, *Burn!* leaves its viewers in no doubt as to the independent existence of Black resistance on Queimada by its treatment of the Santiago episode. The rebel maroon leader, Santiago, needed no duping into revolt, and within the film's first ten minutes he has paid for his actions with his life: the viewer is forced to endure a horrific torture and execution scene as Santiago is garroted and beheaded. However, the manner of Santiago's execution speaks to the constant challenge the colonists faced in suppressing resistance. Santiago must be beheaded as well as garroted since the island's Black population are said to believe in reincarnation, which "requires a whole human body." A population that does not fear death, it is inferred, are even more difficult to keep in subservience. The Santiago episode is a horrific one that makes clear that slavery was far from a benign, paternalistic institution as some of its liberal apologists notoriously claimed, but it is also an episode that makes clear that the maintenance of slave society required a constant disciplining, punishing, and suppressing of resistance that emerged regardless as to whether or not imperial powers sought to co-opt it for their own ends.

"Our First Cry of Freedom" | 45

In a further demonstration of the power and vitality of Black agency, the film, in its denouement, demonstrates that Dolores ultimately triumphs over his would-be puppeteer, Walker, since Walker can no longer manipulate his protégé who has now outgrown him. This maturation, Pontecorvo has explained, was intended to herald symbolically the future triumph of the Third World, but it also reveals Dolores as an individual who has traveled a journey that we are invited to interpret in Fanonian and Césairean terms.[30] Pontecorvo, Zemon Davis writes, had read Fanon's *Les damnés de la terre*, but here it is the Fanon of *Peau noire, masques blancs* and Césaire's thesis of négritude that speaks to Dolores's triumphant claim to a reenergized subjectivity and an ethical self-confidence.[31] We will return to this argument for a reading of Dolores as an exemplar of a triumphant Fanonian psychological regeneration and Césairean négritude in some detail. But before then, consider also the film's final scene for its unequivocal representation of Black agency. After Walker is killed, the camera pans over many Black faces and figures, revolutionaries in waiting whose expressions and presences do not require speech: the oppressed are not mere pawns to be manipulated and will always seek to assert their agency (fig. 1.3). Contrary to the assertions of Stevenson and Stone, then, *Burn!* communicates that a consciousness of resistance and a capacity for

Figure 1.3. Revolutionaries in waiting, *Burn! Source:* Gillo Pontecorvo, dir., *Quemada (Burn!)* (Produzioni Europee Associati, 1969).

its praxis burns inextinguishably in the minds and bodies of enslaved and subjugated peoples whose ways of being and cultural practices always register a yearning for liberation.

A different critique of the film is advanced by Alyssa Goldstein Sepinwall who writes that the film's "frenzied dance scenes made the enslaved masses seem Other" and that "Pontecorvo's portrayal of mixed-race women in the colony as prostitutes" problematically reinforces racial stereotyping.[32] I suggest, on the contrary, that the dance scenes evoke the possibility of utopian transcendence and communal ways of being, while the film's representations of mixed-race prostitutes function as caustic social critique. Consider the following example: when, early on in the film, Walker inquires, "What can one do here . . . to avoid dying of boredom?" his host takes him to Queimada's brothel, which is reputed to be "the most famous brothel in the Lower Antilles." Queimadan settler society—patriarchal, bourgeois, and foul—is presented here by Pontecorvo in the basest of terms: inescapably degraded and combining racism, sexism, and moral laxity. In contrast to the social and cultural poverty of white settler life, Pontecorvo depicts the cultural life of the island's Black population as vibrant and dignified, involving music, singing, dance, rituals, elaborate and adorned clothing, and carnival festivities (fig. 1.4).

Figure 1.4. Carnival and Black cultural life in Queimada, *Burn! Source:* Gillo Pontecorvo, dir., *Quemada (Burn!)* (Produzioni Europee Associati, 1969).

Moreover, in a later scene, the film again depicts Queimada's white, male obsession with "mulatta" prostitutes to effect damning social and economic critique. Addressing an elite group of the colony's male bourgeois settlers, Walker polemically compares prostitution and marriage with metaphorical rhetoric that Walker concedes might appear "a trifle impertinent." As part of his manipulation, Walker encourages his audience to consider prostitution as simply a form of wage labor and marriage as an economic burden akin to the burden of slavery. Walker's discourse thus troubles arguments that would consider wage labor emancipatory and reveals the impulse toward reification at the heart of bourgeois capitalism. This scene, laced with contempt for the colony's settler class and the human and social degradation for which they are responsible, also serves to demonstrate the catastrophic consequences and ethical insufficiency of considering human relations in the terms of unfettered market fundamentalism, no matter how suavely it is presented as it is here by Brando's Walker.

And, as a final example of unsympathetic critique, consider Ella Shohat and Robert Stam's view that by casting Marlon Brando in the role of the charming imperialist villain, Pontecorvo set "one of the First World's most charismatic actors against a completely inexperienced Third World non-professional actor" with the disastrous result that "the scales of spectatorial fascination" are tipped decisively "in favor of the colonizer."[33] While Shohat and Stam do concede that this casting strategy might be read as a subversion of the Hollywood star system, the analysis fails to consider the productive tension generated by juxtaposing Walker's world view with the film's ideological thrust. In addition, while it would be foolhardy to deny the power of Brando's dazzling performance as Walker, Shohat and Stam's view nevertheless underestimates the considerable appeal of the nonprofessional Evaristo Márquez who, under Pontecorvo's direction, was able to portray Dolores in fascinating and iconic terms. Moreover, and I suggest crucially, also overlooked is the possibility that Brando's charismatic Walker actually constitutes a trap for the viewer who experiences profound discomfort when forced to witness how the beguiling Walker's ruthlessness and professionalism affords a capacity for the infliction of barbaric atrocities. As Danny Peary has noted, "for the first half of the picture, [Walker] is our hero. Pragmatic, intellectual, witty. He seems to genuinely like José and to be concerned about the plight of the Blacks on Queimada."[34] However, in the film's second half, when Walker returns to Queimada to capture Dolores, massacre his men, and burn the island, it becomes apparent that Pontecorvo and Brando have ensnared the viewer whose prior alignment with Walker becomes a source of discomfort. The impact of this entrapment, as Mike Wayne has argued, is dramatic: "The spectator realises that Walker cannot rise above his historical and class location within the colonial apparatus, and that his cynical amoralism conceals his own paralysis: he knows that the economic interests he fights for are vile, but he cannot commit himself to the black struggle."[35] Considered in these terms, the casting of Brando as Walker is anything but problematic. Instead, Brando's portrait of Walker as a man who is charming but despicable, Machiavellian but unable to discard a genuine fondness for Dolores, is a characterization of Conradian finesse that enjoins privileged viewers in the Global North to reconsider their sympathies and the nature and direction of their "spectatorial fascination."

Pontecorvo, Conrad, Jameson: *Burn!* as a Fusion Film

Having sketched the contours of ongoing critical disagreement over *Burn!*, its status as a "fusion" film that bridges "mass" and "high" culture can now be considered. As has already been suggested, *Burn!* rests uneasily in traditional film genre categories. While it contains elements of the romantic adventure movie in the style of a Hollywood "swashbuckler," Euro art cinema, and Third Cinema, it is not exclusively any one of these. Considered in this light, perhaps one of the reasons *Burn!* has proven such a divisive film has had to do with the difficulty—even after more than fifty years—of deciding exactly what kind of film it really is. Of course, *Burn!* is far from the first cultural work that has presented a seemingly intractable problem of classification, and here we can begin to seek a solution by turning to Fredric Jameson's seminal analysis of Conrad's *Lord Jim* and *Nostromo*.[36]

Conrad and Pontecorvo have been linked together before, most notably by the critics Natalie Zemon Davis and Carlo Celli. Davis noted Conradian echoes in *Burn!*, speculating that *Nostromo* had surely been in Pontecorvo's mind during the making of the film.[37] Davis's comparison is indeed a compelling one. While *Burn*'s explicit subjects include the Sisyphean nature of attempting to supress resistance to slavery and racially structured extreme capitalist exploitation, *Nostromo* takes for one of its explicit subjects "the futility of attempting to control a Latin American country from beyond its borders."[38] Celli offers an additional connection between Conrad and Pontecorvo, writing that *Burn*'s chief scriptwriter,

Franco Solinas, had a serious interest in Conrad's presentation and analysis of colonialism, and early drafts of the filmscript even employed flashback sequences reminiscent of those in Conrad's *Heart of Darkness*. Pontecorvo's aim in *Burn!*, Celli writes, was "to present the roots of colonialism in a manner that borrowed heavily" from his chief scriptwriter's interest in Conrad.[39] This intention is apparent from the film's opening scene, which can be interpreted as a cinematic homage to Conrad and which presents "a painted ship upon a painted ocean," a quintessentially double-edged Conradian image that evokes adventure and romance but also capitalist imperialism, slavery, European hegemony, and a symbol of Queimada's vulnerability to gunboat diplomacy.[40] "How many English ships are there?" asks Dolores. "Don't get too ambitious, José," comes Walker's wry reply.

Given these thematic parallels and influence, it becomes clear that we can reasonably consider Conrad as a literary antecedent for Pontecorvo. To an extent, the comparison is obvious: both Conrad and Pontecorvo were able to elevate the action-adventure genre, in its literary and filmic forms, into a vehicle for artworks with intensely political and psychological dimensions, and both identified colonialism as the inescapable structuring reality of their times—"the matrix of all our culture," as Pontecorvo once put it.[41] But the comparison works at more than the level of mere generality. For example, both Conrad and Pontecorvo share an apparent obsession for the portrayal of complex and captivating European imperialist villains. Consider, for example, "reports of Kurtz's gorgeous eloquence" in *Heart of Darkness*, "the admiring caresses lavished by the camera on [Colonel] Mathieu" in *The Battle of Algiers*, and the representation of William Walker in *Burn!* as "cunning, charming and handsome" and as "a free superintellectual."[42] I have already suggested that in *Burn!*, Brando's Walker operates as a trap for the viewer. In passing, I now suggest that considering Kurtz, Mathieu, and Walker in analogous terms may prove a mode of reading that usefully problematizes their portrayal as "brilliant" men. Such a reading certainly accords with Pontecorvo's view that he could not treat either Matthieu or Walker as caricatures.[43] As we will see, this approach contrasts with Steve McQueen's representational strategy in *12 Years a Slave*, which certainly does present the viewer with a character who is a caricature of the evil slave master. Ironically, the ideological thrust of these differing representational tactics is that while Conrad and Pontecorvo's seductive character traps elicit an awareness and a rejection of the naturalization of representations of colonialism and imperialism in cultural discourse and provoke systemic comprehension, McQueen's approach, less persuasively, presents the cruelty of individuals—"bad apples"—as an explanatory rationale for the atrocities of slavery.

Here, however, I connect Conrad to Pontecorvo not primarily because their works display a shared profound interest in colonialism nor for the numerous compelling intertextual resonances and parallels that can be detected in their works, but because their works share a formal heterogeneity, defy classification, and straddle the divide between "high" and "popular" culture *while also* sharing a profound interest in colonialism and its role in the making of the modern world. The complex and unstable cultural space Conrad's writing occupies, which I suggest is analogous to the cultural space occupied by Pontecorvo's films, is elaborated here by Jameson: "[Conrad's] place is still unstable, undecidable, and his work unclassifiable, spilling out of high literature into light reading and romance, reclaiming great areas of diversion and distraction by the most demanding practice of style and *écriture* alike, floating uncertainly somewhere in between Proust and Robert Louis Stevenson."[44] Given the proposition that Conrad floats "uncertainly somewhere in between Proust and Robert Louis Stevenson," we might quite reasonably, thinking comparatively, be tempted to suggest that Pontecorvo's work floats uncertainly somewhere in between the traditions of the great Soviet filmmaker Sergei Eisenstein, the Italian neorealist filmmaker Roberto Rossellini, and the "Golden Age" directors of Hollywood swashbucklers, and that *Burn!* constitutes a unique fusion of "the romantic adventure and the film of ideas."[45] Moreover, just as Jameson argues that the result of "the discontinuities objectively present in Conrad's narratives" is "a bewildering variety of competing and incommensurable interpretive options," we can observe that Pontecorvo's *Burn!* also invites a number of interpretative approaches.[46]

The analysis to this point has already touched upon some of these possibilities and their explanatory potential: the analysis of *Burn!* as a film that dissolves the boundaries between the practices of commercial, artistic, and political filmmaking; the Fanonian reading that elaborates *Burn*'s vision of Black agency and dovetails with a reading of Dolores as an embodiment of négritude; the reading of *Burn!* as postcolonial critique that emphasizes the moment of independence not as the rendezvous of liberation but as a pivot point into a new history of neocolonial domination; and the reading of *Burn!* as a document of late 1960s counterculture. Also consider the explanatory potential of the Freudian reading that would center on the father-son quality of Walker and Dolores's relationship and note that in a twist of the classic Oedipal narrative Dolores achieves revenge over his "father" first via self-sacrifice and second via the murder of the "father" by another Black rebel who the father-Walker mistakes for the son-Dolores. A further Freudian layer is provided by the homoerotic dimension of the Walker–Dolores relationship, which is communicated throughout the film, not least via Brando's highly sexualized presentation of Walker who has a fondness for lavender, a color long associated with eroticism, homosexuality, and LGBTQ+ politics. Repressed sexual desire crackles and flutters, like Walker's lavender scarf in the sea breeze (see fig. 1.1), and the tension is sublimated into the relationship with Dolores in which the power struggle is both personal and political. For the purposes of the argument here, it is worth noting that these psychoanalytic approaches do not displace political readings of the film that avow the transformative potential of Black agency, but rather they reveal a subtext consonant with the political readings that give primacy to Black agency as a motor of history. What is striking about *all* of these possible approaches is that they emerge organically from the film itself. Each of these interpretative options and their ideological implications will now be presented. Each approach, it will be seen, reveals a film of aesthetic achievement and ideological assuredness that is neither doctrinaire nor outmoded. Further, each approach arrives at the same conclusion, revealing a film that by varying internal logics insists upon the role played by the dispossessed in the as yet unfulfilled struggle for human liberation.

Gillo Goes to Hollywood:
Combining Commercial, Art, and Political Cinema

Now the analysis considers *Burn*'s somewhat schizophrenic genesis within "the commercial machinery of a Hollywood studio" but under the direction of a filmmaker with an uncompromising artistic and political vision.[47] After the successes of *Kapò* and *The Battle of Algiers*, Pontecorvo was a feted European filmmaker on whom the Hollywood studios were more than willing to take a risk, notwithstanding the brazenly political quality of his filmmaking and his personal political commitments.[48] Born into a middle-class, assimilated Jewish family in Pisa in 1919, Pontecorvo grew up under Mussolini. In the late 1930s he moved to Paris, where he became acquainted with Picasso, Stravinksy, and Sartre. By the age of twenty-four, he was a retired professional tennis player, a clandestine member of the Italian Communist Party, and the Italian representative of the international communist youth movement. He was also a leader of northern Italy's antifascist resistance in World War II, crossing the border between Italy and the unoccupied south of France to communicate with members of the Italian resistance on either side of the border. This firsthand experience of "armed struggle, popular strikes, and uprisings," Celli writes, would become "the foundation of his subsequent cinematic work."[49] Although Pontecorvo resigned his membership of the Italian Communist Party in 1956 in response to the Soviet Union's repression of the Hungarian Revolution, he remained an independent Marxist. This political commitment found a ready outlet in his early films before Pontecorvo retreated into a long filmic silence.[50] Pontecorvo, following Lenin and Castro, considered cinema "the most important of the arts" while cautioning against an overvaluation of cinema's capacity to effect sociopolitical transformation: "it is not, directly, action."[51] Nevertheless, Pontecorvo admitted his belief that "if you reach a large front of people," cinema can be "very valuable and useful."[52] For Pontecorvo, "cinema which addresses itself to the masses" could be "a way of revitalizing a people's deadened responses" and a means of opposing establishment fictions.[53] So, although Pontecorvo was frank and honest about his need, in his late forties, to provide himself and his dependents with financial stability, it was his belief in the virtues of reaching a wide audience—who could be freed from their alienation by his filmmaking—that explains how Pontecorvo came to make a color motion picture about a Black revolution for United Artists starring Marlon Brando.[54]

The origins of *Burn!* can be traced to Alberto Grimaldi's interest in hiring Pontecorvo to direct a political Western. Grimaldi had produced Sergio Leone's wildly successful trilogy—*A Fistful of Dollars* (1964), *For a Few Dollars More* (1965), *and The Good, the Bad, and the Ugly* (1966)—starring Clint Eastwood. Although Pontecorvo was "initially averse to working in a popular genre like the Western," Grimaldi and Pontecorvo did eventually agree on a project "to adapt the format of the historical action-adventure film to issues of the Third World and colonialism."[55] The goal was to take one of Hollywood's most popular genres and to appropriate and subvert it with densely political filmmaking rooted in Pontecorvo's neorealist training.[56] Years later, in 2003, looking back on his decision, Pontecorvo revealed that he had been confident in his ability to make an action-adventure film that would be the carrier of a revolutionary anticolonial message: "I said, 'Why should we do something we don't like? Let's make an adventure story . . . let's get a great star, let's make it in colour, in the style of the nineteenth-century novel and so on, but let's add our own ideas' which were always anti-colonial."[57] Whether or not Pontecorvo in fact underestimated the constraints that would come with working in Hollywood remains a moot point. To begin with, the executives at United Artists would not countenance allowing Pontecorvo to film in black and white, a prohibition that Pontecorvo elegantly navigated by producing a film that is magisterial in its deployment of color psychology as part of its cinematographic register.[58] Another directive Pontecorvo navigated successfully was the studio's preference for bankable Hollywood stars to play the roles of Dolores and Walker. In particular, they had Sidney Poitier and Steve McQueen in mind.[59] For Pontecorvo, a neorealist who typically cast nonprofessional actors almost exclusively on the basis of their physical presence and appearance, Poitier and McQueen were not appropriate choices.

For the part of Dolores, Pontecorvo considered Poitier's metropolitan style and well-known face unfitting. Instead, Pontecorvo insisted on casting Márquez, a peasant herdsman from San Basilio de Palenque, a village in northern Colombia originally established as a maroon community. Before filming began, Márquez spoke no English, was illiterate, and had never seen a film, let alone acted in one. But Pontecorvo "thought his face was perfect for what [he] wanted" and cast him without even a screen test.[60] Pontecorvo's instinctive genius here bordered on recklessness: "at the beginning, Evaristo [Márquez] was terrible," Pontecorvo remarked later in an interview in which he revealed he had feared he would have to bring in a professional after all.[61] However, after weeks of intensive coaching, Pontecorvo's great gamble began to pay off, resulting in Brando's quip that such was Márquez's rapid growth as an actor that he had surely sent Stanislavsky "spinning in his grave."[62]

However, for the part of Walker, Pontecorvo and his chief scriptwriter, Franco Solinas, had had Brando in mind from the outset of the project. In 1969, Brando did not have the same box-office appeal as McQueen, but Pontecorvo admired Brando deeply and considered him "the greatest film actor in history."[63] Pontecorvo's admiration was reciprocated by Brando, who held *The Battle of Algiers* in high regard and was both eager to work with Pontecorvo and undeterred by the prospect of working alongside Márquez.[64] So, Pontecorvo insisted on Brando and the studio relented. However, Brando and Pontecorvo's working relationship on set was marked by conflict and disagreement that was the product of two stubborn perfectionists with antithetical approaches working together in challenging conditions.⁶⁵ However, their mutual respect endured, and in his memoir published to coincide with his seventieth birthday, Brando wrote that he considered Pontecorvo to be "sensitive and meticulous" and "aside from Elia Kazan and Bernardo Bertolucci, the best director" he ever worked with.⁶⁶ And Pontecorvo, for his part, remained adamant that although he found working with Brando demanding and difficult, he was unique among actors, the only one who "with one expression" could convey "more than ten pages of dialogue."⁶⁷

Aside from Brando, all the film's other characters—save for Teddy Sanchez, who was played by the Italian character actor Renato Salvatori—were ably played by nonprofessionals, with Richard Shelton's performance as the representative of the Royal Sugar Company in Queimada deserving special mention. At the time of filming, Shelton was an administrator for British Petroleum in Colombia, and as one critic noted, he "played himself—convincingly and with ease," enhancing the film's neocolonial bite.⁶⁸ The impact of this largely nonprofessional cast, and the politics of the casting of Brando and Márquez in particular, illustrates the extent to which Pontecorvo had succeeded in bending the conventions of Hollywood to his own artistic and political purpose. Pontecorvo's casting strategy should be understood, as Mike Wayne has argued, as a critique and an unravelling of "the star system using a star, the mechanisms of identification, the hierarchy between actors, the spectator's need for a powerful ego-ideal to empathize with [and dependence on] the star as narrative agent to resolve problems."⁶⁹

However, not all United Artists' prohibitions and wishes could be overcome or dispensed with, and the critic Alan Stone contends that in agreeing to this project Pontecorvo "had made a pact with the devil."⁷⁰ Stone is certainly correct in his assessment that United Artists' editing and final production constituted a "doctoring" of Pontecorvo's vision. For the American and British markets, the film's running time was cut by twenty minutes, resulting in a diminution of narrative coherence. Additionally, for the American and British markets, United Artists changed the title to the sensationalist "*Burn!*" This change, according to Stone, was the product of United Artists' crude calculation "that the rallying cry 'Burn, Baby, Burn!' in American urban riots of that time made it salient."⁷¹ Furthermore, as Joan Mellen explains, the adoption of the imperative "Burn!" for the film's English title is inappropriate linguistically (the correct translation of "*queimada*" is "burnt") and unfitting ideologically since it implies an "endorsement of the tragedy" depicted rather than a statement of "the inexorable fact."⁷²

Also noteworthy is the fact that this was in fact the second title change required by United Artists. The original intention had been for the film's title to be the Spanish "*Quemada*," since the film's colonizers were to be Spanish and the film's historical prelude—the burning of the island to suppress Amerindian resistance—was based upon an episode of sixteenth-century Spanish colonial history. However, United Artists would not permit the release of a film that represented Spain in a negative light. A previous Columbia Pictures film, Fred Zinnemann's 1964 Spanish Civil War drama *Behold a Pale Horse*, had caused offense in Spain, and the Francoist dictatorship had responded by banning the release and distribution of all Columbia Pictures' films in Spain. Therefore, fearing the economic consequences of incurring the wrath of Spain's Francoists, United Artists demanded the substitution of Spain for Portugal.[73] The irony involved in this substitution is rather stunning as at the time of *Burn*'s release in 1969, fascist Portugal was eight years into a thirteen-year war it was waging with increasing desperation against anticolonial forces in its African colonies of Angola, Guinea-Bissau, and Mozambique. Finally, the icing on the irony of this sorry tale of corporate cowardice and tampering is perhaps the fact that it is of course the British who come out of the film looking far worse than even the "Portuguese." However, despite all the cutting and meddling, Pontecorvo was able to accomplish the extraordinary feat of making a film about Black revolution with a clear commitment to Third World politics and anticolonialism from within the repressive environment of Hollywood. In *Burn!*, then, First, Second, and Third Cinema collide to spectacular effect: the thrilling adventure film meets the effective film of ideas by which its director's aspiring auteur vision finds expression.

Pontecorvo's auteur vision perhaps finds its clearest expression in the way in which his films give prominence to sound, and especially to music. In Pontecorvo's filmmaking, music does not merely adorn or complement the visual; instead, Pontecorvo creatively employs music and image in relationship to one another. This emphasis on music results from both passion and musicological knowledge. Pontecorvo emphasized in numerous interviews the critical importance of music in his life and to his practice as a filmmaker. For example, in 1972 Pontecorvo stated that it was music, not cinema, that was his deepest passion in life, that he would have preferred to have become a composer rather than a filmmaker, and that "if films were done without music" he would "probably do some other kind of work."[74] This passion for music led to Pontecorvo's pursuit of musicological training: he studied composition with René Leibowitz, a French composer of atonal music and a disciple of Arnold Schoenberg, but financial constraints caused Pontecorvo to leave these studies incomplete.[75] However, giving up his aspiration to become a composer did not mean the abandonment of music as part of his vocation. Instead, Pontecorvo discovered not only that filmmaking could fulfill "some of the desires" that had impelled him to write music, but also that filmmaking could satisfy his other "mania": photography.[76] What propelled Pontecorvo's mania for photography was, paradoxically, something that he described as "a fight" against the "terrible enemy" of the camera.[77] For Pontecorvo, the camera was an "enemy" because it rendered him a "prisoner of reality" and less free than a painter to realize the image of his mind's eye.[78] Pontecorvo's endless "fight" with the camera resulted in his famously obsessive experimentation with different shooting techniques, with different kinds of film stock, and with multiple methods for developing final prints. This experimentation was all in pursuit of a freer photography by which Pontecorvo could achieve granularity, a painterly aesthetic, and a truth arrived at not by objectivity but by creativity. Giving free rein to these two "manias"—music and photography—would result in Pontecorvo's signature cinematic style: a meticulous attention to "the rapport between music and image."[79] So, while the roots of Pontecorvo's films were to be found "always in music," the full aesthetic impact of his filmmaking was realized by the contrapuntal interplay of music and image, of the "*image sonore*" and the "*image visible*."[80] This mastery can be readily observed in *Burn!* in which Pontecorvo deploys Morricone's rousing score and oratorios and cantatas by Bach in conjunction with images that draw on the heritage of Black revolutionary iconography and communicate the revolutionary potential latent in an oppressed people. These accomplishments have been acknowledged even by the film's less-forgiving critics. Consider Alan Stone's assessment: "In *Queimada* Morricone combines African rhythms with Gregorian chants, creating an original and inspired score. And Pontecorvo, a serious student of Bach who had learned from Eisenstein that a crowd could be a character in film, makes masses of people move across his screen to the rhythms he hears in his head. Nowhere in film is the surging pageant of humanity more compellingly portrayed."[81] Now we will turn to a specific example from *Burn!* to examine in detail this contrapuntal interplay of music and image in action.

In the scene immediately following the assassination of Queimada's Portuguese governor, the camera pans admiringly over Dolores's triumphant and motley rebels (fig. 1.5). At first we observe the rebels through Walker's telescope, and this initial image is made more dramatic by its contrast with that which had immediately preceded it: the hopelessly con-

Figure 1.5. General Dolores and the army of the people, *Burn! Source:* Gillo Pontecorvo, dir., *Quemada (Burn!)* (Produzioni Europee Associati, 1969).

tradictory Sanchez crying "Freedom!" from a white balcony in the capital. This juxtaposition serves as an effective cinematic shorthand by which Pontecorvo sketches and foreshadows the radically divergent meanings of freedom for Queimada's bourgeois settler class and for Queimada's Black population. While Sanchez's version of freedom is liberal, partial, formal, and non-redistributive, Dolores's rebels—anticipating Marx—envision a universal and unconditional "realm of freedom" that will blossom only when "the realm of necessity" has been conquered.[82] This proposition makes material justice a prerequisite for meaningful civil and political freedom and constitutes a turning-upside-down of "the West's prioritization of civil and political rights over social, economic, cultural, environmental, and solidarity rights," a radical reversal with deep roots in Black diasporic political ideology.[83]

We then hear the ocean breaking softly on the shore and the sounds of seagulls as Dolores and his people approach, which we view through Walker's telescope. The camera then cuts to a portrait shot of Walker, who is on horseback. He puts down his telescope and smiles wryly at the impressive sight of Dolores leading so many rebels, an achievement he narcissistically considers his own. But this marvelous sight, which Walker considers the product of his own individual genius, is in fact, as Fredric Jameson has suggested, the "most wondrous" cinematic representation of a collectivity: "a rag-tag and bobtail army of the people itself . . . in carts and on foot, on horse- or donkey-back," clad "in rags and tattered uniforms," and "accompanied by family."[84] The camera then cuts back to and pans across the rebels as Morricone's stirring theme "*Abolição*" begins to play. The opening refrain is played on a church Hammond organ, which is then overlaid, in sequence, by acoustic African percussion, rhythmic electric guitar, and finally the voices of the Alessandro Alessandroni choristers with whom Morricone had collaborated on the scores to a number of spaghetti westerns. The choral voices build in intensity to an imposing crescendo and this striking "*image sonore*"—complex, elaborate, and mature—repeats the dramatic contrast with Sanchez on the balcony, but this time aurally, Sanchez's cry of "freedom" now seeming even more juvenile and jarring in comparative retrospect. Morricone's musical theme reaches its triumphant ending, and the intensity is briefly relieved by a conversation that ensues between Dolores and Walker. Following their conversation, a new interplay of image and music commences: African drums resume, this time accompanied by tribal singing, and Dolores is surrounded by an adoring crowd. Someone from the crowd holds up a baby, which Dolores receives, smiling. The tribal music fades out and is replaced by Bach's St Matthew Passion, which sets the story of the trial, crucifixion, and burial of Jesus to music, as the camera now paints portraits of individuals in the crowd (fig. 1.6).

Figure 1.6. Pontecorvo's cinematographic portraiture: child in the adoring crowd, *Burn! Source:* Gillo Pontecorvo, dir., *Quemada (Burn!)* (Produzioni Europee Associati, 1969).

This naturalistic cinematographic portraiture is reminiscent of the sympathetic representations of poor, ordinary people in the classics of Italian neorealism and the "poetic realism" of French 1930s cinema. As we will see, the representation of Black dignity and individuality via an aesthetics of naturalistic cinematic portraiture is a technique that Tomás Gutiérrez Alea will develop and modify in *La última cena* and is a theme to which we will return in some detail. This emotive interplay of image and sound—of filmic Black portraiture and St Matthew Passion—must also be regarded as a figuration of the Black rebel as Christ. This figuration is a daring and somewhat rare move within the context of cultural forms generated by Black diasporic history, but not one entirely without precedent. Consider, for example, René Depestre's 1967 négritude poem, *Un arc-en-ciel pour l'occident chrétien*, in which Malcolm X is configured in Christlike terms and the discourse of "gentle Jesus" is subverted.[85] In this masterful control of visual and musical rhetoric, by likening Dolores to Christ, Pontecorvo foreshadows Dolores's own execution as well as his resurrection in the form of an unknown rebel, and he likens the colonial British in Queimada to Christ's executioners.

Exploring the ways in which *Burn!* combines, in its making and aesthetic languages, First, Second, and Third Cinema, provides evidence that a mass and commercial culture may yet contain a radical politics.[86] As we will see in the chapter to come on *12 Years a Slave*, even the most adept of filmmakers will not necessarily find ways to negotiate successfully the pitfalls of commercial cinema. But in the case of *Burn!*, we are presented with an example of a commodified art form that undeniably bears the stamp of its craven and pecuniary producers, yet nevertheless finds ways to transcend its social determination, as it elaborates a story of Black resistance in history as a universalist force of transcendent potential.

Third Cinema and Black Revolution:
Burn's Césairean and Fanonian Critique

Finally, we now turn our attention, explicitly, to the elaboration of *Burn*'s Césairean and Fanonian critique that undergirds its Third Cinema politics and its assertion of Black Revolution as a progressive and universalist force. This reveals Pontecorvo's contributions to the development of Third Cinema as a cinema of liberation and supports the view that "the principal characteristic of Third Cinema is really not so much where it is made, or even who makes it, but rather the ideology it espouses and the consciousness it displays. The Third Cinema is the cinema of the Third World that stands opposed to imperialism and class oppression in all their ramifications and manifestations."[87] By this definition, a film made with United Artists' money by an Italian filmmaker need not be disqualified as an example of "Third Cinema" if "the ideology it espouses and the consciousness it displays . . . stands opposed to imperialism and class oppression." It is suggested here that by its deployment of the ideas of Césaire and Fanon, as well as other strategies already outlined, *Burn!* more than satisfies this requirement.

Burn! espouses its Césairean and Fanonian critique by a number of aesthetic and narrative devices, each of which promotes the subjectivization of the oppressed. Prominent among these devices is the drawing on the rich cultural history of iconography generated by the history of Black achievement in the Americas, most clearly—but not exclusively—that of the Haitian Revolution. This is a strategy that had previously been deployed to great effect by both Aimé Césaire and Frantz Fanon. For Césaire, the Haitian Revolution was "the first Negro epic of the New World" and "Haiti [was] the country where Negro people stood up for the first time, affirming their determination to shape a world," while for Fanon, "the plunge into the chasm of the past" was the "condition and the source of freedom."[88] Additionally, Dolores's narrative arc from porter to revolutionary hero is a filmic relation of Césaire's spiritual and political négritude in which derogatory assumptions of Black passivity are repudiated, Blackness is valorized as a creative and liberatory force, and critical participation in the processes of decolonization is promoted. Further, the critics Carlo Celli, Natalie Zemon Davis, and Massimo Ghirelli have all documented the influence of Frantz Fanon's ideas on Gillo Pontecorvo during the making of *Burn!*, while *The Battle of Algiers* is widely regarded as a film that embraces Fanoninst thinking on revolution.[89] Given this influence, it should not surprise us that Dolores's narrative arc also exemplifies the Fanonian thesis that the oppressed must seize freedom themselves since freedom is something that is "beyond the power of any human . . . to endow another human with."[90]

In his visual representation of Dolores, Pontecorvo evokes repeatedly the iconography generated by Toussaint Louverture, the strategic genius behind the Haitian Revolution. Figures 1.2 and 1.7, for example, recall Jacob Lawrence's majestic *The Life of Toussaint Louverture*, a series of forty-one tempera paintings that Lawrence had completed by 1938. The series exemplifies Lawrence's signature modernist style, projects

Louverture as a symbol of Black pride, and should be regarded as a visual companion to Césaire's ideology of négritude.[91] The paintings in Lawrence's series with the strongest compositional affiliations to Pontecorvo's cinematic representations of Dolores in *Burn!* are the seventeenth painting in the series, "Toussaint Captured" (fig. 1.8), which should be considered in relation to Fig. 1.7, and the twentieth, "General Toussaint L'Ouverture" (fig. 1.9), which should be considered in relation to Fig. 1.2. Lawrence's iconic profile portrait of Louverture has since been copied, adapted, and reworked many times—consider, for example, works by the contemporary Haitian artists François Cauvin and Edouard Duval Carrié, as well as the logo of *Jacobin* magazine (fig. 1.10).[92] It is noteworthy that *Jacobin*'s creative director, Remeike Forbes, revealed that when searching for a new logo to present to the magazine's editorial board, his search "was more or less done after rewatching that scene in *Queimada* when the revolutionary leader José Dolores is captured by the British forces."[93] Pontecorvo's representation of Dolores thus forms part of a chain of radical iconography from across the Black Atlantic that continues to contest the tradition of racist, imperial denigration. Consider, by way of further examples, Anne-Louis Girodet's magisterial *Portrait of Citizen Belley* of 1797 and Kimathi Donkor's *Toussaint Louverture at Bedourette* of 2004

Figure 1.7. Dolores captured, *Burn! Source:* Gillo Pontecorvo, dir., *Quemada* (*Burn!*) (Produzioni Europee Associati, 1969).

Figure 1.8. Jacob Lawrence, "Toussaint Captured," *The Life of Toussaint L'Ouverture, No. 17* (1938). Tempera on paper. Aaron Douglas Collection, Amistad Research Center, Tulane University, New Orleans. *Source: Toussaint Captured*, 1938 © Jacob Lawrence Estate / Artists Rights Society (ARS) New York / CARCC Ottawa 2023; Amistad Research Center, New Orleans, LA, USA. Courtesy of the Amistad Research Center, New Orleans, LA / Bridgeman Images.

(figs. 1.11 and 1.12).[94] However, Louverture is not the only iconic Black diasporic figure Pontecorvo's portraiture of Dolores evokes. The image of General Dolores bent over his desk, head in his hands, deep in thought, and tormented by the realization that he will soon have to order his men to return to the plantations, evokes the visual and emotional language of Henri-Cartier Bresson's 1961 photograph of Martin Luther King Jr. (figs. 1.13 and 1.14).

The ideology of négritude, which for Césaire was always incompatible with essentialist politics—"it is a fact that there is a Black culture: it is historical, there is nothing biological about it"[95]—also proves to be a compelling explanatory theory for the narrative arc Dolores travels in the course of *Burn!* By the time Dolores and his rebels are being hunted

Figure 1.9. Jacob Lawrence, "General Toussaint L'Ouverture," *The Life of Toussaint L'Ouverture, No. 20* (1938). Tempera on paper. Aaron Douglas Collection, Amistad Research Center, Tulane University, New Orleans. *Source: General Toussaint L'Ouverture*, 1938 © Jacob Lawrence Estate / Artists Rights Society (ARS) New York / CARCC Ottawa 2023; Amistad Research Center, New Orleans, LA, USA. Courtesy of the Amistad Research Center, New Orleans, LA / Bridgeman Images.

Figure 1.10. *Jacobin* magazine logo. Designed by Remeike Forbes. *Source:* https://jacobin.com/about. Used with permission.

Figure 1.11. Anne-Louis Girodet, *Portrait of Citizen Belley* (1797), Châteaux de Versailles et de Trianon, Versailles. Oil on canvas. *Source:* ArtResource.

Figure 1.12. Kimathi Donkor, *Toussaint L'Ouverture at Bedourete* (2004). Oil on linen. *Source:* Collection of the artist. Used with permission.

Figure 1.13. Dolores at his desk, *Burn! Source:* Gillo Pontecorvo, dir., *Quemada (Burn!)* (Produzioni Europee Associati, 1969).

Figure 1.14. Henri Cartier-Bresson, *Martin Luther King. Atlanta* (1961). *Source:* Foundation Henri Cartier-Bresson / Magnum Photos. USA. Georgia. Atlanta. Pastor's study of Ebenezer Baptist Church. President of the Southern Christian Leadership Conference Martin Luther King. 1961.

down by the British army under Walker's direction, Dolores has long since realized the Fanonian principle that "freedom is something you take for yourself." Like the narrator in Césaire's foundational poetic statement of négritude, *Cahier d'un retour au pays natal* ("Notebook of a Return to My Native Land"), Dolores travels a path from alienation and submission to subjectivization and knowledge of true freedom.[96] When, in the film's first half, Dolores leads a small band of Black rebels in the robbery of Queimada's central bank, Dolores is still operating under Walker's guidance. However, when in the course of the robbery a guard confronts Dolores, searches the cart, and discovers the stolen gold, Dolores instinctively kills the guard to preserve his own life and to ensure the robbery's success. It is a scene in which the viewer is witness to Dolores's increasing confidence and self-assurance. Following the robbery, Dolores makes his way to the maroon village where Santiago had lived, but, unbeknownst to Dolores, Walker has tipped off the authorities as to the location of the stolen gold. Consequently, Dolores finds himself successfully leading the villagers in a battle against Portuguese soldiers who have been dispatched to recapture the gold. Of course, Walker gives himself the credit for Dolores's rapid ride to the status of revolutionary leader:

> WALKER: If I had told you, José, to start a revolution, you wouldn't have understood me, to rob a bank, yes, that was possible. First, you learned to kill in order to defend yourself . . . and later you had to kill to defend others . . . and the rest came by itself.

As Natalie Zemon Davis has noted, we do not have access to Dolores's thoughts while Walker utters these words, but the viewer is entitled to some degree of skepticism as to whether Dolores agrees with this version of how he came to lead a revolution.[97]

By the time of Dolore's capture by the British, however, there is no doubt as to the extent of his spiritual and political growth. He is fully cognizant of the incompatibility of the interests of foreign capital with liberation in Queimada, and he recognizes that when the Queimadan government granted the right of exploitation of its sugar plantations to the Royal Sugar Company for a period of ninety-nine years—renewable—the result was not only that the Royal Sugar Company in practice came to control the entire economy of Queimada, but also that the Royal Sugar Company became the Black population's new master. Dolores also recognizes that, as in the days of slavery, the profitability of the entire system rests upon the continued exploitation of those who cut the cane. For Dolores, now equipped with this understanding, the struggle for liberation has become a radical struggle against the iniquities of capitalism. As one of Dolores's followers explains to Walker, "José Dolores says, that if a man works for another, even if he's called a worker, he remains a slave. And it will always be the same, since there are those who own the plantations and those who own the machete to cut cane for the owners." In these circumstances—and with the British army now called in to slaughter Dolores, his men, and any members of the Black civilian population who get in their way—a defensive and emancipatory violence is the only remaining course of action. Dolores's follower continues: "And then, José Dolores says, that we must cut heads instead of cane." These words signify the radicalization of Dolores's politics and call to mind the revolutionary battle cry of Jean-Jacques Dessalines, the Haitian Revolutionary who delivered the decisive defeat of Napoleon's forces at the Battle of Vertières in November 1803 and promulgated Haitian independence in 1804: *"koupe tèt, boule kay"* ("cut heads and burn houses").

After his capture, Dolores, with crystalline vision, sees through Walker's desperate attempts to justify himself and he refuses to engage even in conversation with Walker. During a break in the journey to the British military camp where his fate awaits him, Dolores addresses a rapt audience of mostly Black soldiers who are in the pay of the British and who assisted in his capture. The presence of divisions among the Black population (and the depiction of British military personnel wearing turbans) indicates another Fanonian lens: the insufficiency of race alone as an explanatory category for the social fractures produced by colonial and imperial oppression. Addressing his captors, Dolores compares imperialism to a "beast" that must be fought, as the genuine freedom of the oppressed is predicated on its defeat:

> DOLORES: And the groans from this dying beast will become our first cry of freedom, one that will be heard far, far beyond this island.

This view that anticolonial and anti-imperial resistance will expose the faux humanism of European bourgeois society and usher in a true, universal humanism while also heralding the spiritual rebirth of the colonized is also unmistakably Fanonian: "When it is achieved during a war of liberation the mobilization of the masses introduces the notion of common cause, national destiny, and collective history into every consciousness."[98]

Having at last captured their enemy, Queimada's elite and the British must now decide what to do with Dolores. General Prada, the president of Queimada since the execution of Sanchez for treason, resolves on hanging, reasoning that the garotte would be "too reminiscent of Portugal" and the firing squad insufficiently solemn. However, Walker, by now jaded and uncertain of his purpose, burdened with the guilt he feels for the impending execution of his former friend, outlines the risk they face in making a martyr of Dolores:

> WALKER: The man who fights for an idea is a hero, and a hero who's killed becomes a martyr, and a martyr immediately becomes a myth. A myth is more dangerous than a man because you can't kill a myth. Don't you agree, Shelton? I mean, think of his ghost running through the Antilles. Think of the legends and the songs.
>
> SHELTON: Better songs than armies.
>
> WALKER: Better silence than songs.

To the end able to manipulate Queimada's elite, Walker persuades Prada to try to tempt Dolores into betraying the cause of Black liberty since "a hero that betrays is soon forgotten." However, secure in his ethical conviction and unable to countenance betrayal, Dolores laughs at Prada's offer of freedom and "a great deal of money." With Dolores's execution now imminent, Walker is overcome by his feelings of shame and dirtiness. He sneaks into Dolores's tent the morning of the execution, cuts Dolores free, and offers him his horse. But Dolores refuses: he declines the opportunity to save himself in the knowledge that his death will advance the cause of Black liberty. Once again, Pontecorvo provocatively accentuates the Christian echoes of Dolores's resolute integrity and revolutionary commitment. Notably, Dolores's refusal to flee can be read biblically in the light of Paul's similar refusal to leave prison in Acts.[99] Further, there are also Christlike dimensions at work in this scene, and socialist interpretations of Christ's understanding of the likely political consequences that would flow from his crucifixion are particularly relevant here. Terry Eagleton, for example, has argued that "perhaps Jesus felt in some obscure way that he could fulfill the will of his Father only through death. The theological point being made by the Gospel writer here is not that Jesus wanted to die, but that his death followed logically from his life."[100] Dolores's portrayal in similar terms would likely have had a powerful resonance given the prevalence of Latin American liberation theology at the time of the film's release. The film's emotional climax thus fuses Fanonian and Christian theological revolutionary traditions to offer a final unequivocal lesson, but it is a lesson Walker simply cannot grasp:

> WALKER: My god man go, your time's running out. Come on, you're free! José, you're free! Free! Don't you understand? [Long pause.] Why? What good does it do? What meaning does it have, José? Is it a revenge of some sort? But what kind of revenge is it if you're dead? I don't know José. It just seems madness. Why?

As the critic Marcus Wood has written, these lines present "so very many questions from a man supposedly in a position of absolute authority and intellectual superiority, who up to this point has had all the answers."[101] These lines, which are Walker's last words in the film, had originally been longer, but Pontecorvo, in a further masterstroke of manipulating the interplay of image and sound, cut two pages of dialogue and replaced them with Bach's cantata *Komm, süsser Tod* ("Come, sweet death") and a lingering close-up of Brando, who "produced a silent gestural performance of such transcendentally expressive acting that even electricians and carpenters present on the set broke out in applause" (fig. 1.15).[102]

Figure 1.15. Walker's incomprehension and loss of power, *Burn! Source:* Gillo Pontecorvo, dir., *Quemada (Burn!)* (Produzioni Europee Associati, 1969).

It was, according to Pontecorvo, the only time in his career that Brando had known two pages of dialogue to be replaced with music.[103] The emptiness and incomprehension that Brando summoned from deep within his psyche communicates the colonizer's "vast bewilderment . . . when finally faced with the rejection of his power to liberate."[104] As Dolores is led off to the gallows, he breaks the silence he has maintained since his capture. His final words taunt Walker and signify Walker's total loss of control over both Dolores and the course of history that will now unfold in Queimada: "*Inglés!* Remember what you said! Civilization belongs to the whites. But what civilization? Until when?" With these final words, Dolores proclaims the future triumph and liberation of the Third World—and with it the dawn of a new and genuine humanism in the world.

Conclusion: A Spectacular and Incendiary Fusion

Burn's aesthetic language and ideological thrust registers the influence of the practices of "First," "Second," and "Third" Cinema and bridges "mass" and "high" culture; this results in a film unique among cinematic representations of slavery. The attention given to the representation of Black agency, the focus on understanding slavery within the context of the history of capitalism, and its utopian yet unsentimental revolutionary politics controvert and render dubious Tomás Gutiérrez Alea's assertion that *Burn!* is only superficially a revolutionary film and that Pontecorvo, as a result of alleged unconscious paternalism, reproduced the repressive "structural dynamics" that were the object of his critique.[105] As Natalie Zemon Davis has put it, *Burn!* "tries to give a general account of shifts in power and class and the rhythm of historical change" while also telling a story that revolves around the rivalry of its two principal characters.[106] But it also does much more than that: with *Burn!*, Pontecorvo somehow managed to find a way to harness simultaneously the spirits of Conrad, Eisenstein, and Rossellini; Césaire, Fanon, and Black Power; and the men and women who made the Haitian Revolution, Marxism-Leninism, and 1960s radicalism, all while spectacularly subverting the format of the Hollywood swashbuckler.

Of course, *Burn!* is not perfect: especially *imperfect* is the US/UK version with its twenty minutes of cuts, which Pontecorvo considered a butchering of his original vision.[107] But *Burn*'s most serious shortcoming—its lack of female perspectives—cannot be ascribed to the meddling of United Artists. Although we witness Santiago's widow mourning her husband and going about her matriarchal duties in the aftermath of her husband's death, we do not gain real insight into the circumstances of her social life, nor is her character's interiority developed. Admittedly, Santiago's widow is only a minor character, but other opportunities are also missed as female roles are generally absent or underdeveloped. For example, female characters within and connected to Dolores's rebel army are lacking, as are female voices from within Queimada's bourgeois settler class. Within the category of slavery films, *Burn!* is not alone in this shortcoming: as we will see, other films considered in this study also either omit female perspectives or include them with an insufficient account of the Atlantic world's gender politics in the age of slavery, which results in misleading or superficial characterization. Nevertheless, despite this serious shortcoming, *Burn!* daringly contests the cultural tradition, which has deep roots in Hollywood, in which the memory of slavery is romantically sanitized. Instead, *Burn!* takes the slavery film as a springboard to produce a searing statement as to the imperative of anti-imperialist revolutionary social transformation.

Burn! refuses to treat slavery in antiquarian terms and equally refuses to treat it as an aberrational evil that was hermeneutically contained in slave societies. *Burn*'s narrative depicts British abolitionism as consistent with its pursuit of imperialist hegemony, and the film thereby refuses the debilitating narrative that abolition was a legally encoded humanitarian gift. Instead, strategically invoking the Haitian Revolution, *Burn!* insists upon Black agency as the central historical force in the story of an as yet incomplete struggle for liberation. *Burn!* communicates the reifying core impulses of slavery *and* bourgeois market capitalism and conveys the message that a meaningful, ethical freedom necessarily includes freedom from all forms of economic domination.

Released with the spirit of 1968 still a fresh memory, to watch *Burn!* after more than fifty years is to experience a reminder of an age in which belief in the progressive possibilities of radical social transformation resonated far and wide. The Marxian and Rimbaldian mantras that collective action and human agency could transform the world and human life had not yet begun to seem an embarrassment within mainstream politics, which had not yet been "dissolved by the global corporate institutions we call late capitalism."[108] But, thankfully, *Burn!* is far from an antiquarian relic. Like its more-celebrated predecessor, *The Battle of Algiers*, *Burn!* has aged well. It remains the closest we have to a film that celebrates the aspirations and achievements of the Haitian Revolution, and in a late capitalist world in which racial and economic justice appear as chimeric as ever, *Burn!* has lost none of its political urgency. After more than fifty years, *Burn!* has become a salutary reminder to refuse left melancholia and the temptations of acquiescence. Tender and utopian, but also critical and grounded in realities, *Burn!* provides an addendum to the oft-quoted dictum usually attributed to Fredric Jameson: "it is easier to imagine the end of the world than to imagine the end of capitalism."[109] That may be so, but José Dolores nevertheless reminds us that it remains "better to know where to go and not know how, than to know how to go and not know where."

Chapter 2

"Cinema Must Be Revolutionary in Itself"

Afro-Cuban Resistance, the Haitian Revolution, and Black Comedy in Tomás Gutiérrez Alea's *La última cena*

Le Blanc est un maître qui a permis à ses esclaves de manger à sa table.

(The white man is a master who has allowed his slaves to eat at his table.)

—Frantz Fanon, Peau noire, masques blancs[1]

Count de Casa Bayona: *¡Esto no es Santo Domingo!*

(This is not Santo Domingo!)

—*La última cena* screenplay[2]

In the mid-1970s, not long after the release of Gillo Pontecorvo's *Burn!*, a Cuban filmmaker by the name of Tomás Gutiérrez Alea turned his attention to Afro-Cuban history and the slave background of Cuba's African-descended population. Like Pontecorvo, Alea had been heavily influenced by the aesthetics of Italian neorealism in the formative stage of his career. Also like Pontecorvo, Alea's filmmaking practice was dedicated to the elaboration of a revolutionary cinema, and in 1976 Alea completed a film that sought to elevate the repressed history of Black resistance to slavery to a position of prominence within Cuban cinematic practice and public discourse. Alea's *La última cena* (*The Last Supper*), a revolutionary statement of Cuban cinema, is an ironic historical drama of slave revolt and religious hypocrisy that has been praised for its intelligence, moral and political complexity, and arresting visual beauty.[3] Its release was a breakthrough moment in the history of Cuba's national film institute, the Instituto Cubano del Arte e Industria Cinematográficos (ICAIC), which had been founded on March 24, 1959, just eighty-three days after the victory of the Cuban Revolution.[4] The ICAIC's mandate was to promote human development via the medium of film with the primary goals of "universal film literacy and universal access to the medium."[5] The importance of film within the revolution is made clear by Susan Lord, who has summarized the ICAIC's goals in the following terms: "to build a nation through images by experimenting with new modes of documentary; historical dramas that were meant to rebuild history (new citizens, new stories, new forms); transformations in contexts of production, reception, and distribution; and the production of discourse in the form of manifestos . . . and cine-debates (forums for discussion of the films)."[6]

Although Cuban films produced by the ICAIC had met with international critical acclaim before, *La última cena* pushed Cuba's reputation as a filmmaking nation to new heights. *La última cena* was a critical and commercial success, a film festival prizewinner, and a box-office hit in various global locales, including Brazil and London's West End.[7] This relative success contrasts with the rather "cool public and critical reception" that, as we have seen, greeted *Burn!* on its initial release.[8] However, in other respects, *La última cena* shares much in common with Pontecorvo's *Burn!*, notwithstanding Alea's negative opinion of Pontecorvo's film.[9] First among these commonalities is Alea's treatment of the Haitian Revolution as a source of inspiration. However, although *La última cena* has generated considerable discussion in both academic and mainstream circles, the film's Haitian dimension has gone largely unnoted.[10] This is perhaps especially surprising given Alea's longstanding interest in Haiti, as evidenced by his 1964 film *Cumbite* ("Cooperative Labor"), which is based on a celebrated Haitian novel, Jacques Roumain's *Les Gouverneurs de la Rosée*.[11] Shot in sumptuous monochrome and set in 1940 in a rural Haitian community, *Cumbite* tells the story of thirty-four-year-old Manuel who, having spent fifteen years in Cuba, returns home to find his community stricken by drought and poverty. Unable to grow crops in the bone-dry, dusty earth, some villagers have resorted to logging trees to sell as timber. Manuel's parents make palm-leaf hats by hand to sell in the city, but they are barely getting by; Manuel's father laments that "there aren't enough heads in the city to sell all these hats." However, in Cuba Manuel acquired the knowledge and skills required to locate and divert water in order to irrigate farmland sustainably. He is also politically conscious and is keenly aware that the only sustainable solution to the community's poverty is the adoption of eco-socialist practices, including recognition that "the water belongs to everyone." However, Manuel becomes the victim of an intergenerational family feud, and he is murdered before the community is able to set aside their divisions and begin the work Manuel had known was necessary. *Cumbite* displays Alea's gift for storytelling and rich characterization, and it communicates that cooperative labor—and international exchange and cooperation—are among the keys to conquering the realm of necessity. Although Alea was himself unsatisfied with *Cumbite* (he considered it lacking "authenticity"), the film does demonstrate an intimate understanding of its Haitian setting.[12] In making *Cumbite*, Alea drew on the advice of the Haitian négritude poet René Depestre, whose influence is apparent in the film's detailed and beautiful representation of vodou and the Haitian prayer for the dead at Manuel's funeral. There can be no doubt that Alea was deeply acquainted with Haitian history and culture. Therefore, departing from previous critical treatments, this chapter makes the ideological resonance of the Haitian Revolution in *La última cena* central to its analysis in order to demonstrate that in narrating a historically documented episode of slave resistance in late nineteenth-century Cuba in relation to the Haitian Revolution, *La última cena* is attentive to a transnational, Pan-Caribbean history of resistance in which freedom and liberation necessarily extend to freedom from economic domination. It is argued that Alea articulates exactly how slavery as a regime of labor exploitation intricately relates to capitalism, that his ironic method reveals Hispanic Catholicism's sophistry vis-à-vis slavery, and that he identifies in the history of Black resistance to slavery an emancipatory principle of enduring and universal value.

Alea, affectionately known in Cuba as "Titón," was a preeminent filmmaker during Cuba's postrevolutionary period. By the time of his death in 1996, he was widely regarded as "the doyen of Cuban *cineastas*."[13] Alea undertook his formal training as a filmmaker between 1951 and 1953 in Rome's Centro Sperimentale di Cinematografia—a film school known for its commitment to Italian neorealism—which, as we have seen in the context of Pontecorvo's work, emerged in the context of resistance to fascism and can be characterized by a frequent reliance on nonprofessional actors, techniques drawn from documentary filmmaking that it often mimics, and a political vision that owes much to Sartre's theory of *littérature engagée* ("committed literature").[14] However, while critics have noted that the politics and aesthetics of Alea's early films in particular are indebted to Italian neorealism (the aforementioned *Cumbite* is the high-water mark of Alea's neorealism), his filmmaking practice drew on a wide range of cinematic styles and auteurs, including Soviet cinema, the French New Wave, and Cinema Novo, while Buñuelesque themes are readily apparent in his works.[15] His theoretical influences were also wide-ranging and include Frantz Fanon's anticolonial writings and Bertolt Brecht's critical writing on theater and aesthetics.[16] Further, Alea was a central figure in debates over cultural Marxism in Cuba to which his theoretical writings, as well as his films, were a key contribution.[17] His aesthetic and narratological innovations are elaborated in his writings and actualized in his films. Chief among these innovations is a dialectical synthesis of Aristotelian identification and Brechtian alienation that has as its goal the production of a revolutionary cinema that engenders critical discernment.[18] His work has also been praised for its nondoctrinaire political commitment, and his dedication to the revolution's ideals was apparent from both his filmmaking practice and his public statements. For example, in 1978 Alea remarked that "Cuban cinema came into being with the revolution, and is a cinema consistent with the revolution."[19] Nevertheless, he did not refrain from critique when the revolution's ideals miscarried, and he was also a prominent defender of the artistic independence of Cuba's national film industry. As the film historian and critic Michael Chanan reports, Alea "used his friendship with Castro to ensure the [ICAIC's] autonomy from external censorship."[20]

This independent intellectual spirit is also registered in Alea's considerable range, which spans both documentary and fiction films that are often marked by black comedy, social satire, and ironic political critique.[21] These span such diverse subjects as political corruption, homophobia, sexism, the sociology of race and class, and the nature of radical social transformation. Alea gained international renown for his 1968 FIPRESCI prizewinning film, *Memorias del subdesarrollo* (*Memories of Underdevelopment*), which tracks Sergio, an alienated "bourgeois misfit," who elects to remain in Cuba after Castro's revolution while his wife, family, and friends choose to relocate to Miami.[22] Critics have noted that Alea's portrait of the handsome and articulate Sergio, an aspiring writer, initially encourages emotional identification, but this is then ruptured by the exposure of Sergio's accommodation to the contradictory and repressive social mores to which he is accustomed and by which he lives—a prime example of Alea's dialectical manipulation of Aristotelian identification and Brechtian alienation in filmic praxis.[23] As we will see, the main character in *La última cena*, the enslaver Count de Casa Bayona, is exposed by a comparable strategy. The Count strives to reconcile his status as an enslaver with his Christian faith. As Paul Schroeder has noted, the Count "sincerely wants to become more authentically Christian, but the vanity and the self-righteousness of his class, both of which he has internalized, are obstacles to that end."[24] Both Sergio and the Count, rather like Pontecorvo's Walker in *Burn!*, are thus corrupted by their inability to transcend their class locations, which are constituted in relation to the hegemony of American power in the case of Sergio and slaveholding colonialism in the case of the Count.

La última cena is in some ways eccentric when set against Alea's overall corpus of work and stands out for several reasons, first among which is its use of color, which by the mid-1970s had become a common feature of Cuban filmmaking.[25] Just as Pontecorvo had always worked in black and white until *Burn!*, *La última cena* was Alea's first color film. A further characteristic that sets *La última cena* apart from the majority of Alea's other films is its chronological setting in the final decade of the eighteenth century on a Havana sugar plantation. As such, *La última cena* foregrounds the history of plantation slavery in Cuba in the late eighteenth and early nineteenth centuries, which was booming in the wake of the revolution in neighboring Saint Domingue.[26] Crucially, however, the film also foregrounds Cuba's African slave heritage, a subject that had been overlooked and misrepresented in the historical writing of the Cuban "pseudo-republic" of 1902–1952.[27] In this endeavor, Alea was part of a group of filmmakers and historians working in Cuba's national film institute who from the late 1960s onward had begun to explore Black Cuban history and culture. Initially, this work took the form of documentary films that profiled the African roots of much Cuban music.[28] Then, in the 1970s, a series of films emerged that continued this recuperative work by directly addressing the subjects of slavery, slave resistance, and abolition in order to construct an assertive and representative picture of Black Cuban history and culture. As the critic Zuzana Pick explains, this project "undertook to restore black [Cuban] heritage to its rightful historical place."[29] Members of this collaborative group whose work addressed slavery included the Afro-Cuban filmmaker Sergio Giral (whose trilogy of slavery films is the focus of the next chapter) and the historian Manuel Moreno Fraginals (with whom Alea collaborated in the making of *La última cena*), as well as Alea himself. Moreover, the timing of Alea's rescuing of Afro-Cuban history in *La última cena* was contemporaneous not only with efforts from within the ICAIC to consider Cuba's Black heritage but also with Cuba's principled military engagement in Angola. This intervention was named "Operation Carlota" by Castro in memory of an enslaved woman who had led an uprising on a nineteenth-century Cuban sugar plantation, Carlota Lucimí, who is also known as "La Negra Carlota." In his autobiography, Castro later outlined the significance of this symbolic tribute:

> The name is both a symbol and a tribute to the thousands of slaves who died in combat or were executed during the first slave insurrections in Cuba. It was in those uprisings that women such as Carlota were forged. She was a Lucimí [an Afro-Cuban of Yoruba ancestry] slave on the Triunvirato sugar-cane plantation, in what is now the province of Matanzas, and in 1843 she led one of the many uprisings against the terrible stigma of slavery, and she gave her life in the struggle.[30]

By symbolically linking Cuba's mission in Angola with Cuba's heritage of slave resistance, Castro summoned a solidarity with Angola and acknowledged Cuba's Black diasporic roots while pursuing a mission demonstrative of the revolution's internationalist ethic and spirit. The operation itself provided emergency assistance in 1975 to Agostinho Neto's socialist government, the *Movimento Popular de Libertaçao de Angola* (the MPLA), who were facing an imminent catastrophe. With the demise of the left-wing revolution in Portugal in August of that year, the MPLA had lost a crucial ally, while American money and weapons had been flooding into Angola to assist the antisocialist National Front for the Liberation of Angola (the FNLA), the MPLA's principal military and political rival. Then, on October 14, a military force comprised of some 1,000 South African–trained FNLA guerrillas and 150 white soldiers and officers invaded Angola from South Africa. Reinforcements in the form of an additional 1,000 South African Defense Force soldiers swiftly followed. Cuba's response, undertaken independently and without having consulted the Soviet Union, was to provide the MPLA with 480 military instructors and 4,000 soldiers by the end of the year. The intervention, Richard Gott has argued, was undertaken "entirely without selfish motivation."³¹ Moreover, it proved to be "dramatic and effective" and resulted in both an MPLA-Cuban victory and the rise of Cuba in the African political imaginary.³² The high-profile operation, one of Castro's most ambitious foreign interventions, must have been on the minds of all those working at the ICAIC from late 1975 onward. While Alea's *La última cena* does not make any allusion to Angola or Operation Carlota, the intersecting interests of the Cuban state and the ICAIC at this historical moment are indicative of the extent to which an internationalist worldview and pan-African discourse had permeated Cuban society.³³ This discourse cannot be disentangled from the attention devoted to the Haitian Revolution in *La última cena*. Indeed, *La última cena* is remarkable for its strategic invocations of the Haitian Revolution. While this subject is rarely explicitly mentioned, it is intricately embedded in and around the film's narrative and imagery in constant and internecine ways. A crucial effect of the film that has been ignored is the extent to which Alea's tangential but elaborate treatment of the Haitian Revolution finally places Cuban history in the context of a wider Caribbean history. At a historical moment in which the Cuban state was acting decisively in Africa and efforts to revalorize Cuban Black history and culture were occurring in the ICAIC, Alea's *La última cena* urged its viewers to consider Cuba's shared Black diasporic history. Inviting the viewer to think comparatively and transhistorically by juxtaposing Haitian and Cuban revolutionary history, *La última cena* opened up new horizons for Black internationalist discourse.³⁴

The Christian Parodics of Alea's Method

The plot of *La última cena* is based on a single paragraph taken from *El Ingenio* (*The Sugar Mill*), a groundbreaking work of scholarship by the Cuban historian Manuel Moreno Fraginals.³⁵ In Fraginals's telling of the historical events, one Holy Week in the late 1780s [*sic*], an aristocratic Havana plantation owner, the Count de Casa Bayona, "decided in an act of deep Christian fervor to humble himself before [his] slaves" and "One Holy Thursday he washed twelve Negroes' feet, sat them at his table, and served them food in imitation of Christ."³⁶ However, far from mollifying the enslaved workers or reconciling them to their enslaved status, the Count's twelve chosen slaves interpret Christ's teachings as a call to universal social equality. Consequently, the slaves' response to their master's antics is to organize an uprising and to burn down the sugar mill, thereby demonstrating their selfhood and asserting their agency.[37] The Count's reaction to the insurrection is brutal and predictable: the ordering of his *rancheadores* ("slave catchers") to hunt down and execute the rebels. Thus, the events of this particular Holy Week, which began with the Count washing the feet of twelve of his slaves, end with the Count ordering that the same slaves be caught and executed and that their severed heads be stuck on spikes mounted on a hilltop. These historical events, which Alea transposes from the 1780s to the 1790s and hence into the shadow of the Haitian Revolution, culminate in a scene that evokes Aimé Césaire's withering critique of the hypocrisy of Christian colonialism and its "reddened waters."[38] The Count pronounces his intention to build a church in honor of the enslaved workers' overseer who was killed in the uprising. Alea has the Count make this pronouncement from the very same hilltop that is now testament to the barbarity of colonial slavery, which is clearly an intensely ironic gesture. The Count is encircled by a grotesque apostolic parody—eleven severed human heads (fig. 2.1).

Figure 2.1. The Count's grotesque apostolic parody, *La última cena*. *Source:* Tomás Gutiérrez Alea, dir., *La última cena* (1976), Cuba. Instituto Cubano del Arte e Industria Cinematográficos.

The depravity of the scene is carefully composed and reveals the intricacies of Alea's parodic and symbolic method. The deep-focus shot draws attention to the illusory proximity of the cross in the mid-picture to four of the severed heads. This ensures that the viewer cannot avoid seeing simultaneously both the most important sign of the Christian faith and the murderous truth of slaveholding colonialism. The composition and deep focus also juxtapose the severed heads against palm fronds, another Christian symbol that Alea treats with colossal irony. In the Christian iconographic tradition, palm fronds and branches are emblematic of victory, peace, and salvation and are associated with moral justice and virtue. Consider, for example, the description in Revelations (7:9) of "a great multitude [of peoples] before the throne, and before the Lamb, clothed with white robes, and palms in their hands."[39] Consider also Psalms (92:12), which proclaims that "the righteous shall flourish like the palm tree."[40] Finally, recall that the advent of Easter Week is marked by "Palm Sunday," the day on which, according to the Gospel of Saint John (12:13), the people "took branches of palm trees, and went forth to meet [Christ entering Jerusalem] and cried Hosanna."[41] Here, however, Alea's cinematography treats the palm fronds as decorations for the severed heads. The camera angle even makes it appear as if two of the heads are not mounted on spikes but rather are resting on elaborate palm-frond collars that recall the ruffled collars of late eighteenth-century colonial dress, which the Count wears throughout the film. Thus, by both brutal neorealist representation and intricate aesthetic symbolism, the scene presents a picture of Cuba's colonial past as a degenerate hell that evokes Conrad's treatment of the Belgian Congo in *Heart of Darkness*.[42] It also foreshadows Francis Ford Coppola's filmic transportation of Conrad's novella into the Vietnam War in *Apocalypse Now*, the original version of which was released in 1979, three years after the release of *La última cena*.[43] The hell of Kurtz's camp, which like the Count's hilltop also abounds with severed heads and mutilated human bodies, is one of cinema's most notorious portraits of the unrestrained human barbarity that is coexistent with the drive to imperial mastery. The Count's hilltop in Alea's *La última cena* prefigures Kurtz's camp, and like Coppola's masterful adaptation, it communicates the intrinsic barbarism of colonial and imperial projects. However, the impact on the viewer of these two scenes can be distinguished. While the presentation of Kurtz's camp produces a visceral revulsion, the barbarism of Alea's scene is overlaid with an intense irony, and this provokes both horror and the activation of the viewer's critical faculties.

With the execution of eleven of the enslaved rebels/apostles, only one remains at large—the aptly named Sebástian, who serves as a poignant symbol of the inevitability of resistance and of its eventual triumph. Further, Sébastian's characterization illuminates the Christian parodics of Alea's method. To begin with, the name "Sébastian" was certainly neither innocently chosen nor arbitrary. Sébastian is of course the name not of one of Christ's disciples but of "a third-century saint, a Roman soldier martyred by the arrows of his fellow officers [whose] sufferings were a favourite subject for medieval artists."[44] However, this bare-bones definition mistakes the doctrinal significance of Saint Sebastian's death and grossly underestimates his fascinating, unstable, iconographic history, which is certainly not restricted to medieval art. In fact, Saint Sebastian has inspired a stunning range of tributes, representations, and evocations in a multiplicity of media. These span canonical Western visual art from the medieval period to Salvador Dalí and Damien Hirst, classical and pop music, and an array of literary and filmic depictions.[45] Perhaps the most sensitive consideration of Saint Sebastian and his cultural afterlives is to be found in the writings and drawings of Federico García Lorca. In a public lecture and poetry reading he first delivered in Madrid in March 1932, Lorca remarked that he considered "one of man's most beautiful postures" to be "that of Saint Sebastian," whose vulnerability he likened to the poet's relationship to the world.[46] Lorca's lecture remark that evening should not surprise us, since it arose from many years' deep contemplation. Some five years earlier, in correspondence with Dalí dating from August 1927, Lorca had reflected on his and Dalí's respective artistic visions of the saint. There, Lorca explained that he was profoundly moved by Saint Sebastian's "*grace* under torture" and that he considered Saint Sebastian to be "the loveliest figure in all of art."[47] Alea's masterful construction of Sébastian as a heroic Black rebel cunningly plays on this cultural inheritance in ingenious ways. A number of attributes emphasized in Saint Sebastian's iconographic history can be identified as especially relevant to Alea's characterization of Sébastian as a model of Black survival and resistance.

First, as a triumphant image of transcendent suffering, Saint Sebastian, who was lashed to a stake and shot with arrows by the orders of the Roman Emperor Diocletian, symbolizes a capacity to endure ritualized torture and punishment. Despite suffering horrendous injuries—he was left at the stake and presumed dead—Sebastian did not die of his arrow wounds but lived to evangelize and die another day. He was nursed back to health by Saint Irene of Rome, and on his recovery, he did not go meekly into the night but rather verbally assaulted Diocletian in public for his cruelties to Christians. Diocletian once again ordered Sebastian's execution, which this time proceeded successfully—Sebastian was clubbed to death. Sebastian's story of undeterred opposition to the established order is thus a potent one in the context of slaveholding society. Second, in his death Sebastian became the patron saint of athletes as a result of his extraordinary capacity for suffering, his powers of recovery, his endurance, and his strength. As a result, many visual representations of Sebastian—and Sebastian is possibly the most-painted martyr in the Christian tradition—emphasize masculine athleticism and the body beautiful. All this helps to explain how and why Sebastian is probably the only Christian saint who has gone on to become an enduring gay icon.[48] The heritage of this iconographic tradition is also potent for Alea's project in which the rebel/apostle/saint Sébastian is also characterized as athletic, attractive, and physically strong. Sébastian spends a good deal of the movie running, and when he does so, the mise-en-scène and associative imagery goes to great lengths to celebrate his body as powerful, athletic, and attractive. This adoption of the visual iconography of Saint Sebastian to a Black subject recalls Carl Fischer's 1967 photograph of Muhammed Ali as Saint Sebastian, the composition of which was based on the fifteenth-century Italian artist Francesco Botticini's dynamic and affective painting of Saint Sebastian (fig. 2.2). Fischer's photograph was a product of his long-running collaboration with art director and designer George Lois, who would later use it to produce *Esquire* magazine's iconic April 1968 cover. Fischer's photograph thus served as the basis for what the writer, journalist, and radio-show host Kurt Anderson considers as "the greatest magazine cover ever created." The substance of Anderson's high praise for the magazine cover applies equally to the Fischer photograph, which makes "a political statement without being grim or stupid or predictable. It's not just a great idea, but visually elegant, economical, perfect."[49] As fate would have it, the April 1968 issue of *Esquire* magazine hit the newsstands the very same day that Martin Luther King was assassinated: April 4, 1968. This fateful timing augmented the image's already-powerful resonance and helped to ensure its reception as a forceful visual statement of dissent and an essential image of late 1960s American counterculture.

While the general background to the *Esquire* photoshoot was the maelstrom of protest and struggle over race and religion in the United States in the late 1960s, Ali's conviction for draft evasion in April 1967 ensured the image's incendiary impact. Having conscientiously objected to serving in the US military in the Vietnam War, Ali had been sentenced to five years in prison, fined $10,000, stripped of his world heavyweight

Figure 2.2. Carl Fischer, "Muhammad Ali as Saint Sebastian." Photograph 1967 (photographed), ca. 2004 (printed). Victoria and Albert Museum, London. *Source:* "Muhammad Ali as Saint Sebastian," 1967 © Carl Fischer Estate / Artists Rights Society (ARS) New York / CARCC Ottawa 2023.

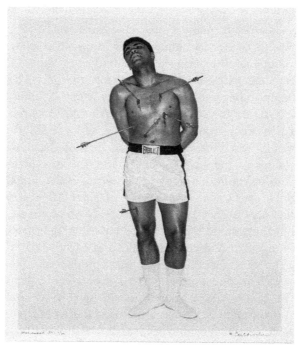

title, and suspended from boxing. Ali subsequently appealed to the US Supreme Court against his conviction, and at the time of the photoshoot he was awaiting the court's decision.[50] After Ali's death in 2016, Lois reported that during the photoshoot Ali named each of the arrows after his various persecutors, among them President Lyndon B. Johnson, Defense Secretary Robert McNamara, and the commander of the United States forces during the Vietnam War, General William Westmoreland. The power of the Fischer–Lois image of Ali as Saint Sebastian remains unmistakeable, and Alea's channeling of this iconographic inheritance is striking.

Both Alea's filmic Sébastian and the Fischer–Lois figuration of Muhammed Ali as Saint Sebastian present images of the Black body as beautiful, despite the tortures inflicted upon it. Both also evoke the sense of "grace under torture" that entranced Lorca. The attribution of grace to the tortured Black subject is also an effective strategy by which the torturers' *lack of grace* is conveyed. They both also communicate an antiestablishment message of moral virtue and physical strength and reveal a willingness to use Christian doctrine to expose Christian hypocrisy. Further, perhaps the most incendiary element of the message that is elicited by Alea's canny reconfiguration of the Saint Sebastian story is that it casts the Count as the anti-Christian Emperor Diocletian, even as he aspires to become a better and truer Christian. And, as we will see, Diocletian is not the only Roman executioner to whom the Count will be likened. As the reviewer Philip French remarked, after the insurrection, "the Count returns not as self-elected Christ but as brutal Pilate to crucify his disciples."[51]

La última cena opens with the camera panning slowly over medieval frescoes: we see close-ups of an infant bearing a crucifix, Christ and the Virgin Mary, a rosary, and thorny pink roses. By dwelling on these images, Alea communicates the centrality of bodily suffering and sacrifice to his narrative via the conventions of Hispanic Catholic iconography: the rose and thorns represent the blood and flesh of Christ, while a crown of thorns symbolizes Christ's suffering and sacrifice. The camerawork is accompanied by polyphonic, Renaissance choral music—a motet—the deployment of which contrasts with Pontecorvo's use of Bach at key junctures in *Burn!* Pontecorvo's pairing of Bach's music with celebratory and emotive cinematographic images of the Black revolutionary José Dolores is suggestive of a belief in the possibility of a transcendent, radical universalism. Pontecorvo's pairing of Dolores and Bach and the political project we can ascribe to it can be readily aligned with Susan Buck-Morss's identification of the Haitian revolutionaries who sang *La Marseillaise* as tantalizing evidence, "however transitory," of "the concrete meaning of freedom" and the realization of Hegel's philosophy of absolute spirit.[52] Alea's use of music from the European classical tradition, on the other hand, offers a more skeptical assessment. For Alea, the relationship between sacred Christian art, Black history, and the possibility of a transcendent, radical Enlightenment—and the consequent redemption of the project of universal history—is much less clear than it was for Pontecorvo. What is clear from this opening, however, is Alea's heavily ironic attitude that uses both sacred music and splendid religious iconography to mount a powerful critique of the manner in which the full resources of the aesthetics of baroque Christianity were used to justify the slave system. Alea is here creating his own anticolonial critique, one that runs in parallel with Aimé Césaire and Frantz Fanon's denunciations of the faux humanism of European so-called civilization.

Consider, for example, Césaire's argument presented in his *Discourse on Colonialism* that "the dishonest equations Christianity = civilization, paganism = savagery."[53] These false equations, Césaire compellingly argued, ensured abominable consequences for colonized peoples and contributed to the creation of a "collective hypocrisy" that obstructs an honest answer to the question: "What, fundamentally, is colonization?"[54] Later in the film, Alea employs non-European music to mount a different historiographical and ideological point. While sacred music from the Roman Catholic tradition is used at key junctures throughout the film, Alea's musical choice when Sébastian escapes is evocative of popular West African world-beat music and is characterized by the sounds of hand drums and rhythmic call-and-response vocals. This ensures a dramatic acoustic contrast and emphasizes the cultural currency and inheritance of diverse African musical traditions in modern Cuba.

The ironic tranquility of the film's opening that was established by the use of European artistic celebrations of the benevolence and central love of Christ's message is abruptly shattered by the violence of the first scene. A subtitle informs the viewer that it is Ash Wednesday, one of the most somber days in the Christian liturgical calendar. On this day, Christians of a variety of denominations including Catholicism receive black ash in the sign of the cross on their foreheads. The ashes, which are obtained by burning the palm fronds from the previous year's Palm Sunday, remind Christians that according to their faith all humankind is sinful in nature, that "there is none righteous, no, not one" (Romans, 3:10), and that "dust thou *art*, and unto dust shalt thou return" (Genesis 3:19).[55] With the ubiquity of sin and suffering thus foregrounded, and the view that humankind is not deserving of God's mercy, an appropriate stage has been set for the entrance of the Count's overseer. A set of wooden double doors are slammed open toward the camera, which looks out from a dark and filthy barrack for enslaved workers, a dwelling that seems more akin to an animal enclosure than a habitation fit for human beings. The structure of dwellings for enslaved populations probably varied vastly, and given that almost no slave dwellings survive unless they were constructed as part of the "Casa Grande," such as Jefferson's Monticello "dependencies," the historically right or wrong way to construct a slave cabin is shrouded in uncertainty. Nevertheless, it is notable that the foul and claustrophobic living quarters for the enslaved represented in *La última cena* are a far cry from the pristinely prettified slave huts of more recent Hollywood movies addressing slavery, such as *12 Years a Slave*. The plantation overseer,

Don Manuel—a robustly built, muscular, and olive-skinned man of early middle age—bursts into the barrack holding a riding crop. Sebastián has escaped, and Don Manuel accuses an enslaved man resting in the barrack of aiding Sebastián in his attempt. Don Manuel seizes the enslaved man by his clothing, the man protests his innocence, and Don Manuel throws him to the ground. The dim gloom of the scene is manufactured by the dull palette and Alea's careful control of the lighting, which is limited to a mere glimpse of natural light from the small window seen above the overseer's head. That this masterful cinematic control of color and light produces a glow above the overseer's hat, which resembles a saint's halo, should be understood as a further example of Alea's parodic technique and his penchant for savage irony (fig. 2.3).

The runaway's meagre bedclothes are identified and presented to the wildly barking sniffer dogs so the fugitive can be tracked, captured, and punished. Thus, from the very first scene *La última cena* makes clear that the institution of slavery was founded on systemically orchestrated violence and terror. Yet, it also makes clear that one of the most traumatic and challenging experiences confronting the slave power is the act of self-liberation by the enslaved. Alea poses the question: What is the difference

Figure 2.3. Don Manuel in the slave hut, *La última cena*. *Source:* Tomás Gutiérrez Alea, dir., *La última cena* (1976), Cuba. Instituto Cubano del Arte e Industria Cinematográficos.

between a runaway and a human reclaiming stolen liberty? Within the system of this small sugar plantation, as the film will also make clear, the notion of a paternalistic, benevolent master is a terrifying and of course unrealizable paradox.

La última cena clearly elaborates the complicated ways in which the hierarchical structure of the plantation system, and its concomitant forms of labor specialization, generates a fractured community of radically unequal individuals with incommensurable worldviews. One notable aspect of the social analysis is the way it extends to consider the mental isolation existing within different strata of the slave power itself. For example, the Count delegates matters of terror, brutality, and torture to the overseer, Don Manuel, who is charged with maintaining discipline on the plantation and the recapture of runaways. When Don Manuel begins to tell the Count, who has just returned on horseback from Havana, about the fact of Sebastián's running away, his master is uninterested. The Count cuts Manuel off; he refuses to acknowledge the reality of the slave world he reigns over. He has neither the desire nor the capacity to recognize that one of the day-to-day dirty realities of plantation life is dealing with incessant slave resistance. Such recognition would necessarily require at least an implicit admission of the capacity of the enslaved for a political practice of dissent. In turn, this would of course destabilize the Count's conviction that Blacks were ideal slaves. The Count's worldview emerges as a fantasy that remains coherent only to the extent to which it maintains a blindness to certain realities relating to the unstoppable force of slave autonomy. These are, of course, realities to which his overseer, and other plantation middle managers, are routinely exposed. Hence, when Don Manuel in a subsequent scene attempts to explain to the Count that the only way to counterbalance the fall in production caused by affording the enslaved time off for religious holidays is more frequent whippings, the Count does not dwell on the matter long enough to recognize any contradiction. Instead, the essence of his curt response is to tell the overseer that matters of torture are his business and his business alone. The maintenance of such a strictly compartmentalized perspective ensures that the Count remains ignorant of the fact that the logic of the plantation system is that all social relations are rendered subordinate to its demands. Further, in closing his mind to the reality under his nose of slave resistance and of the dependence of productivity on practices of torture, the Count is, by extension, also closing his mind to the revolutionary events occurring just 700 miles away across the Windward Passage on the French colony of Saint

Domingue. For the Count, the facts of slave resistance and of the Haitian Revolution were unthinkable and to be actively disavowed in order that he might continue to deceive himself as to the fundamental barbarism not only of slaveholding but also of proto-capitalist colonialism.[56] Alea's perspicuity here identifies the sugar plantation and slavery as central to not only pan-Caribbean history but also global modernity.[57]

Having introduced at the outset the subject of the struggle of the enslaved for their freedom and the efforts of the overseer to deny them such freedom, Alea situates this dichotomy alongside another: the contradictions between the Count's religious faith and his economic interests as the owner of the mill and plantation. Alea uses dramatic irony to reveal the absurd shortcomings of the Count's fanatical religious humanism while simultaneously uncovering the Count's spiritual anguish and his chaotic moral consciousness. Various set-piece dramatic vignettes bring out these ethical confusions. For example, in one scene the plantation's priest conveys to the Count his concerns regarding a creeping moral lassitude that has invaded the plantation. In the priest's analysis, the overseer is not God-fearing and the enslaved are not receiving the necessary religious instruction due to overwork. Moreover, while the Count is bathed, pampered, and massaged by an enslaved domestic worker, the priest gently rebukes him for his drinking and, euphemistically, for spending so much time with enslaved women. In response, the Count admits that he is uneasy and unable to find peace and that, "aunque sea de día, ando como perdido en un laberinto lleno de tinieblas" ["even by day, I walk lost in a maze of darkness"]. The Count is materially rich but spiritually impoverished. Slave societies everywhere, it is implied—Cuba, Saint Domingue, and throughout the Americas—are debased and rotten, and no individual can escape the taint of slavery, the Count included. Shortly after his admission of aimlessness, the Count, together with his overseer and his priest, is taken on a tour of the mill by the engineer, Monsieur Duclé, a "mulatto" refugee from the revolution in Saint Domingue. The Count and the engineer discuss the purchase of a new, technologically advanced sugarcane press—a three-beamed English model—the origin of which serves to evoke the multinational aspect of the Atlantic slave system. Far from being an outmoded relic of a feudal order, Alea shows us that enslaved labor both used and drove capitalist technological improvements. Monsieur Duclé approves of the more-advanced technology—"no hay duda que el trapiche horizontal terminará por imponer" ["there is no doubt that the horizontal press is the future"]—but he notes, in a foreboding tone, that the new press "necesitará de seguro más caña" ["will definitely need more cane"] and that more cane will require greater numbers of enslaved workers. This, Duclé muses, will tip the demographic power on the island in the favor of the enslaved Black population. While the Count is unfazed by this prospect, remarking, "No se preocupe, señor Duclé. Nosotros aquí sabemos tratar a los negros" ["Don't worry Mr. Duclé. We know how to treat the Blacks here."], Duclé's silence in response suggests that his experience in Saint Domingue weighs heavily on his mind. The opening of the subsequent scene resonates ambivalently with the Count's blithe words: Sebastián, who had attempted to escape from the plantation, has been caught by the mounted *rancheadores* and is thrown to the ground at the count's feet. Punishment from Don Manuel is swift and brutal: addressing Sebastián, he states, "A ver si ahora te quedan ganas de escaparte otra vez" ["Now, let's see if you feel like running away again"], before he cuts off his left ear and tosses it to the dogs, who quickly devour it. The Count is nauseated by the scene but does not object to Don Manuel's brutality. The scene serves to reiterate that the application of systemic terror underpinned plantation slavery and serves as one of a number of dramatic counterpoints in the film to the attempted formal benignity of the lengthy "last supper" sequence that is the film's centerpiece.

The following day—Maundy Thursday, the fifth day of Holy Week and the day on which the Christian rite of foot-washing takes place—the Count instructs the overseer to pick out twelve enslaved workers who will be his "disciples" and dinner guests in his parodic reenactment of Christ's last supper. Among the Count's chosen ones is Sebastián, and the Count insists on his release from the stocks where he is presently held. The twelve slave-disciples are then brought to the chapel where, while the slaves wait for the Count to wash their feet, the priest offers instruction on the glory and generosity of God who permits His followers to dine at His table. This scene is punctuated by cinematographic portraits that the critic Penelope Gilliat considered "startlingly beautiful" and evocative of "Rembrandt's portraits."[58] However, I suggest that the lineage of the light effects and staging of these cinematic portraits can be traced not to the Dutch Golden Age but to Spain and the lush, violent, polarized paintings of Zurbarán and, especially, of Velázquez. Critics have remarked that Velázquez's painterly style strove not to reproduce "reality as it appeared to the eye" but rather aspired "to catch [a] characteristic impression."[59] This technique, which made Velázquez an enamored figure in Paris among the nineteenth-century founders of impressionism, has been acclaimed for its capacity to capture a depth of character and atmosphere that eludes painting in the range of traditions that stress precision aspiring to perfection.⁶⁰ Germane to the discussion here are the commonalities in the techniques and effects of Alea's and Velázquez's portraits, notwithstanding their differences of medium and chronological separation. Consider, for example, the effect of Alea's almost exclusive reliance on natural light and candlelight rather than artificial set lighting.⁶¹ The effect, which we can observe in figure 2.4, is the soft illumination of faces against a backdrop that ranges in palette from an inky blackness to grays and browns (fig. 2.4).

This cinematographic style imparts the ambience of theater production and recalls the dark, shadowy tone of a Velázaquez portrait. Consider, for example, Velázquez's portrait of his enslaved assistant, Juan de Pareja (fig. 2.5). The extremely limited palette—predominantly there are black, grays, and browns—is reminiscent of not only the portrait shots that precede the supper scene but also shots from other scenes, including the opening scene in the slave hut already analyzed (see fig. 2.3). Moreover, the play and contrast of light and shadow across the face in Velázquez's portrait of Juan de Pareja resembles Alea's cinematic portrait of Sebastián to an uncanny degree (fig. 2.6). Prominent facial features—the forehead, cheekbones, and nose—of both subjects catch the muted light while the right side of their faces and necks disappear into shadow. A further similarity can be observed in the exquisite treatment of shading across their clothing. The

Figure 2.4. Alea's cinematic portraiture that evokes Velázquez, *La última cena*. Source: Tomás Gutiérrez Alea, dir., *La última cena* (1976), Cuba. Instituto Cubano del Arte e Industria Cinematográficos.

Figure 2.5. Diego Velázquez, "Portrait of Juan de Pareja," c. 1650. *Source:* Metropolitan Museum of Art, New York.

Figure 2.6. Portrait of Sebastián, *La última cena*. *Source:* Tomás Gutiérrez Alea, dir., *La última cena* (1976), Cuba. Instituto Cubano del Arte e Industria Cinematográficos.

folds of Pareja's distinguished attire and Sebastián's simple, stained smock serve to create intimacy and a sense of ephemerality. The dark tones that dominate both portraits make it impossible to make out some details: Juan de Pareja's hair and Sebastián's chest under his chin and neck are obscured by insufficient illumination. However, far from being detrimental, these "imperfections" enhance the aesthetic impact of these two portraits since the viewer's imagination must supply some visual details to "complete" the portraits. The pertinence to this analysis of the argument presented by the Cuban filmmaker and writer Julio García Espinosa, in his seminal 1967 essay "Por un cine imperfecto" ("For an Imperfect Cinema"), is striking. García Espinosa argued that in the Third World, technical and aesthetic perfection were inappropriate goals for filmmakers for reasons of both resources and politics. García Espinosa's claim was that whereas technically and aesthetically "perfect" commercial cinema produces passive spectators, "imperfect," revolutionary cinema demands an active audience to achieve completion. The argument thus enables the consideration of Cuban and Latin American "imperfect cinema" as a filmic form that approximates elements of Velázquez's aesthetics.[62]

While both Velázquez's "Juan de Pareja" and Alea's filmic portrait of Sebastián portray their subjects with great dignity, it is an unavoidable fact that Alea's Sebastián also presents an image of an abused, deformed, and tortured man. With his eyes swollen nearly shut and a bloodied bandage wrapped around his head and over the wound caused by his mutilation, Alea's Sebastián nevertheless remains an image of defiance. Up to this point, Sebastián has not uttered a word; he is to be judged on his actions, which indicate an undeterred belief in the possibility of the negation of subjugation via resistance. The series of cinematographic portraits of the twelve enslaved men waiting in the chapel also has the effect of dramatically individualizing the enslaved. Each portrait is powerful testimony to the suffering of the enslaved, but Alea's genius is to capture suffering while carefully preserving agency, as in the portrait of Sebastián. When the Count washes the feet of the twelve enslaved men at the front of the church, the tension is palpable, and Alea does not overlook the comic potential of this bizarre ritual. Indeed, the film as a whole can be interpreted as "a tour de force of black comedy."[63] The first slave to have his feet washed cannot help himself from bursting into a fit of uncontrollable laughter. Finding the whole affair comic-absurd, and perhaps ticklish to boot, the enslaved man's inconvenient reaction to the Count's highly choreographed, hubristic imitation of Christ threatens to derail the Count's best-laid plans. Then, after the Count reluctantly—and for just a split second—kisses his bathed foot, the man shakes his head in bewilderment (fig. 2.7). It is clear that these enslaved men will not meekly play their assigned roles in the Count's show.

To the overseer's discomfort, Sebastián is next to have his feet washed by the Count, and as the Count prepares to kiss Sebastián's bathed foot, the overseer walks out of the church in disgust. He proceeds straight to the engineer's quarters, where he quite accurately states, "Yo no entiendo nada pero aquí está pasando algo muy raro" ["I don't understand it, but something very strange is going on here"], before he rhetorically asks Monsieur Duclé, "¿Adonde vamos a parar?" ["Where will this take us?"]. Don Manuel then reveals his astonishment that the Count kissed Sebastián's feet before marveling at Sebastián's recuperative healing powers and his indefatigable nature. Notably, these are both qualities Sebastián shares with Saint Sebastian. Don Manuel's comments prompt Duclé to make the film's first explicit reference to the Haitian Revolution, which is a red rag to the overseer:

> M. Duclé: Beba, beba. Beba mientras pueda hacerlo. No sabe lo que pasa cuando los negros se alborotan. En Santo Domingo . . .

Figure 2.7. The Count kisses his slaves' feet, *La última cena*. Source: Tomás Gutiérrez Alea, dir., *La última cena* (1976), Cuba. Instituto Cubano del Arte e Industria Cinematográficos.

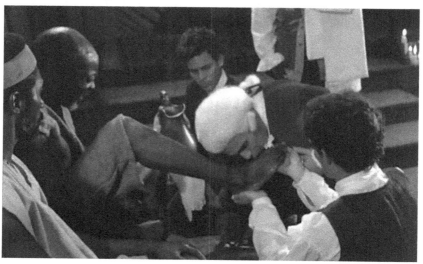

(Drink, drink. Drink while you can. You don't know what it's like when the Blacks rise up. In Santo Domingo . . .)

Don Manuel: Ah ¡siempre por el mismo camino! Santo Domingo.

(Ah! Always on about the same thing! Santo Domingo.)

M. Duclé: Porque lo conozco. Ahí habían más negros que blancos y mulatos. Ahora solamente hay negros. A mí tampoco me gustaría ver mi cabeza sirviéndole de pelota a un juego de negritos.

(Because I know it. There were more Blacks than whites and mulattos there. Now there are only Blacks. I wouldn't want to see my head used as a ball for little Blacks to kick around either.)

And with Duclé's words and grim laughter, the camera pans to Don Manuel, foreshadowing his killing by the enslaved rebel in the forthcoming uprising. Once again, the Haitian Revolution is an event that must be silenced and disavowed: Don Manuel does not want to hear any talk of it.[64] And with those words, the scene ends and the film's extraordinary centerpiece, the fifty-five-minute supper scene, begins.

From Supper to Revolution

Before turning our attention to an analysis of the supper scene—the film's focal point—it is instructive to pause momentarily on the matter of its duration since this reveals certain matters pertinent to Alea's filmmaking strategy and the politics of Alea's filmic form. In Hollywood certainly, a scene of fifty-five minutes' duration in which the dialogue is allowed to "work itself out" would be uncommon in the extreme. Indeed, as Stanley Aronowitz noted some time ago in analysis that reveals the influence of Herbert Marcuse and E. P. Thompson, "American films are characterized by rapid camera work and sharp editing whose effect is to segment the action into one- or two-minute time slots, paralleling the prevailing styles of television production. . . . The prevailing modes of film production rely on conceptions of dramatic time inherited from the more crass forms of

Figure 2.8. The Count's Last Supper, *La última cena*. Source: Tomás Gutiérrez Alea, dir., *La última cena* (1976), Cuba. Instituto Cubano del Arte e Industria Cinematográficos.

commercial culture."[65] Consequently, the "passivity of the spectator" is achieved and time and space for deliberation on the part of the viewer is dramatically diminished or even eliminated altogether. The fifty-five-minute supper scene in *La ultima cena*, on the other hand, is evidence that Alea's filmmaking strategy is working toward the polar-opposite extreme. In refusing fragmentation as filmic technique, Alea conjures a strategy that results in what Fredric Jameson has called "a more totalizing way of viewing phenomena."[66] By allowing the conversation of the lengthy supper scene to unfold as a temporally ordinary activity, Alea provides his viewers with time to reflect critically on the meaning of the dialogue, the occasion represented, and the peculiarities of the individual characters and their unevenly situated positions within the micro-system of the Count's plantation and the macro-system of Atlantic slavery. The politics of Alea's form is thus structurally underscored by this lengthy theatrical set piece, which affirms the film's ideological thrust: that freedom and liberation cannot be passively received, the egoism of the Count's religiously inspired charity, the richness of Cuba's African heritage, and the political agency of the enslaved. As such, the legacy of the Haitian Revolution inevitably simmers away throughout. The enslaved men who sit at the Count's table display their humanity with every gesture, word, and expression; among them there are tellers of stories and fables, musical performers, and dancers. Without ever descending into sentimentality, Alea's orchestration of the supper scene powerfully conveys the sickness of a world-system that wantonly wastes such an abundance of human talent, knowledge, and experience. The Count's enslaved dinner "guests" are deeply individualized: they are no anonymous mass and they are given carefully constructed individual voices and histories, and this serves to communicate a diversity of experience while also conveying the challenge of constructing a politics of solidarity among the enslaved given the hierarchical and stratified structures enforced-upon enslaved populations. For example, there is an enslaved houseworker who cannot bear the prospect of being sent back to the field "con todos los negros sucios, estos" ["with all these dirty Blacks"].[67] Social divisions resulting from the prior statuses of the enslaved are also communicated: among the Count's supper guests there is African royalty—Bangoché, a Yoruban king, who we learn was captured in war and sold into slavery in Guinea.

The supper scene also constitutes further evidence of Alea's subversive comic-ironic touch. Alea was not the first filmmaker to parodically recreate the Last Supper, and a number of critics have noted that the centerpiece to Alea's film recalls Luis Buñuel's subversive 1961 film *Viridiana* and its famous drunken-banquet scene, which freezes into a tableau that resembles Leonardo da Vinci's *The Last Supper*.[68] However, whereas Buñuel's re-creation of the Last Supper conveys an ambience of "carnage" and an "absurd orgy," the black humor of Alea's re-creation has a meditative, and of course a savagely ironic, quality.[69] Aspects of the scene also elaborate the film's meditation on the nature and politics of freedom and bondage with intelligence and emotional clarity. During the scene, an elderly enslaved man named Pascual approaches the Count to ask for his freedom. He explains that he is old and worn out and of little use now as a field slave. Indeed, Pascual personifies the human capacity to endure the inflictions of cruelty as well as its debilitating consequences. To his surprise, the Count grants Pascual his freedom, though his initial joy quickly sours: he breaks down for not knowing what to do with his newfound liberty. The Count quizzes him: Where will he go and what will he do? These are questions to which Pascual has no answers. The Count's cruel taunts—"¡Vean ustedes, acaba de obtener su libertad y no sabe qué va hacer con ella!" ["Look everyone! He's just got his freedom and he doesn't know what to do with it!"]—compound Pascual's existential grief. Pascual's realization that he may not be able to redeem or salvage what remains of his life serves to demonstrate that the scale and depths of slavery's monstrosity will forever be a stain on human history: it is a crime for which all measures of compensation are inadequate and for which there can be no true justice. However, Pascual's experience suggests the political imperative for the enslaved is not to achieve a negotiated emancipation, but rather the total destruction of a social order premised on human domination. The example of the Haitian Revolution thus lingers, ever present in the film's presentation of self-emancipation by means of revolution as the only possible route to political and psychological regeneration for the enslaved. The exchange between the Count and Pascual thus recalls the thesis articulated by Frantz Fanon–recently recapitulated and elaborated by Marcus Wood—that freedom granted by permission constitutes a "horrible gift." Wood argues that Fanon searched "deeply into the appalling aporia lying within the myth that freedom can ever be given by any master to any slave" since freedom is "beyond the power of any human . . . to endow another human with."[70]

The counterpoint to Pascual's story is Sebastián. Throughout the supper scene, Sebastián remains a picture of quiet defiance as he allows his peers and the garrulous (and increasingly drunken) Count to dominate the conversation. Seated directly on the Count's right-hand side, and with the bloodstains still fresh on his bandaged head, his mere physical presence sustains a simmering dramatic tension. When the Count asks Sebastián the question, "Quien soy?" ["Who am I?"], he refuses to call his enslaver by his name, title, or anything at all (fig. 2.9). This refusal of recognition is a climactic moment in the supper scene, and it has been interpreted by the critic Dennis West in the terms of Hegel's master-slave dialectic: "the master depends on his bondsman for acknowledgment of his power, indeed for assurance of his very selfhood."[71] But the Count does not receive any such acknowledgment or assurance. Instead, Sebastián spits on the Count's face from point-blank range, an act that constitutes a rejection of the Count's faux civility, a refusal of the terms on which their relationship is based, and an assertion of Sebastián's autonomy and his power to withhold recognition.[72] The Count's response is to raise his arm in readiness to strike him with the nearest thing he can lay his hands on—ridiculously, this is a spoon, and this deepens the Count's humiliation. However, the Count recovers his composure, lowers the silver spoon in his right hand, and does not strike Sebastián.

Figure 2.9. The Count and Sebastián at the supper table, *La última cena*. Source: Tomás Gutiérrez Alea, dir., *La última cena* (1976), Cuba. Instituto Cubano del Arte e Industria Cinematográficos.

Still consciously modeling his behavior on Christ, the Count exclaims that he can forgive Sebastián for his actions. The Count utters: "Un día como hoy, Cristo se humilló ante los hombres. No tiene nada de grandioso que un amo se humille ante sus esclavos. Ven, bebe. ¡Beba! ["On a day like today, Christ humbled himself before men. There is nothing remarkable about a master humbling himself before his slaves. Come, drink. Drink!"]; he then likens Sebastián to Judas, who spat in Christ's face just as Sebastián spat in his master's face. This interaction serves as a corrective to the view articulated by Oscar Wilde (and subsequently frequently quoted, paraphrased, and repeated) that "the worst slave-owners were those who were kind to their slaves, and so prevented the horror of the system being realised by those who suffered from it."[73] This interaction between the Count and Sebastián makes clear that the presumption that the enslaved will be duped and pacified by "kind" treatment severely underestimates the self-knowledge of the oppressed and their capacity for resistance. Sebastián's simmering revolutionary consciousness certainly needed no sparking by an enslaver's cruel behavior.

The tension between the Count and Sebastián is defused somewhat by the appearance of an enslaved domestic worker bringing bread to the supper table, and it becomes clear that the Count intends to lead his slave-disciples in a version of the Holy Communion. This set piece serves as a further opportunity for Alea to reveal the dishonesty of any equations of paganism and savagery, Christianity and civility. In the midst of explaining the Eucharist, the Count is interrupted by a bewildered slave who asks in disbelief, "A lo Cristo ¿se lo comieron?" ["What happened to that Christ? They ate him?"], a subversive-comic exchange that recalls a similar episode in Peter Shaffer's 1964 play *The Royal Hunt of the Sun*.[74] The religious instruction of the enslaved in Latin America was indeed a responsibility of enslavers, and the fact that a number of enslaved men on the Count's estate did not know of the Eucharist is itself an indication that he has been lax in providing instruction. The Count then tells the story of Saint Francis, the moral of which, according to the Count, is that "de todas las cosas buenas del Espíritu Santo que Cristo considera sus amigos la mejor es avergonzarse uno mismo y soportar penas e injurias por amor a Cristo. . . . Sólo el dolor es lo único verdaderamente nuestro y eso es lo único que nosotros podemos darle a Dios con alegría" ["of all of the good things about the Holy Spirit that Christ loves, the best is humbling oneself and suffering hardships and insults for His love. . . . Sorrow is the only thing that is truly ours to give to God with joy"]. Then the Count proceeds to expound upon a hodgepodge of stock racist justifications for slavery: "El negro está mejor preparado por la naturaleza para resistir el dolor con resignación" ["The Black man is by nature better able to put up with pain"]; and "¿Cuándo han visto ustedes a un blanco cantando mientras corta caña? El negro, en cambio, siempre canta. Y eso es bueno porque con el canto uno se olvida de lo que está haciendo. Se alegra el espíritu." ["Have you ever seen a white man singing when he cuts cane? The Black man, in contrast, is always singing. And that's good because when you sing you forget what you're doing. It gladdens the heart."]. And, more specifically: "Dios hizo las cosas de tal modo que el negro tiene como una disposición innata para el corte de caña" ["God gave the Black man an innate ability for cutting cane"]; and "Puede decirse que el negro ha nacido en medio de la caña" ["You could say that the Black man was born in the cane field"]. Then, having dominated the conversation for so long, the Count passes out at the table and Sebastián speaks for the first time in the film. He tells a creation myth in which the central characters are "Truth" and "Lie": Lie beheads Truth with a machete and places his own head on the body of Truth. Sebastián then explains that ever since then, the body of "Truth" has been deceiving people. Sebastián's creation myth serves as a rebuttal of the entirety of the Count's discourse and of all justifications for his enslaved status. Sebastián finishes his speech by declaring his commitment to the pursuit of his freedom, and his words—which are testimony to the power of the "marvelous" to sustain political will—foreshadow his eventual escape:

> SEBASTIÁN: Sebastián se hace palo en los montes, se hace pescado en los ríos, se hace piedra, se hace *susundamba*. ¡Vuela! Nadie me puede agarrar. A mí nadie me puede matar.
>
> (Sebastián will turn himself into a tree in the woods, a fish in the rivers, he will change into a stone, he will become a *susundamba* [an owl]. Fly away! Nobody can catch me. Nobody can kill me.)

The inspiration behind these words of Sebastián would appear to belong to the character of the vodou priest turned slave rebel Makandal in Alejo Carpentier's classic novel of marvelous realism and the Haitian Revolution, *El reino de este mundo* (*The Kingdom of This World*).[75] Working in different mediums, both Alea and Carpentier appear to have gazed from Cuba across the Windward Passage to Haiti to seek aesthetic and historical inspiration for their representations of resistance and the possibility of social transformation. Then, with Sebastián's words of marvelous dissent still hanging in air, the Count, drunk and barely conscious, is carried away by Edmundo, one of his enslaved domestic workers.

The following day, Good Friday, Don Manuel awakens the enslaved for work. Pascual attempts to tell Don Manuel that he is now a freeman having been granted his liberty by the Count at the previous night's supper. Don Manuel dismisses Pascual's claim as nonsense and he insists that the enslaved, Pascual included, must get to their work in the fields. It is the final catalyst for the uprising: as Don Manuel prepares to strike Bangoché, the enslaved collectively resist their overseer. Bangoché fights back and Sebastián quickly joins in the struggle. Within seconds they have restrained and captured Don Manuel as a hostage. Initially, the uprising is a demand not for freedom but for a modicum of justice, and it takes the form of a workers' rebellion: having been promised Good Friday off as a religious holiday, the enslaved refuse to work. These initial demands recall the attempts of the formerly enslaved population of Saint Domingue under the leadership of Toussaint Louverture to negotiate better treatment rather than the immediate end of slavery in the early stages of the Haitian Revolution. And just as in the case of Haiti, a negotiated peace is beyond the vision of the enslaving class. News of the uprising rapidly reaches the Count, who assembles an armed band of slave catchers who begin to hunt down and kill the slaves. Reasonably sensing the necessity of a ruthless, preemptive violence of self-defense, Sebastián kills Don Manuel. The Count's discovery of his overseer's body prompts one of his most remarkable analogical contortions, as he likens this cruel and vicious man to Christ. Whereas at the previous evening's supper the Count had admitted to his slaves that Don Manuel "jamás podrá parecerse a Jesús Cristo" ["could never be like Jesus Christ"], now, on finding his corpse, the Count inquires of the priest, "Padre ¿a que hora murió Cristo?" ["Father, at what time did Christ die?"], to which the Priest responds: "A esta misma hora, señor" ["At this very hour, sir"]. Further, Don Manuel's death brings thoughts of the Haitian Revolution rushing to the Count's mind. Hours later, in the plantation church where Don Manuel's body is now lying in state, the Count angrily insists "¡Esto no es Santo Domingo!" ["This is not Santo Domingo!"]. However, the merciless hunting down and slaying of the slave rebels certainly recalls the atrocities of the Haitian Revolution. Cuba may not be Saint Domingue, but Alea communicates the parallels for all to see: grotesquely uneven slave societies beholden to the Atlantic world economy and a racial conflict the logical end point of which is genocidal war.

One by one, the Count's *rancheadores* succeed in their murderous enterprise: the defenseless Pascual is brutally murdered by two members of the Count's band while another dies in an attempted escape leaping to his death into a gorge, believing that he will sprout feathers and wings and fly to freedom. Only Sebastián evades capture. The film's dramatic final scenes are of Sebastián on the run—a defiant fugitive from slavery reclaiming stolen liberty. The organ music and baroque Christian music is replaced by African drumming and non-lexical singing. The musical substitution is an indication of Sebastián's rejection of a faux civilization and an embrace of his African origins. Though we do not know whether Sebastián is an African-born *bozal*, the shift in music also indicates Cuba's musical-cultural bond with Africa. Césaire famously claimed that Haiti was "the most African of the Antilles," but here Alea affirms that Cuba also shares African roots.[76] Alea's film thus poses the question: At what point

"Cinema Must Be Revolutionary in Itself" | 103

does the incorporation of the African element into the Cuban national imaginary take place?

As Sebastián continues to run—with the drumming and singing becoming ever more intense—Alea intersperses highly emotive images of freedom in nature. There is a bird in flight, water running over rocks in a riverbed, rocks tumbling into a gorge, a herd of wild horses, and then, finally, there is Sebastián, in profile, bloodied and exhausted but still running, and now free (fig. 2.10). Such imagery must be regarded as a filmic language of magical realism that communicates not a human right to freedom, but the immanence of freedom in nature and humankind—a freedom entirely antithetical to the bondage of labor under both proto-capitalist slaveholding colonialism and capitalist modernity. Further, in connecting slave resistance to an aesthetics of magical realism and an ontology of the marvelous, *La última cena* again invokes the origins of the Haitian Revolution, the character of Makandal whose magical "escape" is vividly narrated in Carpentier's *El reino de este mundo*, and the Bois Caiman vodou ceremony that preceded the uprising on the northern plains, the initial catalyst to the revolution in August 1791.[77] Like Carpentier's *El Reino de este mundo* before it, Alea's *La última cena* thus suggests

Figure 2.10. Sebastián: free, *La última cena*. Source: Tomás Gutiérrez Alea, dir., *La última cena* (1976), Cuba. Instituto Cubano del Arte e Industria Cinematográficos."

that slave resistance could be informed by "magical" beliefs as well as rational thought. Thus, the achievement of *La última cena* is not only its affirmation of the agency of enslaved Blacks and maroon populations but also its evocation, via an aesthetics of the marvelous and the magical, of a radical conception of anti-capitalist freedom in the abstract *and* in its material reality in the Haitian Revolution.

Conclusion: "Cinema Must Be Revolutionary in Itself"[78]

In conclusion, I wish to suggest that engaging with the radical aesthetics and representational politics we find in *La última cena* enables us to construct a narrative of slavery and abolition in which slave resistance— and the impact of the Haitian Revolution—assumes a role center-stage. Revisiting Alea's *La última cena* also serves as a corrective to a new wave of widely celebrated historical scholarship that has sought to reassess slavery's relationship to capitalism.[79] The chief claims and arguments of these post-2008 histories of capitalism, collectively dubbed the New History of Capitalism (NHC), unequivocally affirm "plantation slavery as an inherent element of global capitalist accumulation."[80] The NHC also places emphasis on commodities as explanatory categories, capitalism's coercive violence, and the reifying core impulses of slavery and capitalism. However, Peter James Hudson has perspicaciously observed that the New Historians of Capitalism have "selectively cited, completely ignored, or borrowed without acknowledgment" a radical intellectual tradition that took slavery and capitalism for its subject, even while it repeats many of the claims of these earlier scholars, including C. L. R. James, Eric Williams, W. E. B. Du Bois, Walter Rodney, and Manuel Moreno Fraginals.[81] The unwavering emphasis on capitalism in Alea's *La última cena* clearly marks it as ideologically belonging to this radical tradition and constitutes further evidence that in some circles a conception of slavery's intricate relationship with and fundamental importance to capitalism has a long history. As such, this body of work reminds us that situating Haiti's and Cuba's revolutionary traditions in comparative critical context—as Alea's *La última cena* challenges us to do—holds the promise of revealing deep causal explanations. Further, in Alea's hands, the subject of slavery becomes the basis for an elaborate meditation on revolutionary politics and the possibility of true liberation. Alea's *La última cena* links the brutalities of slavery to capitalist economic forces and thereby exposes the impossibility of social justice under capitalism. Also revealed via Alea's spectacular ironic aesthetic register is the inevitable failure of Christian humanism as a means of forging social bonds that might transcend the divisions of race and class in slave society given its complicity with the interests of the plantocracy and its insufficiency as consolation for systemically induced suffering. Instead, invoking the Haitian Revolution, not as a horrifying example but as a crucial landmark on the way to the realization of a free and dignified future, *La última cena* insists on the necessity of revolutionary social transformation and the dissolution by the oppressed of race- and class-based social hierarchies if the universal human desire for freedom is to be realized. This insistence takes cinematic form beyond its status as a medium for historical representation. Instead, it positions cinema at the vanguard of the revolution and makes good on Alea's declaration that "cinema must be revolutionary in itself."

Chapter 3

Sergio Giral's *"Negrometrajes"*

Subverting Sentimental Abolitionism and Reconstructing the History of Slavery

Sergio Giral's trilogy of Cuban slavery films—*El otro Francisco* (1974), *Rancheador* (1976), and *Malualua* (1979)—were popularly known in Cuba as Giral's *"negrometrajes."*[1] The term, which translates literally as "Black-length films" and euphemistically as "Black feature-length films," was a dubious pun on the terms *corto-metraje* (short-length film) and *largo-metraje* (feature-length film). When asked how he felt about this label that had been given to his films, Giral's rather nonchalant reply was, "It seemed funny to me, and that's how the label stuck. I didn't see it as a derogatory thing because at least it was a way to name it."[2] While the term *negrometraje* was used to identify any Cuban-made film focused on Afro-Cuban themes (other notable examples include Tomás Gutiérrez Alea's *La última cena* discussed in the previous chapter and Sara Gómez's posthumously released *De cierta manera*), the label is most closely associated with Giral's work.[3] Giral, who has resided in Miami since 1992, was one of only three Black filmmakers working at the Instituto Cubano del Arte e Industria Cinematográficos (ICAIC) in the 1960s and 1970s.[4] The films Giral made throughout his tenure at the ICAIC, from 1961 to 1991, sought to highlight racial problems in Cuba, demonstrate the historical growth of Afro-Cuban subjectivity, and vindicate Black Cuban history. Giral's slavery trilogy, which foregrounds Black resistance and a diversity of perspectives, is the centerpiece of this project spanning three decades. By prioritizing these hitherto overlooked historical realities, Giral's trilogy exposes the ideological context of the received historiography of slavery and abolition and contributes to the fulfillment of the ICAIC's mandate to produce "historical dramas that were meant to rebuild history."[5] The trilogy has been regarded as a "welcome tonic to the cloying melodrama of American period films like *Gone with the Wind*" that erased Black agency as part of their romantic sanitization of the institution of slavery.[6] Giral's trilogy also constitutes further evidence of the centrality of Cuban film in the flourishing of the new Latin American cinema movement that emerged in 1967 and that can be characterized by its commitment as well as its theoretical and aesthetic originality.[7]

Giral was a friend and colleague of Tomás Gutiérrez Alea and the two collaborated on numerous occasions, including on *El otro Francisco*.[8] However, Giral, whom the British Film Institute describes as an "Afro-Cuban auteur" and "a giant of Cuban cinema," has not received the same degree of critical attention as that of his more-celebrated contemporary.[9] Born in Havana in 1937 to a Black Cuban American mother and a middle-class white Cuban father, Giral was raised in Cuba and maintained dual Cuban and American citizenship. After graduating from high school in 1954, the seventeen-year-old Giral moved to New York City to escape the "deplorable" socioeconomic conditions in Cuba under the Batista regime.[10] In New York City, the Giral family initially lived in the Bronx before settling in Manhattan. Giral busied himself learning English but found that only menial work ("washing dishes, scrubbing floors") was available to him.[11] Giral reports that even for an American citizen such as himself, life in New York City in the 1950s was far from easy for a Black Latin American immigrant.[12] However, Giral was drawn to the visual arts, and he found New York's cultural life alluring. For two years he took painting classes at the Art Students League of New York, an antiestablishment art school that boasts among its famous alumni Jacob Lawrence, Georgia O'Keefe, Jackson Pollock, and Mark Rothko. Giral also became, in his own words, "pretty involved with the Beatniks" in Greenwich Village.[13] The village's bohemian jazz joints and cafés were his scene, his "idols" were Allen Ginsberg and Jack Kerouac, and Jean-Paul Sartre was his "guru."[14] The Giral of this period was young, creative, and experimenting with his sexuality (for two years in his Greenwich Village days he lived with his male lover of the time). However, Giral was struggling to get by. He was "barely surviving" and he had "no answers" to the question of how he could keep body and soul together while pursuing a vocation that was of genuine interest.[15] When Fidel Castro made his first speech as the revolutionary leader of Cuba from a balcony in Santiago de Cuba on January 2, 1959, it was Giral's twenty-second birthday. Castro's speech must have made quite an impression on Giral, who was in Cuba for the occasion as he had traveled home for the Christmas holidays. Indeed, Giral would later state that almost instantly he "fell in love with the revolution" that would change the course of his life.[16] Eager to contribute to its early program of social justice, Giral made the decision to do "the opposite of what a lot of other Cubans were doing then"—he decided to stay.[17]

As he began to settle in Cuba, Giral discovered that "little by little" the revolution gave him the answers for which he was yearning.[18] They were answers with "many contradictions," but Giral discovered that these contrary answers were "sufficiently rich" for him to dedicate himself to the Revolution.[19] At first, Giral embarked on a program of studying agricultural engineering. He was striving to make himself useful, and in those early months of the revolution the overhaul of Cuba's agricultural sector dominated public political discussions. In May 1959, Castro announced a much-anticipated series of land and agrarian reforms, which included the establishment of the Instituto Nacional de Reforma Agraria (INRA, the National Institute for Agrarian Reform) and the formation of agricultural cooperatives. The development of Cuba's agricultural system was a priority for the revolution, but Giral found himself unsuited to a career in this sector. Instead, Giral was attracted to the newly established national film institute, and he resolved to find a way to contribute to the creation of a revolutionary culture through filmmaking.[20] Giral's earlier training as a painter and his upbringing meant that he was well equipped to realize this ambition. His life from early childhood had been an education in film. His father—an artist himself and a member of the Cuban Democratic Party, which was overthrown by Batista's coup d'état—had been a cinephile and had taken the young Giral to the movies with him regularly. In fact, Giral claims that he saw "every picture shown in Havana during the 40s and 50s."[21] Hollywood films provided him with a "basic education" in film while Italian neorealism and French realism entranced him and became his early inspirations.[22] By 1961, Giral had maneuvered himself into a position in the ICAIC. He had received an invitation to work in the ICAIC, which had come by way of a Spanish Cuban friend from his days waiting tables in Greenwich Village, Néstor Almendros, who was working at the ICAIC and was on his way to becoming one of the world's most-renowned cinematographers.[23] Although when he started at the ICAIC Giral still considered himself to be a painter and he had no filmmaking experience, he seized his opportunity to contribute to the Revolution in a creative capacity.

Giral describes his filmmaking "apprenticeship" at the ICAIC as "autodidactic" in method and character. This was the common path for the great majority of new filmmakers in the ICAIC who learned on the job and "began making documentaries right away in order to learn how to make films."[24] The earliest film for which Giral is credited as director is the 1967 short documentary *Cimarrón* ("Maroon").[25] This film takes the form of an interview with Esteban Montejo, who was Cuba's last-surviving fugitive from slavery and who was 107 years old at the time of filming. Giral's short film offered a dramatic reimagination of his life and struggle for freedom.[26] This early film reveals the subject matter to which Giral would return throughout his career. It also provides an early indication of his interest in manipulating genre and reworking historical, literary, and cultural materials to offer commentary on the subjects of race, class, and Afro-Cuban identity and heritage. Giral's 1986 feature film *Plácido* is a further illustration of Giral's commitment to reworking in filmic form the raw materials of Black Cuban history. *Plácido* narrates the story of the Afro-Cuban poet, Gabriel de la Concepción Valdés—known as Plácido— who was executed following the ferociously suppressed Black rebellion of 1843–1844 known as "La Conspiración de La Escalara" ("The Conspiracy of the Ladder").[27] Plácido subsequently became an emotive symbol of Black resistance in Cuban folklore. While Plácido's life story offers perhaps ideal material for a gripping historical feature film, unfortunately Giral's rendition was judged "too histrionic" and failed to capture the attention and imagination of audiences as his slavery trilogy had done.[28] However, Giral's 1990 feature film *María Antonia*, which would prove to be the last film Giral made in Cuba before he returned to the United States, also probes Afro-Cuban history and was a much greater success.[29] Set in prerevolutionary 1950s Cuba, *María Antonia* reworks Eugenio Hernández Espinosa's popular 1965 Afro-Cuban theatrical adaptation of Bizet's opera *Carmen*.[30] Giral's own assessment is that it his most-accomplished film, depicting deprivation and racism in its 1950s setting but also offering commentary on their persistence in contemporary Cuba in the final scene, which transposes social and racial inequalities from the 1950s into the present. Presenting the eponymous Mariá Antonia as a tortured soul and a creolized Carmen, the film also gives prominence to the Afro-Cuban religious and cultural practice of *santería*.[31] However, it is Giral's trilogy of slavery films from the 1970s for which he remains most renowned, although even the trilogy has received only limited critical attention within North American and European circles.[32]

Like Alea's *La última cena*, Giral's slavery trilogy assertively presents Black Cuban history and recuperates the inheritance of Afro-Cuban experience and should be situated within the institutional context of the ICAIC, which in the 1960s and 1970s was making efforts to foreground Afro-Cuban themes.[33] This institutional commitment was shaped, in part, by the Havana Cultural Congress of 1968, a major event that addressed the theme of "The Intellectual and the Liberation Struggle of the Peoples of the Third World."[34] The Cuban state's engagement in Angola was also, of course, a shaping contextual factor. Black Cuban history, Black nationalist politics, and Pan-Africanism were thus enjoying an unprecedented degree of visibility in everyday Cuban life—a propitious context for the reception of Giral's trilogy. Each film in the trilogy presents a perspective that had traditionally been marginalized within the Cuban historiography of slavery prior to 1959. In *El otro Francisco*, sentimental, bourgeois perspectives vis-à-vis slavery and abolition are turned upside down. In *Rancheador*, the perspectives of various poorer whites—smallholder farmers and slave catchers—are brought to the fore to emphasize the insufficiency of race, when taken in isolation, as an explanatory category by which to comprehend the social dynamics of oppression in slaveholding Cuba.[35] And in *Maluala*, the strategic and political dilemmas faced by the leaders of Cuba's maroon communities are emphasized as part of the film's depiction of the growth of Afro-Cuban consciousness. By this foregrounding of perspectives that had previously been sidelined, the trilogy recovers the history of slave resistance in nineteenth-century Cuba, asserts Black subjectivity, and narrates a counter-history of Cuban slavery and abolition. However, although we can speak of the trilogy as one in ideological terms, the films are not a trilogy in a narrative sense. Each film can be viewed independently, the plots are not interdependent in any way, and the films can be watched in any sequence. Further, the trilogy is notable for the variety of its narratological, aesthetic, and technical experimentation from film to film, rather than for the adoption of a unified filmic language. Consequently, each film develops its own aesthetic register, character, and rhetorical style.

For example, *El otro Francisco* offers a socioeconomic analysis of slavery and class struggle in nineteenth-century Cuba by explicitly undermining and critically retelling the first antislavery novella in the Americas, Anselmo Suárez y Romero's sentimental and sensationalist *Francisco*.[36] Romero wrote *Francisco* in 1838–1839 under a climate of severe censorship designed to inoculate the Cuban public from all talk of independence, and the novel was proscribed by Madrid's censors and remained unpublished, other than in samizdat journals, until 1880.[37] While Suárez's novel was a vehicle for the author's sentimental abolitionism, Giral's objectives were much more far-reaching. Adopting the techniques and format of "docudrama" filmmaking—including freeze frames and the use of a critical, didactic narrator who directly addresses the viewers—*El otro Francisco* narrates a story of Black subjectivity in relation to the history of Black Cubans' struggle for freedom and equality that provides a rigorous sociological examination of Romero's earlier novel. The effect is the displacement of the novel's ideological mood and logic and the generation of a critical skepticism in relation to its historical veracity. This method of didactic exposition, aesthetic self-assurance, and narratological creativity has drawn high praise from scholars and critics. For example, the critic Dennis West considers *El otro Francisco* to be one of the ICAIC's "most stylistically innovative features."[38] *Rancheador* and *Maluala*, on the other hand, employ the aesthetic and rhetorical strategies of popular adventure-fiction films and fuse the conventions of that format with radical politics. Hence, *Rancheador* offers a principled statement on the necessity of preemptive defensive violence in the context of the structural violence of nineteenth-century Cuban slave society. *Maluala*, on the other hand, elaborates a story that foregrounds Black autonomy and self-liberation set in the *palenques* (communities of fugitives from slavery) in the mountains of Cuba's Sierra Maestra. Conjuring in filmic language the coexistence of the past and the contemporary, the rational and the magical, *Maluala* combines magical realism with political drama. Nevertheless, despite their varied aesthetic registers, the trilogy is unified by the foregrounding of Black agency and an insistence on the formative role slavery played in the creation of Cuban and global modernity. As such, and in common with Pontecorvo's *Burn!* and Tomas Gutiérrez Alea's *La última cena*, Giral's trilogy elaborates a representation of Atlantic slavery as fundamental to the nineteenth-century capitalist world-system. Also in common with *Burn!* and *La última cena*, the imaginary horizon of Giral's trilogy envisions an anti-capitalist freedom born of the highly contingent experience of the African slave trade and the plantation system in the Americas.

El otro Francisco: The Prologue

Ever since its release in 1974, *El otro Francisco* has attracted the attention of international critics who have found themselves impressed despite their expectations. For example, Vincent Canby, writing in the *New York Times* in 1977, considered *El otro Francisco* an "unusually fresh example of the sort of didactic movie making that often leaves a lot to be desired" and a "demonstration of the great vitality of the contemporary Cuban film industry."[39] The award of the FIPRESCI Prize at the 1975 Moscow Film Festival is evidence that Canby was far from the only critic to hold *El otro Francisco* in high regard.[40] Shot in black and white, *El otro Francisco* opens in dramatic fashion: we see the eponymous Francisco (fig. 3.1), an enslaved Black man, and Dorotea, an enslaved "mulatta," gazing longingly at each other before they embrace passionately in a riverside forest clearing.

Immediately, it is apparent that Francisco and Dorotea's emotional anguish is an instance of the cruelties inflicted by slavery on individuals longing for romantic love. Dorotea is unable to hold back her tears as

Figure 3.1. The eponymous Francisco, *El otro Francisco*. *Source:* Sergio Giral, dir., *El otro Francisco* (1974), Cuba. Instituto Cubano del Arte e Industria Cinematográficos.

she reveals to Francisco that she allowed their master, Ricardo, to rape her in order that Francisco be saved. Wracked by guilt and punished by patriarchal slave society, Dorotea declares that she did everything she could have done for Francisco but that now she must travel to Havana with their mistress, Ricardo's mother, and that she cannot bear to see Francisco ever again. This news devastates Francisco and, seeing his pain, Dorotea rushes away with tears streaming down her face, the emotional burden overwhelming her. Francisco, alone with his feelings of despair in the forest, rages and lashes out at the tall grasses and tree branches. He eventually collapses to the ground in turmoil and, to the accompaniment of dramatic orchestral mood music, Francisco resolves to hang himself. Some days later, drawn by the buzzards that were circling a tree, Francisco's body is discovered by the master and the plantation overseer. Francisco's suicide is thus presented as an instance of death as a form of freedom from pain and suffering, which is a well-rehearsed trope in Black diasporic cultural production.[41] When Dorotea learns of Francisco's death—the news reaches her via a letter from Ricardo to his mother, who then relays the news to her—she is overcome with grief, "wastes away," and dies only a few years later.

This narrative of star-crossed, enslaved lovers whose relationship is thwarted and their lives destroyed by the behavior of a depraved enslaver is one that would be familiar to readers of sentimental antislavery writing. And indeed, at this juncture the film reveals that this is precisely what this opening has been. The film cuts to a well-to-do, fashionable Havana literary salon where the novelist Anselmo Suárez Romero is reading from his freshly completed manuscript, *Francisco*. Shortly thereafter, the frame freezes and a narrator directly addresses the film's viewers. The impact of this direct address is to shatter the film's naturalism and to reveal the film's theoretical investment in a Brechtian cultural politics and narratological form. The narrator declares that the film will proceed as an investigation into the ideas presented by, and the critical limitations of, Romero's celebrated sentimental antislavery novella. The narrator informs the viewer that Domingo Del Monte—a historical figure who was the host of the literary salon, a bourgeois intellectual, and a social reformer (but nevertheless a slaveholder)—had suggested to Romero that he should pen "a novel to lay bare the plight of the slaves."[42] Romero's reading is met with adulation, applause, and a standing ovation. He is warmly embraced by a number of men present at the salon, including Del Monte, and he receives the praise of a number of women. The appearance of these finely dressed and fastidiously coiffured participants in Del Monte's literary salon could not form a more striking contrast with the simple and worn attire of Francisco and Dorotea. Champagne is served on silver trays and the narrator informs the viewer that the novel's overwhelmingly positive reception in this circle leaves no doubt that it satisfied the demands of these bourgeois reformist ideologues. At this juncture, Giral leaves it to the viewer to discern the hypocrisies of this well-meaning bourgeois collective, but the narrator explicitly poses the fundamental question that will animate the rest of the film: "Is a real view of the slave provided by the author through his character, Francisco? Let us see if the rejoicing over the novel was justified or if it failed to show *un otro Francisco*." In this manner of Brechtian critique, Giral begins his inquiry, drawing attention to the sociopolitical context of Cuba's literary history via its focus on Romero's original novella and framing his film as a historical investigation into what Francisco "might have been like, what kind of life he would really have led, had he been a historical figure."[43] After this prologue, the opening credits appear, which in an expression of Pan-Caribbean revolutionary solidarity acknowledge "The Haitian Group" (referring to a collective of Haitian residents in Cuba at the time, likely including the writer and activist Martha Jean-Claude). Linking Cuba's national history to Haiti's antislavery revolutionary heritage has the effect of emphasizing Cuba's and Haiti's affinities as Black diasporic nations—a perspective that, as we have seen, would prove fundamental to Tomás Gutiérrez Alea's *La última cena*. Thus, from the outset, Giral's *El otro Francisco* unsettles the identification of Cuba as a "Latino" or "mulatto" society rather than as a Black diasporic society. Giral's granting prominence of place to Cuba's Haitian Group in the opening credits is also consistent with the film's situating of slavery in Cuba in its wider Caribbean and global contexts, rather than in its narrower Spanish colonial context. This comparative perspective encourages an understanding of slavery and slave resistance in transnational terms and makes clear that Cuba and Haiti should both be understood as locations of historical Black agency and that more binds these two nations together than drives them apart.

El otro Francisco: Ricardo's Plantation

With the sentimentality of Romero's version established, the film proceeds to narrate the story of "the other" Francisco. Giral's script brings the viewer up to speed quickly: through a conversation between Ricardo and the plantation overseer, we learn that Dorotea is Ricardo's mother's favorite slave and that she serves her as a seamstress and as her maid. Ricardo has just discovered that Dorotea is pregnant with Francisco's child, and this provokes Ricardo to instruct his overseer to mete out abominably cruel tortures: sadistic whippings and the rubbing of urine, alcohol, salt, and gunpowder into Francisco's wounds. This opening recalls the rhetorical strategy taken in C. L. R. James's *The Black Jacobins*. There, in the first chapter, which is accurately and ironically titled "The Property," James documented the innumerable, inventive, and cruel means and methods of slave torture.[44] This catalogue of torture serves as indisputable evidence that slavery was founded on an intricate system of terror and that apologists for empire cannot explain nor excuse slavery as benign, paternalistic, or civilizing. The impact of this strategy in *El otro Francisco* is highly comparable: without subjecting the viewer to gratuitous horrors, Giral unequivocally conveys the physical and emotional traumas and coercive violence on which slavery depended.

The camera then cuts to Francisco among a group of enslaved workers cutting sugar cane in the fields while singing a work song when, suddenly, Francisco collapses from exhaustion. Later the overseer will claim that Francisco "staged a faint" to escape working—such everyday forms of resistance were a commonplace frustration for the planter class. However, Francisco's queasiness and exhaustion are clearly conveyed as authentic, as is his physical unsuitability to the harsh demands of working in the cane fields. Following this scene, the narrator interjects to provide information on both Francisco and Dorotea and their roles on the plantation. We learn that Francisco was taken from Africa at the age of ten. He is an enslaved domestic worker who has always stood out for his excellence in this role—his malleability, loyalty, and good nature. He is, the narrator proclaims, "free of vice." Then the narrator formally introduces Dorotea: we learn that her mother nursed the young Ricardo and that her beauty, innate goodness, and kindness made her seem to Francisco "an ideal companion to lighten his slave's burden." The companionship and physical intimacy that Dorotea could provide is thus apprehended as ameliorative. This recalls a notion that was in circulation in the wake of the Haitian Revolution: that allowing enslaved populations greater familial and romantic freedoms might suppress the growth of revolutionary sentiments. Accompanying this description is a portrait shot of Dorotea that is illustrative of the film's treatment of her character, which is far less progressive than the film's other elements (fig. 3.2).

Figure 3.2. Portrait shot of Dorotea, *El otro Francisco*. *Source:* Sergio Giral, dir., *El otro Francisco* (1974), Cuba. Instituto Cubano del Arte e Industria Cinematográficos.

As the critic Julia Lesage has noted, "the only instance where *The Other Francisco* cannot overcome traditional cinematic iconography to make a social point is in the depiction of Dorotea. She is a 'beautiful woman' in the traditional cinematic sense."[45] To Lesage's point, we can add that this portrait shot, in its casual but nevertheless carefully composed elegance, is comparable to the 1990s black-and-white portrait fashion photography of Peter Lindbergh. Reading the image sympathetically, we might suggest that this cinematographic portraiture is an indication of Giral's painterly eye for composition and evidence of a laudable aspiration to portray Dorotea in all her individuality. Such a reading would assign to this image a progressive politics since it could be argued that it forms an effective contrast with the various longstanding derogatory and racist traditions in which enslaved persons of African descent have been represented in deindividualized and anonymized terms. However, Lesage's critical interpretation highlights the shortcomings of Giral's representation of Dorotea and his representation of enslaved women more generally. The problem, Lesage persuasively writes, is that "the established photographic conventions for treating female beauty are so stubborn to overcome [and] Dorotea's image rarely moves beyond those conventions."[46] The film's troublesome depiction of the rape of Dorotea by Ricardo elaborates the point. The rape scene itself, with its shots of "twisted thighs" on crumpled bedclothes, provides "only a conventional voyeuristic depiction," and the subsequent freeze-frame extreme close-up of "Dorotea's face with tears in her eyes" is notable merely for its conventional "beauty and pathos."[47] The insufficiency of the analysis of the situation of women under slavery remains evident even as the film strives to make it one of its central pillars. Especially regrettable for a film committed to the recuperation of the numerous and varied forms of slave resistance is its overlooking of multiple forms of *female* slave resistance. Lesage, relying on Angela Davis's work, points out that we can attribute many different acts of resistance directly to enslaved women who were working in the domestic environment—women such as Dorotea. These acts of resistance included aiding and abetting runaways, poisoning food, committing arson, and planning escapes. In sum, Davis writes, the enslaved woman was "the custodian of a house of resistance."[48] While diverse forms of female Black agency are strongly registered in the second and third installments of the trilogy, *Rancheador* and *Maluala*, this perspective is regrettably absent from *El otro Francisco*.

The narrator proceeds to provide further information on Francisco and Dorotea's relationship, apprising the viewer with sociohistorical detail as necessary to foster a critical perspective. We learn that Francisco had requested his mistress's permission to marry Dorotea but that such permission was refused, a historically unlikely outcome since marriage was encouraged for reproductive and moral purposes. We then learn that Francisco and Dorotea embarked on a clandestine affair for two years, at the end of which Dorotea became pregnant. In response, the mistress commands the whipping of Francisco and, contrary to the slavery codes that stipulated that slave owners should keep slave families together, she sends Dorotea to a French mistress in Havana where she is to work as an enslaved domestic worker assigned to the laundry. Throughout this part of the narrative, the romantic aspect of this story is accentuated by soft music. However, abruptly the picture freezes and the music stops: Giral rouses the viewers from the dreamy, uncritical state into which he had lulled them. Suddenly, the viewer becomes aware of their manipulation by Giral and realizes that the intense drama of this romance, the soft music, and the beautiful portraits had deceived them into accepting an extremely limited understanding of the realities of slave life. As Francisco assists Dorotea into an ornately decorated carriage, presumably to be taken away to her new mistress, the Brechtian narrator asserts: "Francisco and Dorotea act in keeping with the novel's romantic selling point; but the 'real facts' of slave life and love were different." Following the narrator's interjection, Giral proceeds to show us—in brief, self-contained episodes that contain further narratorial direct addresses to the viewers—examples of *how* slave life differed from Romero's depiction. The picture then immediately cuts to a scene in which an enslaved Black woman on a riverbank is sexually assaulted by a white man. The lack of sound estranges the viewer from the scene, which is brief, and the camera remains at a distance, which proves a more effective representational strategy than the approach employed in the depiction of Dorotea's rape. Meanwhile, the narrator continues, explaining that relationships among enslaved people and the sexual lives of the enslaved were profoundly circumscribed and limited by their status. Moreover, there were far fewer enslaved women than there were enslaved men, and the sexual abuse of enslaved women by the planter class was rife.[49]

Giral then connects the institutionalized sexual abuse of enslaved women to the practice of self-induced abortion under slavery. An enslaved woman is shown preparing a homemade remedy that she drinks to abort her pregnancy. The scene contains no dialogue, and the woman is entirely alone. The only sounds are those of birdsong, hand drums, and the playing of a conch shell (a traditional slave musical instrument). As the scene unfolds, the intensity of the music, which is correlated to the woman's suffering, increases dramatically. The effect is to shock without numbing the viewer's capacity to understand as well as to feel. The scene concludes with the woman collapsed on the ground, convulsing with agonizing uterine contractions. As the critic Julia Lesage notes, Giral here shows the condition of enslaved women via a representative individual, but he "does not let us inside slave women's consciousness as the novel lets us inside the minds and feelings of the aristocrats and the two house slaves. Romantic subjectivity and emotional life, according to the film, belong to the leisured class."[50] The abortion scene is one of the film's rare depictions of female agency that for Cuban viewers at the time of the film's release would almost certainly have called to mind contemporary legal changes in Cuba vis-à-vis women's reproductive decision-making rights. State opposition to abortion had ended in 1965 in response to high levels of maternal morbidity resulting from self-induced and back-alley abortions. In 1972, access to abortion was liberalized. Seven years later, in 1979, universal, medicalized, and free abortion was fully legalized. Abortion politics and legislation in Cuba have thus for long been progressive within a hemispheric American context, and in the wake of the US Supreme Court's 2022 decision to overturn *Roe v. Wade*, Cuba's position on this issue in contrast to that of the United States is even clearer.[51] We see the enslaved woman asserting control over her own body while the physical trauma of the abortion is evident and the emotional trauma is clearly implied. Yet, this scene does not strive to emotionally manipulate the viewer, and the rhetorical strategy can be distinguished from the theatrical staging of slave suffering crudely designed to elicit sympathy as in much abolitionist literature. Instead, the suffering of this enslaved woman is used to make the viewer aware of multiple levels of causation and culpability. The institution of slavery is doubly indicted: first, because in the context of racial slavery rape is apprehended as a strategy for the aggressive assertion of white male dominance and consequently is understood as being endemic to social relations under slavery (notwithstanding the shortcomings of the depiction of the rape of Dorotea by Ricardo); and second, because the enslaved woman is aborting the fetus to avoid bringing a new life into conditions of slavery. However, by extension, capitalism is also indicted by virtue of Giral's identification of slavery's function within the capitalist world-system. And further, because the scene can be paired with the earlier sequence in which a slave woman was assaulted and raped on a riverbank (as well as Ricardo's rape of Dorotea), the individual rapist's culpability is also condemned. The systemic gendered and racialized violence of slavery is thus imparted, while a clear focus on individual suffering and culpability is maintained.

Un otro Ricardo

As well as providing the viewer with an image of "another Francisco," Giral offers a perspective on Ricardo that is absent from the Romero novel. "In the novel," the narrator states, "Ricardo is moved only by his passions, but was that the reason he set out to cause pain to Francisco and Dorotea? Millowners of the times had other motivations. There's *another Ricardo [un otro Ricardo]* whom the author does not show us." So, who is this "other Ricardo"? In the words of the narrator, he is, like other members of the planter class, "a slave lord," entering modern capitalism with a "deep class consciousness" and a keen sense of the possibilities afforded by technological advances. The Ricardo Giral presents us with is a capable manager of a business who is able to enter into dialogue on the subject of slavery with a diversity of interlocutors including engineers, economists, and clergymen. In the spur of the moment, *el otro Ricardo* can produce a cogent defense of the political economy of slave-based sugar production premised on what he regards as the absolute necessity of increasing productivity ad infinitum. So, as Ricardo strolls through his plantation with other members of the planter class, he is quite at ease discussing costs and savings and entering into debates over the merits of taking advantage of technological advances.[52] This "other" Ricardo is visibly excited by the prospect of replacing his ox-driven mill with an English Fawcett and Preston steam-driven mill when it is presented to him by an English company agent. This scene, which clearly influenced Tomás Gutiérrez Alea's presentation of a similar scene in *La última cena*, demonstrates that technological advances serve to intensify the exploitation of enslaved people while also revealing the transnational dimensions of the Atlantic slave system. Giral is at pains to inform the viewer that just as Romero's production of a sentimental antislavery romance fails to communicate the political economy of Atlantic slavery, the emphasis on early nineteenth-century British abolitionism as philanthropically motivated fails to comprehend England's economic interests in breaking down the colonial mercantile system to open up more markets for English businesses. As we saw earlier, this is precisely the strategy that drives the narrative in Gillo Pontecorvo's *Burn!* Thus, with clarity and concision, via the characterization of this "other" Ricardo, Giral identifies slavery as a system of capital accumulation, situates it within the global economy of trade and exchange, and conveys that its beneficiaries, scattered throughout the Atlantic world, were easily masked by deeply layered production and commodity chains.

Giral's elaboration of this "other" Ricardo continues in a dinner scene at which there is some spirited discussion among various enslavers as to whether advancing technology will eventually render enslaved labor unnecessary. Whether wage labor would be more efficient, profitable, and ultimately preferable to dependence on enslaved labor is discussed and debated. Ethics and consideration of the well-being of enslaved people have no place in this discussion, although some of this is perhaps explained by the gap between the legal discourse surrounding slavery and the actual practices of slavery. The situation of formerly enslaved people in the English colonies is considered with the conversation revolving around one question only: Which is the more efficient mode of extracting surplus value from the labor force? The formal "freedom" that "free" labor grants is entirely incidental to the debate. It is also noteworthy that the lingering aftermath of the Haitian Revolution makes itself felt during this scene. The lone advocate for "free labor" and "economic progress" is rounded on by the others, all of whom fear that such "progress" will usher in the end of their privileged positions as "slave lords" in Cuba. The specter of Haiti haunts them deeply: the example of the once "flourishing" colony of Saint Domingue that has become a fearful "republic of Blacks" is used to put a definitive end to all talk of free labor and abolition as conduits to progress.[53]

El otro Francisco: The Threat of Black Revolution and Brecht versus Lukács

Following the dinner scene, another Brechtian direct address from the narrator follows: Francisco's narrative is about to be shown in a dramatically new light. The narrator informs the viewer that Ricardo halted Francisco's tortures after his rape of Dorotea. The film then replays, without the sound, the scenes presented earlier in the prologue: Francisco and Dorotea's passionate embrace, Dorotea's anguished revelation that she allowed herself to be raped by her enslaver to save Francisco, and Francisco's consequent despair and suicide. The narrator then boldly asks—as a means of opening the film's most-explicit examination of the theme of Black agency—whether "a typical slave of the time" would have reacted as Francisco did. The film then cuts to a scene in which Romero is being interviewed about his novella. In response to the question, "Is Francisco a typical slave?" Romero's response is striking: "He is absolutely not typical: how could a slave suffer as much as Francisco and not be rebellious? He's a freak, a singular exception who helps me denounce the horrors of slavery by contrast with the cruelty of the masters." In sum, according to Giral's Romero, Francisco has a remarkable "mildness and Christian resignation so hard to find in slavery." Romero's words reveal Francisco to be a rhetorical device and the mirror image of the lusty, sadistic Ricardo. Francisco's meek goodness is the antipode of the slavers' overbearing viciousness. The veracity of all this, Giral will challenge. Having used Romero's own words to establish the historical improbability of the virtuous Francisco's docility, the narrator opens the next segment of *El otro Francisco* with the following words:

Maybe behind the good intentions of Suárez Romero and other sincere anti-slavers there moved class interests that pursued with the ideal image of the slave not only an improvement in the owners' conduct. Perhaps the real aims of the capitalist ideologists and the British Empire in suppressing the slave trade weren't only philanthropic. Let's take the novella as the starting point to look at the real situation of slavery and the true picture of a slave mill of the times.

"The real situation of slavery" is immediately presented as one of unending resistance on the part of the slaves. A defiant enslaved man named Crispin now comes to the fore in the narrative. Crispin, who is played with gusto by Samuel Claxton—who also played leading roles in *Rancheador, Maluala,* and *La última cena*—has been captured in attempting to escape. Bound in ropes and being led by a mounted *rancheador,* Crispin is delivered to the plantation overseer for punishment, his face a portrait of indignation and defiance, and a counterpoint to Romero's placid Francisco (fig. 3.3).

Figure 3.3. Crispin, played by Samuel Claxton, *El otro Francisco. Source:* Sergio Giral, dir., *El otro Francisco* (1974), Cuba. Instituto Cubano del Arte e Industria Cinematográficos.

He is placed in the stocks, but the following day he is released to cut cane wearing a slave collar with a bell. During a brief rest break that day, Crispin talks rousingly to Francisco, telling him of a *palenque* just beyond the mountains where Blacks are free, equal, and able to marry, raise children, and live harmoniously in the absence of enslavers and overseers. When Francisco mocks him, retorting that this idyllic place is as fictional as the myth that Guinea can be reached in death, Crispin urges his companion to come to a meeting that evening at which plans for a rebellion will be laid. During the slaves' nighttime meeting, the film's ambience and aesthetic register embarks in a dramatically new direction. Numerous slave voices are heard, and African drumming and dancing takes place, giving license to an infectious current of insubordination. The effect is to expose Romero's sentimental love-triangle novella as a white fantasy that willfully ignores the realities of slave autonomy. Instead of presenting the enslaved as docile, Giral offers an account of slavery in which Black agency and resistance are central and are animated by a vision of emancipation as a first step toward social justice.

At the meeting, a rich living culture is on display. While Ricardo and his fellow planters considered the slaves only in terms of their labor value, at the meeting they are individualized and demonstrate a capacity for creativity and solidarity and an awareness of occurrences of slave resistance from beyond Cuba's borders. At the meeting, the chief orator exclaims to his enrapt companions: "There's a land that the Blacks call Haiti, where we're free already, where the masters have run away over the ashes of their houses!" It is a powerful representation of the impact of the Haitian Revolution spreading across the region, transcending linguistic barriers and inspiring enslaved populations throughout the Americas.[54] The following night there is a further meeting at which there is more singing, drumming, and dancing. It becomes apparent that the instigators have carefully planned an uprising: a vanguard group of enslaved rebels have set the plantation buildings alight, and during the ensuing chaos they make their escape. Yet, the next day, in an intense sequence, *rancheadors* on horseback with hunting dogs pursue and capture two of the escapees in a scene set to rhythmic, percussion-based music. Slave society, it is suggested, is always in a state of disciplinary violence, defensive violence, and counterviolence.

Then, the narrator interjects to explain why this tradition of Cuban Black resistance was not a subject of interest to Romero, Del Monte, and the island's bourgeois antislavery reformers. The dependency on free

Blacks, and even some poor whites, was so great that it was feared that news of Black resistance might destabilize the colony's social hierarchy. To further explain the domestic complexities of antislavery politics in Cuba at this time, Giral then stages a brief conversation between Del Monte and Richard Madden, an Irish doctor and ardent abolitionist who as British consul in Havana was, inter alia, tasked with reporting on the observance of the Anglo-Spanish Treaty of Madrid of 1817, which had granted the British navy the right to inspect Spanish ships suspected of slaving.[55] In their conversation, Del Monte explains to Madden that there was no appetite in Madrid for abolishing slavery in Cuba (or anywhere else in the Spanish Empire) and that among the colony's reformist population a fear of the potential for Black insurrection was holding back the cause of independence. Little wonder, then, that Romero elected to focus the attention of his antislavery novella on romantic themes and a meek and mild slave protagonist rather than to seek to recuperate the tradition of slave resistance in the colony.

Giral's characterization of Richard Madden and his role in the narrative also affords insight into the politics of *El otro Francisco*'s Brechtian form and its relation to other modes of representing slave resistance on screen. The critic Julia Lesage has argued that Giral's Madden reveals *El otro Francisco* as a "cinematic response to *Burn!*" This is because, Lesage argues, Giral's Madden parallels the character of William Walker in Gillo Pontecorvo's *Burn!* Lesage concurs with critics of *Burn!* who have considered that Marlon Brando's "skilled and attractive" performance of Walker as "a romantic antihero . . . undercuts the film's political analysis."[56] Lesage also agrees with critics who maintain that "*Burn*'s drama hinges as much on the pathos of Walker's story as it does on the depiction of oppression." Contrastingly, Lesage argues, Giral's *El otro Francisco* charts a different mode of cinematic storytelling that is more suited to the expansion of the viewer's curiosity and critical consciousness: "In *The Other Francisco* Giral uses Madden only to represent a certain locus of power, a privileged access to information, and an advanced ideological position. *The Other Francisco* stands as a cinematic response to *Burn!* and counters *Burn*'s mode of narration and characterization. The information in Madden's interviews is what is essential in *The Other Francisco*, not the 'feelings' of the man."[57]

It is true that Madden and Walker can be likened to one another insofar as they are both agents of the British Empire, they are both working to contrive circumstances conducive to the growth of English capitalism, and they both serve the same class interests. However, attention to Walker's interiority (a category that includes but cannot be reduced to only his "feelings") does not diminish *Burn*'s ideological impact as is alleged here. On the contrary, while Giral relies on a Brechtian narrator to provide explanation of how Madden's mission to Cuba reveals the naked hypocrisy of Britain's foreign-policy actions in the nineteenth-century Caribbean, Pontecorvo relies on Brando's abilities as a Stanislavskian method actor par excellence to portray the hypocrisies of Walker's mission to Queimada. Contrary to Lesage's analysis, I suggest that Giral and Pontecorvo's modes of narration and characterization in these two films can be ideologically aligned and therefore that Brechtian and Stanislavskian principles can be adopted in such a manner that they become ideologically compatible. There is in fact plenty of evidence to support such a proposition. Within Brecht studies there is increasing recognition that after 1948 Brecht himself acquired a "growing affinity for Stanislavsky's acting and directing techniques" and that by 1953 Brecht had begun "to see Stanislavsky as a 'partially' dialectical director."[58] Indeed, in his final years Brecht adapted "Stanislavsky's emphasis on realistic observation and detail (i.e., naturalism), on empathy, and even on audience identification with characters" while continuing to insist "on the critical demonstration of social significance."[59]

Moreover, Lesage's response to the differing modes of narration and characterization represented by these two films by Giral and Pontecorvo can also be understood as an expression of a preference for Brechtian rather than Lukácsian aesthetics. The famous disagreement between Georg Lukács and Brecht was, at its core, a heated debate over the politics of two contrasting aesthetic approaches to literature and a difference of opinion as to the capacity of each approach to capture reality in all its depth and complexity. I suggest here that the coordinates of their debate can be mapped onto the comparison Lesage makes between *El otro Francisco* and *Burn!* Responding in 1938 to an essay on expressionism by Ernst Bloch published in the same year, Lukács argued that progressive twentieth-century literary writers aspiring to depict contemporary reality in all its complexity, such that "relations between appearance and essence" might be grasped by the reader, should not reject the European literary tradition of the nineteenth century, but on the contrary should consciously build upon it.[60] In the elaboration of his argument, Lukács paid particular attention to Thomas Mann whom he acclaimed as a successor to Walter Scott, Balzac, and Tolstoy. For Lukács, Mann was a "true realist" and a writer who "towers as a creative artist and in his grasp of the nature of society."[61] Lukács argues that Mann's *The Magic Mountain* should be regarded as a twentieth-century novel that demonstrates knowledge of "how thoughts and feelings grow out of the life of society and *how experiences and emotions are parts of the total complex of reality.*"[62] However, for Brecht, "true realism" was to be sought by other means. Brecht's counterargument, here précised by Fredric Jameson, was that "if the novels of Balzac or Tolstoy were determinate products of a particular phase of class history, now superseded, how could any Marxist argue that the principles of their fiction could be recreated in a subsequent phase of history, dominated by the struggles of another and antagonistic class?"[63] Instead, for Brecht, "a living and combative literature" that demonstrates "the causal complexes of society" and unmasks "the prevailing view of things as the view of those who are in power" need not be yoked to the practices of the past.[64] Brecht's own innovative aesthetic solutions to this problem are well known. His project of a political "epic" theater sought to engender detachment and a critical view via alienation effects (*Verfremdungseffekt*: literally "a way of making strange"), although, as we have noted, in the latter stages of his career he combined his approach with elements of Stanislavsky's method.

While both Lukácsian and Brechtian approaches (and indeed all aesthetic approaches) will always fall short of representing in its completeness the Leninist ideal of the "totality" (the containment of all aspects, relationships, and mediations of historical objects), the high stakes of the debate (the demystification of all social, historical, and cultural processes as a prerequisite for the generation of a revolutionary socialist consciousness) help to explain its ferocity. While Giral's approach can be aligned with Brecht, Pontecorvo's approach can be aligned with that of Lukács. Recall that in making *Burn!*, Ponteocorvo set out "to present the roots of colonialism in a manner that borrowed heavily" from Joseph Conrad, a writer, like Thomas Mann, in whose work the literary traditions of the nineteenth and twentieth centuries merge and then reemerge anew."[65]

Following the Madden interview, Giral conveys the tragic reality of almost all slave rebellions—that of defeat. Crispin has been captured and killed, and the overseer mutilates his body "so that he has no interest in coming back to life." This barbaric act recalls the beheading of the Black rebel Santiago after his execution in *Burn!* Intended to terrorize, both episodes communicate the extreme lengths to which the slave power was compelled to go to suppress incessant resistance that could be sustained by spiritual beliefs, including that of reincarnation. However, Crispin's capture and murder does not signal the end of the representation of Black resistance in *El otro Francisco*. On the contrary, in the film's remaining twenty-five minutes, slave resistance is Giral's unwavering focus. The film's emotional timbre has transitioned through passion, to oppression, and now finally to the power of collective resistance.[66] Working through these transitions, the film demonstrates definitively the limitations of Romero's novella and the profound mistake of turning the history of abolition into a triumphant morality narrative. While Ricardo is raping Dorotea, the enslaved begin to put a carefully planned rebellion into action, and this time Francisco is a key conspirator. The insurrection begins when Francisco sabotages the sugar-mill grinder by thrusting a machete blade into the cogs. The mill is badly damaged and no longer functional—it will take days to repair. Ricardo hurries to examine the scene and orders the overseer to identify the slave responsible. He singles out Francisco, who is whipped savagely. Giral presents Francisco's indefatigable resistance in the face of unmitigated tortures as the crucial missing pieces in Francisco's story as presented by Romero. The narrator describes these omissions in the novella as a form of "censorship" and asserts that thwarted romantic love is insufficient as explanation for Francisco's suicide.[67] With the "other" Francisco's story now told, the dramatic finale of *El otro Francisco* can begin. The narrator explains that while suicide was one form of slave resistance, there were of course others. High-tempo drumming and percussion music resumes, the individual drumbeats and percussive sounds building suspense, tension, and expectation as the camera cuts to a new scene. A group of rebel slaves are running through a forest holding flaming torches, the speed of action represented visually corresponding to the high-tempo music. The rebels are then shown setting the cane fields alight, and the rebellion quickly gains momentum (fig. 3.4).

The overseer is assaulted and strangled. Suddenly, weaknesses in the slave power are revealed and the transformative potential of Black collective action is revealed. The narrator then establishes that an insurrection such as this was not an isolated event by providing a catalogue of major rebellions that occurred between the years 1812 and 1843:

> Long before and then after the Suárez Romero novella, a wave of uprisings shook plantations across Cuba: 1812: uprisings in mills at Puerto Principe, Holguin, Bayano Trinidad & Havana led by Jose Antonio Aponte; 1825: rebellions at mills and

Figure 3.4. Rebels burning the cane fields, *El otro Francisco. Source:* Sergio Giral, dir., *El otro Francisco* (1974), Cuba. Instituto Cubano del Arte e Industria Cinematográficos.

ranches in Matanzas, 24 estates sacked and burned, 15 whites and 43 Blacks killed; 1830: uprising at a coffee plantation near Havana; 1835: uprising at the Carolina Mill and a coffee plantation; 1837: insurrection in Manzanillo and Trinidad mills; 1842: uprising at the Loreto Mill near Havana and a coffee estate in Lagunillas; 1843, January 27 and 28: uprising in the Alcancia mill in Matanzas followed by a coffee estate and a ranch and four other sugar mills, plus the builders of the Cardenas-Jaruco railroad; November 5 of the same year: uprising at the Triunvirato mill in Matanzas that spread to the slaves at four other mills.

Immediately following these words there are brief, appalling scenes of retaliatory punishments and executions. Giral neither idealizes nor romanticizes resistance or violence. The focus instead is on the recuperation of Black agency as a liberatory force in Cuban history without occluding the agonizing difficulties and brutalities Black resistance faced. The scenes depicting this counterviolence of the slave power is then opposed by further scenes of Black resistance. Finally, Giral cuts to a panoramic landscape shot of the lush Cuban hills and mountains, the geographic heart of emancipatory struggle throughout Cuban history, from Indigenous Indian resistance, to Black resistance, to Castro's 26th of July Movement.

Rancheador: "The Hills Eat the White Man"

Released two years after *El otro Francisco*, Giral's second *negrometraje* from the outset establishes a tone that is quite distinct from its predecessor. Unlike *El otro Francisco*, *Rancheador* is filmed in color, and it conjures the tension of an action-adventure film alloyed with the intrigue of a political drama that demonstrates the alliances and antagonisms forged between the enslaved, fugitives from slavery, poorer whites, enslavers, and colonial bureaucrats. Indeed, the ambience of *Rancheador* is closer to Pontecorvo's *Burn!* than it is to *El otro Francisco*. However, in common with *El otro Francisco*, *Rancheador* demonstrates Giral's penchant for reworking textual historical source materials (it is based on the diary of a nineteenth-century Cuban slave catcher), recuperates Black agency as an emancipatory force in Cuban history, and functions as a disdainful exposé of the sanctimonious cant of bourgeois liberal abolitionism. Thus, *Rancheador*'s didactic purpose can be aligned with that of *El otro Francisco*—the rejection of fantastical but ideologically dominant modes of imagining slavery and abolition and a dramatic revision of the perception of the Black subject. The film undertakes this project by giving prominence of place to several interrelated themes. First, the film demands recognition of slave autonomy: slave self-liberation is presented as a conduit to a revitalized Black subjectivity. Second, the film symbolically presents the wilderness ("*el monte*") as a place in which the profoundly unequal social relations violently established and maintained by the slave power can unravel. And third, the film devotes considerable attention to the lives of poorer whites—the *rancheador* and his possé as well as the smallholder farmers who in the course of the film are evicted from their land and homes.

As mentioned, *Rancheador* is based on the diary of a nineteenth-century Cuban slave catcher whose viciousness became notorious: Francisco Estévez.[68] Estévez's diary of 1837–1842 is notable for several elements that find expression in Giral's adaptation. These include: Estévez's frustration at being so heavily outnumbered by runaways and their seemingly supernatural capacity to evade recapture; the resilience of maroon communities; the incorporation of the viewpoints of others; and the communication of Estévez's precarious dependence on the enslavers whom he serves.[69] Estévez's diary was thus ideal source material for Giral to convey the constant challenge posed to the slave power by slave self-liberation. Indeed, this constant struggle between emancipatory and repressive forces provides Giral with the raw materials for the film's opening shots. *Rancheador* opens with four Black men, two of whom are armed with rifles, running across a field of tall grasses. The camera then cuts to Estévez the *rancheador* on horseback, galloping through the Cuban hills to the sound of 1970s funk music. The drama of a chase sequence—four Black fugitives from slavery making a bid for freedom being pursued by Estévez the *rancheador*—thus serves as the film's opening hook. In these opening scenes, Estévez appears to enjoy an unfettered freedom in the wilderness, a free agent of the slave power who is impervious to danger. This opening impression, however, will be delicately deconstructed and exposed as false. The first hint of Estévez's vulnerability in the wilderness is provided by the communication of his dependence on enslaved trackers. We then learn that two fugitives from slavery, Mataperro and Melchora, have been a constant thorn in the side of the local community of enslavers, evading recapture and threatening the prosperity of the planter class. Melchora in particular, a female runaway, is a significant threat since her leadership of a free Black community, a *palenque*, has become the stuff of legend on the surrounding plantations. Throughout the film, the sound of drums from Melchora's *palenque* penetrates the aura of colonial order and control, audibly exposing the lie of its impregnability. While Melchora never appears in the film and we never see her *palenque*, her mythlike presence dominates the film, providing a backdrop of Black liberty that communicates the possibility of a radically different future. While we noted *El otro Francisco*'s regrettable failure to represent female Black agency, *Rancheador* should be acclaimed for its depiction of female Black agency as a galvanizing, inspirational force. Further, in addition to Melchora's centrality to the film, in *Rancheador* Giral does not miss the opportunity to represent enslaved female Blacks as coordinators of resistance. Consider, for example, a domestic scene in which an unnamed enslaved woman presents Mataperro with a kitchen knife and silently urges him to assassinate Estévez (fig. 3.5).

Figure 3.5. An enslaved woman's act of resistance, *Rancheador. Source:* Sergio Giral, dir., *Rancheador* (1976), Cuba. Instituto Cubano del Arte e Industria Cinematográficos.

Estévez's pursuit of the four runaways leads him and his men to a set of slave shacks on a plantation belonging to a local enslaver named Dubois, whose Francophone name may indicate that he is a Saint Domingue refugee, like Alea's Monsieur Duclé in *La última cena*. Estévez's crude, aggressive, and domineering character is immediately apparent. He is an ideal henchman for the slave power, his lack of refinement and grace positive qualities in the context of his line of work. He is tall and physically imposing, despite his advancing middle age and paunch. He revels as a tyrant in the power he wields—intimidation and terror are his stock-in-trade. At the slave shacks, Estévez orders his enslaved tracker to search the huts and brusquely dismisses the protests of Dubois's overseer, Felipe, who wishes to have his own men conduct the search. However, Estévez and his men are ambushed, and his tracker is killed by a rifle shot from inside one of the shacks. Chaos ensues and a skirmish breaks out, during which Estévez orders the burning of the slave shacks, contrary to Felipe's pleading, to flush out the runaways hiding inside. As the runaways emerge from the flames, Estévez's men open fire. By the end of the melee, seven slaves have been killed and a further seven have been captured, one of whom is Mataperro. "Receipts"—left ears—are taken from the deceased, and these gruesome mutilations are even more barbaric because of their portrayal as routine.

This early scene of brutality is the first indication of the problems that will arise as a consequence of Estévez's uninhibited aggression. Following the skirmish, at a meeting chaired by the local colonial official, Captain Infante, Dubois demands compensation for his loss of seven enslaved workers. However, Don Lucas Villegas, the narcissistic and manipulative enslaver for whom Estévez works, defends his *rancheador*. The problem, Villegas argues, is not Estévez and his men but the destabilizing presence of maroons from Melchora's *palenque* in their midst. Melchora's rebels have been raiding the local plantations, freeing slaves, and engaging in illegal trade with both enslaved communities and white smallholder farmers. During daylight hours, runaways have been hiding among enslaved populations on the local plantations, including on Dubois's plantation, before retreating back to the hills and their *palenque* at night. The situation Giral sketches is one in which colonial control is far from total and Black resistance is incessant, emerging, retreating, and reemerging—hydralike—from unknown places.[70] The meeting concludes with Villegas getting his way: there is to be no compensation for Dubois, and Estévez and his posse are formally instructed to locate and eliminate Melchora's settlement. For this task Estévez needs a new tracker, and thinking him ideal for the task, he negotiates Mataperro's release. Garroting Mataperro would be a pity, Estévez explains to Villegas, considering how well he knows the hills. As the critic Aisha Z. Cort writes, "as a recaptured runaway, Mataperro has not only been to *el monte* [the wilderness], but he has learned its secrets; its routes, tricks, treasures, and promises."[71] All this Estévez knows and prizes. Mataperro is thus offered a reprieve from execution if he will agree to serve as an enslaved tracker for Estévez. At first Mataperro rejects the offer, but faced with no alternative, he reluctantly agrees. However, Mataperro's agreement signals not submission but confirmation of his status as a clarion of Black agency.

While at the outset of the film it appeared that Estévez held all the cards, now his double dependency is revealed: he is beholden to the planter class and Madrid's colonial bureaucrats (who will abandon him when they consider him a liability and beyond their control) *and* reliant on Mataperro to guide him to Melchorra's settlement. Though Mataperro remains enslaved, in *el monte* it is Mataperro, not Estévez, who wields the power. Moreover, as they journey through the wilderness, Mataperro's confidence, composure, and dignified bearing—ably conveyed by Samuel Claxton's charismatic screen presence and poise—accentuates the shift in the balance of power that has taken place between the two men (fig. 3.6).

Mataperro's calm demeanor is in stark contrast to Estévez's agitation. Unsettled and frustrated but also curious, during a rest break Estévez questions Mataperro: What does the incessant drumming coming from Melchorra's settlement communicate? From where does Melchora get her power? How has she been able to evade recapture so successfully? Like Pontecorvo's Walker in *Burn!*, for a man ostensibly in charge, Estévez's incomprehension is stunning. Instead, it is Mataperro who has all the answers, as well as confidence in the triumph of Black liberation:

> MATAPERRO: When the *rancheador* hunts the Black, Melchora turns into a bird and flies away . . . into a snake and creeps

Figure 3.6. Mataperro, *Rancheador*. *Source:* Sergio Giral, dir., *Rancheador* (1976), Cuba. Instituto Cubano del Arte e Industria Cinematográficos.

away, into rain to wipe out the tracks of the slaves. No one can find her. She changes the hills so the white man will get lost. The hills eat the white man.

The imagery of Mataperro's speech, which conveys how slave resistance could be informed by "magical" beliefs, is reminiscent of the connecting of slave resistance to an ontology of the marvelous via an aesthetics of magical realism that we encountered in Tomás Gutiérez Alea's *La última cena*. The motifs of Mataperro's speech also prey on Estévez's insecurities: Mataperro's declaration of Melchora's capacity to turn into a bird and fly away is especially resonant given Estévez's propensity to call out in frustration that "niggers can't fly!" whenever tracks appear simply to stop and vanish. Moreover, Mataperro's belief in Melchora's human-animal shape-shifting abilities as well as her capacity to draw on the powers of the natural world suggests a reverence for the natural environment. The implicit proposition is that of a harmonious relationship between the politics of Black liberation and the natural world, which can be contrasted with the impulse of slaveholding European capitalist modernity to dominate nature. The world that the slave power has created, it is inferred, is distinctly *unnatural* and, as a result, the people empowered by this world are estranged from nature. For this reason, whereas the free Blacks in the hillside *palenques* enjoy a communion with the natural world, the planter class and their allies who have sought only to instrumentalize the natural world have ironically forgotten its primacy to human life and society.

Rancheador: The Eviction of the White Smallholders and Mataperro's Triumph

As well as giving priority to slave resistance and communicating the fragility of the slave power when confronted with the realities of slave autonomy, *Rancheador* also elaborates the social divisions among Cuba's settler classes. Poor white farmers are accused repeatedly by Estévez of trading with fugitive slaves while the farmers look resentfully on the wealthy planter class who wish to drive the farmers off their land. The local farmers who produce crops for subsistence and local markets are regarded by the enslavers as obstacles to the further development of their sugar-cane plantations. The only question for the likes of Villegas is how to take possession of this land. Villegas's solution is to decide that the farmers settlements lack legitimacy: the farmers do not in fact hold title deeds to the land on which they live and work, and their use of the land is a hindrance to the processes of capital accumulation. Therefore, by Lockean logic, Villegas can decide that no consent is required to seize the land—which in fact belongs to him as the mill owner—and he calls on Estévez to dispossess the farmers. Villegas instructs Estévez to pause his pursuit of Melchora and to "persuade" the farmers to leave the land. Villegas offers Estévez a bribe, to which Estévez smiles and declares, "I can never say no to you."

Predictably, however, Estévez and his men encounter resistance. The assertion of Villegas's dubious property rights requires the use of force and violence. One farmer, Morales, from whom Estévez had purchased provisions earlier in the film, refuses to leave, calling Estévez and his men "Villegas's dogs." Morales insists that he and his family have the right to remain on the land that sustains them. Giral's representation of Morales and his family is designed to arouse our sympathy. Morales is seated on a simple wooden chair, his wife and daughter are standing in the doorway, and three other children, two of whom are very young, are sitting on the ground (fig. 3.7).

Figure 3.7. Morales and his family, *Rancheador*. Source: Sergio Giral, dir., *Rancheador* (1976), Cuba. Instituto Cubano del Arte e Industria Cinematográficos.

The tired faces of the members of the Morales family in this shot are unmistakable. Their home is modest as is their clothing, which is simple, worn, and dirty. The careful composition extends to the drab lighting, which drains color and energy from the shot. Cumulatively, all this conveys rural poverty, a life of toil and hardship, and a brutalizing and precarious existence. The Morales family clearly presents no threat, but Estévez's response to Morales's defiance is to order one of his men to shoot and kill him. The cold-blooded murder of Morales instantly triggers an outpouring of grief and fury among Morales's family. The scene can be productively compared to the earlier scene in which Estévez and his men murdered seven of Dubois's slaves. While the killing of the slaves is more gruesome to watch (particularly in the aftermath of the murders when the slaves' bodies are mutilated), both scenes are profoundly traumatic and communicate that the poor whites and enslaved populations had a shared enemy in the planter class.

The murder of Morales scandalizes the local community. Once again, Estévez has overstepped the bounds of what is permissible even in degraded slave society. Villegas is furious that Estezez did not heed his instruction to act "tactfully," to which Estévez responds with exasperation, "Did you really think they would just agree to leave peacefully?" Ever the negotiator, however, Villegas can see a solution: Villegas tells Estévez to give up the member of his crew who shot Morales. Estévez duly complies but is wracked by feelings of guilt and betrayal, and he feels responsible when his former colleague is executed by the garrote. Although he escaped prosecution himself, in the wake of Morales's murder, Estévez has fallen out of favor and his reputation in tatters. He wallows at home, seeking solace in the bottle and in sexually abusing an enslaved Black woman. However, when a band of maroons from Melchora's *palenque* raid Villegas's plantation one night, burning down various mill buildings and freeing a number of slaves, Estévez suddenly finds himself charged once again by Villegas with the capture of Melchora and the destruction of her *palenque*. Estévez and his possé head back into *el monte* once more to resume their search for Melchora, again aided by Mataperro. However, following the Morales affair, Estévez is a changed man. He is driven by anger, resentment, and a misplaced desire for vengeance, and what little self-restraint he once possessed has now entirely evaporated. Estévez and his men round up and capture runaways and enslaved men and women alike, torturing and killing indiscriminately for information pertaining to Melchorra and her whereabouts. Consequently, Captain Infante is inundated with complaints from incensed enslavers. The final straw comes when Captain Infante receives testimony from Juan Lope, hitherto the most-loyal member of Estévez's gang, corroborating the many complaints about Estévez's behavior. Captain Infante then requests that the Junta relieve Estévez of his duties as *rancheador* and institutes a new possé to be led by Lope, charging them with the duty of capturing Estévez and bringing him before the law.

But Estévez remains in the wilderness, obsessed with tracking down Melchora. However, his authority is beginning to fade: his men hear rumors that he has been relieved of his duties as *rancheador* and that he is now a wanted man. One by one, his men begin to desert, and after Estévez and his men are ambushed in the jungle by unseen assailants, only Estévez and Mataperro remain. The camera cuts to a snake slithering through the jungle, which recalls Melchora's ability to transform herself into a snake as in Mataperro's "the hills eat the white man" speech. The sounds of the jungle—the squawks and cries of birds, the chirping of crickets, and a percussive instrument that evokes the sound of a rattlesnake—confirm that Estévez and Mataperro are now deep in *el monte*. In the chaos of the ambush, Estévez loses his horse and, like Mataperro, is now alone and on foot in the jungle. Exhausted, Estévez stumbles upon a jungle pool where he sees his horse. He approaches to recapture it, but Mataperro bursts out from the jungle and draws a machete. The two men face each other in a final gladiatorial set piece in which Mataperro kills Estévez, thereby finally achieving self-liberation. Melchora's prophecy has come to pass: "the hills eat the white man." The film's final scenes are an image of triumphant Black liberty and an inversion of the film's opening. Now Mataperro rides on horseback through the Cuban jungle and hills before the camera pans out to a landscape shot (figs. 3.8 and 3.9). *Rancheador's* final shot thus mirrors *El otro Francisco's* final shot, evoking once more *el monte* as a site of resistance and struggle.

Maluala: Giral's Homage to Cuba's *Palenques*

The final installment in Giral's trilogy of films representing slave resistance, *Maluala*, is an homage to the history of Cuba's free Black, self-emancipated communities. Released in 1979 to widespread praise on the world film-festival circuit, *Maluala* received prizes in Brazil, Cuba, and the former Czechoslovakia.[72] As did *Rancheador*, the film achieves a high-energy ambience with the feel of an action-drama, and this has

Figure 3.8. Mataperro: triumphant Black liberty, *Rancheador*. *Source:* Sergio Giral, dir., *Rancheador* (1976), Cuba. Instituto Cubano del Arte e Industria Cinematográficos.

Figure 3.9. Mataperro in *el monte*, *Rancheador*. *Source:* Sergio Giral, dir., *Rancheador* (1976), Cuba. Instituto Cubano del Arte e Industria Cinematográficos.

been noted by various critics. Writing for the BFI, the critic Ashly Clark has observed that *Maluala* bears echoes "of both the elemental grace of Sergio Leone and the brusque power of Gillo Pontecorvo."[73] This grace and power is complemented by the opening score, written by the Cuban composer Sergio Vitier, which reveals the influence of US Blaxploitation soundtracks of the period.[74] The musical artists who contributed to the scores of Blaxploitation movies include such luminaries as Curtis Mayfield, Marvin Gaye, and Tina Turner. Drawing on the heritage and popularity of such artists, Vitier's *Maluala* score incorporates the syncopated beat and groove we readily associate with African American funk, R&B, and soul music, which is then overlaid with distinctly Cuban vocals, acoustic drums, and percussion. This uplifting score should be contrasted with the mournful solemnity of Hans Zimmer's score for *12 Years a Slave*, which we will consider in the next chapter. These contrasting musical scores are also indicative of the divergent ideological messages of Giral's and McQueen's slavery films. While for McQueen the overriding message imparted centers on guilt, sentimentality, and atrocity, Giral's project aspires to celebrate Black diasporic achievement and creativity, assert pride in Black culture and history, and communicate an understanding of Atlantic slavery as a coordinate in the story of the unfolding of global capitalism.

From the outset, *Maluala* establishes a Black Cuban point of view and emphasizes the actuality of Black Cuban agency in history. Further, *Maluala*'s Black Cuban subjects are presented as active participants, not passive peripheral figures, in the contested spaces of a rapidly globalizing capitalism. This is most clearly expressed in the opening scene's communication of the involvement of Cuba's Black maroon population in the transnational trade networks of the nineteenth century. It is a river scene, and three Black men are aboard a raft that they are punting downriver toward an oceanfront beach. One of the men is Coba, the leader of Bumba, which is one of the region's largest *palenques*. The three men are en route to a rendezvous with Haitian traders who have established business links with Coba and representatives of many of Cuba's other Cimarron communities. Coba had been hoping to obtain rifles in exchange for coffee, but this time he must make do with damask from India, silk from the far east, and decorative items from Venice. Coba's shrewdness of character is quickly established, as is the existence of Black autonomy that has eluded Spanish suppression. After the rendezvous, Coba and his men return to Bumba, which is presented as a vibrant, bustling place where the rhythms of hand drums resound as Bumba's maroon citizens go about their everyday tasks.

The scene then cuts to a conversation between the colonial Governor and Captain Fromesto, the two senior-most Spanish-colonial officials in the film. From their conversation, we learn of their grave concerns that the island's Black population has been inspired by the events of the Haitian Revolution as well as Spain's colonial defeats in Latin America. Coba and another maroon leader, Gallo, have presented the Governor and Fromesto with a petition demanding "land and liberty" for the colony's Black population, both maroon and enslaved. The Governor and Fromesto are especially concerned by reports that the Black population has access to subversive, revolutionary print material. Stamping out this access thus becomes one of their obsessions, and this marks them out as enemies of a democratic public sphere in which the exchange and development of ideas might take place. It also demonstrates that Cuba's population of Black rebels are the film's true agents of a radical Enlightenment.[75] In a plot detail that evokes C. L. R. James's account of Toussaint Louverture's development of a revolutionary consciousness, the Governor and Fromesto discuss the problem of the circulation of proscribed print material among the colony's Black population. A book has been discovered in the ruins of a grand *palenque*. Although we do not learn the title of the book, given the mention of Haiti and the context of the film's plot, a volume of Abbé Raynal's *Histoire des deux Indes* appears to be a likely candidate.[76] Raynal's book, which was first published in six volumes between the years 1770 and 1779, was a popular prerevolutionary, antislavery text that circulated widely in the Caribbean despite its inclusion on the Roman Catholic Church's Index of Forbidden Books. Raynal's famous *Histoire* sent chills down the spines of the Atlantic World's enslaver class and colonial bureaucrats since it contains the famed "Black Spartacus" passage in which Raynal predicted the emergence of a Black avenger. This passage, C. L. R. James alleged, was read "over and over again" by Toussaint Louverture, who drew inspiration from it before his rise to power and subsequent transformation into the Haitian Revolution's great military and political leader.[77] Captain Fromesto and the Governor are more than aware of the precedent set in Haiti and of the threat that the unnamed book represents. The circulation throughout the Atlantic World of revolutionary ideas via printed materials in conjunction with a literate Black population in Cuba instils anxiety and alarm in Captain Fromesto: "I think of Haiti and fear . . ." he remarks before allowing his thoughts to trail off. Fromesto's preferred solution to the tinderbox of maroon communities, revolutionary ideas, and incessant slave resistance is subjugation via extreme violence. The Governor, however, has different ideas, and he outlines an underhanded approach that will sustain the narrative and action of *Maluala*.

The Governor pens a letter—a treaty proposal—to be circulated among the island's free Black population. The Governor is willing to grant freedom to the chiefs of the various *palenques* on certain conditions. These conditions stipulate that the freed chiefs will in return have to work as "free soldiers" of the Spanish government and assist in the tracking down of runways who violate the terms of the treaty. While the chiefs will be granted their freedom on the signing of the treaty, the ordinary members of the *palenques* are to be required to earn their freedom after a period of "dignified work." The treaty is a poisoned chalice intended to sow division and dissent among the Black populations of the *palenques*. On receiving news of the treaty and its terms, Coba and the other *palenque* leaders are outraged. Coba finds the concept of "freed slaves chasing after runaways" grotesque. "Tell the Governor that I have been informed" is his dismissive retort. Other chiefs, including Gallo—the leader of Maluala, the largest of the *palenques*—also reject the terms. In their discussion, they note that the Governor's letter fails to respond to their demands for land and universal freedom. As was also the case for the newly emancipated Blacks in revolutionary Haiti, for the maroon communities of Cuba, tangible freedom without a right to land and the freedom to labor for oneself was unthinkable.[78] As Gallo states, "freedom has to be on our land and for everybody." Gallo's opinion can also be aligned with the Bolshevik critique of "paper laws that are of no use" to oppressed peoples unless they are accompanied by changes in material circumstances.[79] For Gallo, true liberty is to be sought in lived reality: "No paper gives freedom. All are free and equal on the mountain." However, the principle of freedom and equality on the mountain is no guarantee of prosperity: life in the *palenques* is hard, and three of the chiefs resolve to accept the Governor's invitation to the palace for discussions. Ultimately, the trio—Pascual, Luis, and Francisco—accept the Governor's terms and become, as the Governor puts it, "obedient African warriors who will bring glory to Spain." However, by the film's end, Pascual, Luis, and Francisco will all come to regret their decision and prove less than "obedient."

Pleased with his capture of Pascual, Luis, and Francisco, the Governor now aims to turn Coba and Gallo, the two rebel chiefs the Spanish fear the most. A Priest is dispatched to make clear that the Governor's treaty proposal is in fact nothing other than gunboat diplomacy: "The Governor will destroy everything if you don't agree," the Priest explains. Sure enough, in response to their failure to accede to the terms of his proposal, the Governor orders Fromesto to lead the forces under his command on a path of ruthless destruction. The *palenque* of the female chief, Ma-Sunta, is destroyed and her people massacred. Citizens of Bumba are ambushed on the river and brutally slain. Again, the history of the Haitian Revolution is an analogue for the film's action, Fromesto's brutal tactics calling to mind the atrocities inflicted by the French army in Saint-Domingue acting under General Rochambeau.[80] When the conflicted Coba finally submits to the Governor's terms, his decision is largely a popular one among the people of Bumba and is greeted with dancing and celebration. However, not all of Coba's people are impressed, and some, including Feliciano, refuse to resign themselves to serving the King of Spain by tracking down runaways. Feliciano departs for Gallo's Maluala, remarking that "Coba saved his skin and sold his soul." Coba is angered but soon recognizes that his decision was a misjudgment: leading his ostensibly free people out of Bumba, Coba sees "free" Blacks laboring on the construction of a new road. The optics are indistinguishable from slave labor and Coba reneges on the agreement. With Coba's breaking of the treaty, the stage is set for the film's climactic action: the Governor orders Fromesto to lead a military expedition to raze Bumba and Maluala to the ground. Fromesto's lust for violence appears on course for satisfaction. Bumba is duly destroyed, and Fromesto's men set off in pursuit of Coba as he scrambles up a rocky escarpment in a scene that recalls the manner of Dolores's eventual capture by the British in Pontecorvo's *Burn!* However, unlike Dolores, Coba evades capture. Instead, he leaps to his death from the clifftop, denying Fromesto gratification. Coba's story is thus fashioned as a tragedy—the charismatic Black leader who, burdened with moral responsibility for his people, makes a profound political miscalculation and pays for it with his life. As such, Giral's treatment of his defiant but conflicted hero warrants comparison with Césaire's treatment of the Haitian and Congolese revolutionaries Henry Christophe and Patrice Lumumba.[81]

With Coba dead, Fromesto turns his sights on Maluala, but his forces meet fierce resistance. Fromesto's men are ambushed: rocks and boulders rain down on them, volleys of arrows and rifle shots cut them down, and they are forced to retreat to the safety of the city. But in the city the Blacks are celebrating. News of Maluala's victory has reached the city before Fromesto and his routed soldiers. There is drumming, singing, and carnival costumes. The scene cuts to the Governor, slumped in his chair, a picture of defeat. Surrounded by Black Cubans celebrating on the city streets, Fromesto appears as if on the edge of mental collapse. The camera pans closer and rotates around him, the lens language signifying Fromesto's belated recognition of the undeniable realities of Black autonomy, Black culture, and Black resistance in Cuba. This recognition destabilizes his entire world view, and he screams out in a state of despair. The film ends with a freeze-frame image of Fromesto's face that in its coloration (the orange tones of the upper background), its mood, and its sinuous composition (note the tornadolike funnel of smoke in the upper left of the shot, the orange wavy horizontals in the background, the curves of Fromesto's clothing, and the curls of his hair) recalls, more than any other image, Edvard Munch's iconic painting of terrible human anguish and alienation: *The Scream*[82] (figs. 3.10 and 3.11). *Maluala*'s final defiant message—which fuses psychiatric and sociological analysis in a manner that resounds with Fanon's richly evocative thesis of Third World revolution—is unequivocally that while Black resistance will result in the individual and collective liberation of the oppressed, the violence perpetrated by the slave power is the cause of individual and collective breakdown, mental disorder,

Figure 3.10. Fromesto's Scream, *Maluala*. *Source:* Giral, Sergio, dir. *Maluala*. 1979. Cuba. Instituto Cubano del Arte e Industria Cinematográficos.

Figure 3.11. Edvard Munch, *The Scream* (1893). *Source:* National Museum of Art, Norway.

and the brutalization of the oppressors as well as the oppressed. Moreover, given that we can identify Giral's freeze frame of Fromesto's scream as a response to Munch's "canonical expression of the great modernist thematics of alienation, anomie, solitude, social fragmentation, and isolation," we can map comparatively the psychopathologies and material suffering of the age of slavery and the age of modernity.[83] Giral's parting shot, then, is that not only did slavery make the modern world and the modern subject, but the agonies of modernity were portended by those of slavery.

Coda: Giral in Miami

Following the success of his slavery trilogy, Giral made three more feature films before emigrating back to the United States in 1991. *Techo de vidrio* ("Glass Ceiling"), a film that suggested the persistence of racism in socialist Cuba, was completed in 1981 but would not be released for a further six years. Then came *Plácido* in 1986, followed by *María Antonia* in 1990, the year that marked the beginning of the economic catastrophe that swept Cuba in the wake of the disintegration of the Soviet Union and the demise of the Communist states in Eastern Europe. Richard Gott has observed that the economic storm Cuba weathered in the 1990s, euphemistically dubbed the "special period," constituted "the most dramatic and significant change" Cuba had undergone "since the island had first become a sugar-based economy in the wake of the revolution in Saint-Domingue in 1791."[84] Such was the scale of the economic disaster that across the island "horse-drawn carts and carriages replaced cars and lorries [and] 300,000 oxen replaced 30,000 Soviet tractors" while "malnutrition—unknown in Cuba for generations—became widespread."[85] Given the scale of the catastrophe Cuba was confronting, and considering the ease with which Giral was able to move back to the United States given his status as a dual US–Cuban citizen, his decision to leave Cuba behind and to give up his career as a filmmaker at the ICAIC for a life in Miami is entirely explicable and hardly surprising. However, it is striking that the reasons Giral himself provided for his decision to return to the United States make no mention of the conditions in Cuba at the beginning of the "special period." Instead, Giral chose to explain his decision in terms of increasing political disenchantment: "The romantic ideals that had brought me to the island as a young man had slowly evaporated over time. I found the country's double standards perpetuated the racism, social inequality, and political repression that it pretended to cure."[86] In this regard, the fate of *Techo de vidrio* may well have been a pivotal moment that, together with his increasing awareness of the Cuban state's persecution of homosexuals, shook Giral's revolutionary commitment to the core.[87]

Critics have often remarked that the ICAIC was a haven for open-minded filmmaking and have also noted that films critical of the Cuban state were indeed made and released (consider, e.g., Tomás Gutiérrez Alea's *Memorias del subdesarollo* of 1968 and Pastor Vega's *Portrait of Teresa* of 1979, as well as many films released in the 1980s).[88] However, the ICAIC's treatment of *Techo de vidrio* demonstrates that this freedom was not unfettered. When he spoke of *Techo de vidrio* in the 1980s, Giral was extremely guarded in his comments. He shouldered the blame for its nonrelease himself, described it as "a failed film," and remarked that addressing contemporary topics was a "very difficult" endeavor.[89] However, as Aviva Chomsky has noted, after his move to Miami in 1991 Giral was prepared to speak more plainly and to accuse the ICAIC of censorship:

"My film, *Techo de vidrio*, was censored from the onset and ended up in the memory hole."[90] The contrast with Giral's earlier acclamation of the "complete artistic freedom of expression" he enjoyed in the ICAIC is remarkable: "We have tremendous artistic freedom. From the outside, people always miss the point here. The issue of artistic freedom is somehow always wielded against us when people start talking about freedom of expression (which should always be placed in quotation marks in any part of the world anyway)."[91] While the case of *Techo de vidrio* should prompt us to treat Giral's words here (from 1986) with appropriate skepticism, Giral's observation that freedom of expression is fettered everywhere is certainly pertinent to this project. The paucity of Hollywood films representing Black slave resistance and Danny Glover's well-documented failure to interest Hollywood's financiers in backing a film on the Haitian Revolution is illustrative of nothing if not the fact that in "the land of the free," projects aspiring to represent Black agency in history still face significant barriers that all too often prevent their realization. Consequently, within the mainstreams of North American and European public knowledge and consciousness, the historic actuality of Black achievement has but a dimly lit presence. As such, like Pontecorvo's *Burn!* and Alea's *La última cena*, Giral's slavery trilogy has lost none of its urgency, and it remains a resource for those committed to the recuperation and recognition of the role of Black agency in antislavery, anti-imperialist, and anti-capitalist struggle.

In Miami, Giral has lived an openly gay life, worked as an art and film critic, and established his own film and video company.[92] From his Miami base, Giral has made documentaries about Cuban filmmakers in exile (*La imagen rota*, 1995), gay and lesbian activism in Miami (*Chronicle of an Ordinance*, 2000), and Cuban music (*Al Bárbaro del Ritmo*, 2004), while 2010 saw the release of Giral's first fiction film in twenty years, *Dos Veces Ana* ("Two Times Ana"), a comedy that tells the story of two Hispanic and biracial Anas whose lives intersect. While the ideological impetus of these recent films undeniably represents a shift in the tenor of Giral's work, it is nevertheless the case that Giral's late style does not constitute an eschewal of his earlier works that he has continued to defend.[93] Giral's trilogy of "*negrometrajes*" remains a glorious and defiant refutation of the neglect of Black Cuban agency and subjectivity in the historiography of slavery and abolition.

Chapter 4

The Slave Narrative in Hollywood

Steve McQueen's Adaptation of Solomon Northup's *Twelve Years a Slave*

In the first three chapters of this study, I have argued that we can identify a radical restoration of Black agency in the works of a trio of committed filmmakers: the Italian Gillo Pontecorvo and the Cubans Tomás Gutiérrez Alea and Sergio Giral. I will now argue that these works form a revealing contrast with recent popular films, mostly produced with the backing of major Hollywood studios, that have taken slavery for their subject. While Hollywood's longstanding aversion to the subject of slavery has certainly not been overcome and the representation of Black resistance remains taboo, it must nevertheless be admitted that since the turn of the twenty-first century there has been a dramatic upsurge in popular cinematic works of widely varying quality and ideological intent focused on Black history and the legacies of slavery.[1] However, my focus here is on Steve McQueen's *12 Years a Slave* of 2013, as it rapidly became regarded as not only an instant modern classic but as *the* definitive feature film about slavery.[2] The film—an adaptation of Solomon Northup's 1853 account of his kidnapping, enslavement, and eventual return to liberty—is the first cinematic adaptation of a slave narrative, and it immediately garnered overwhelmingly positive reviews.[3] Consider David Denby's assessment in the *New Yorker* that *12 Years a Slave* is "easily the greatest feature film ever made about American slavery" and Peter Bradshaw's view that the film constitutes a triumphant "essay in outrage and injustice, and a visualisation of an end to tyranny."[4] Such effusive reception established McQueen's status as a preeminent commodity in both art-house and mainstream cinema circles. Never before had a Turner Prize–winner gone on to become an Academy Award–winner. However, such endorsement coexisted with reservations and unease, and I will be referring to the thoughtful dissent that followed.

Before crossing over to cinematic feature films, McQueen had worked predominantly in the mediums of video art installations and photography while he also produced sculptural works. His oeuvre has always been diverse in subject matter as well as in medium. While much of McQueen's work has focused on Black diasporic themes (consider, most recently, *Small Axe*, an anthology of five films made for television that premiered in 2020 and which are set in London's West Indian immigrant communities between the 1960s and 1980s), McQueen has also completed major projects on subjects as varied as the IRA hunger-striker Bobby Sands and the destructiveness of sex addiction in the age of the internet.[5] The aesthetic and political sensitivity that is a hallmark of McQueen's approach to such diverse subjects, which frequently forces the viewer to confront the precariousness of life, the "dynamics of bodies drawn into abject states," and the pain and suffering of others, has been repeatedly recognized by critics.[6] This widespread critical success confirms McQueen's standing as one of Britain's most-influential artists of the twenty-first century, a fact also reflected in the great many prestigious accolades and prizes McQueen has been awarded over the years.[7] In November 2013, following the release of *12 Years a Slave*, *Art Review* magazine noted the unprecedented nature and scale of this success, observing that McQueen has crossed over "from art-house to mainstream cinema without compromise" and that "no real precedents exist for such hugely successful straddling, or collapsing, of worlds. Nor for the impetus McQueen has delivered to both, whether helping legitimate cinematic aesthetics within art or bringing an artist's mindset and ethical realism to Hollywood."[8] However, notwithstanding McQueen's undoubted gifts as a multimedia artist at home in both the gallery and the cinema, the argument here is that McQueen's *12 Years a Slave* inadvertently elides the formative role slavery has played in the creation of the modern self and the modern world while also rendering Black resistance to slavery invisible. Furthermore, McQueen's adaptation implicitly presents racism as anachronistic rather than as a vector of continuing systematized oppression. This is especially ironic given that McQueen's wider oeuvre—especially his art films and video-installation work—has criticized contemporary racialized labor exploitation, its roots in colonialism, and chattel slavery's intricate relationship to capitalism.

To substantiate these claims, I proceed along two lines of inquiry. First, I compare McQueen's adaptation to Solomon Northup's text to identify systemic patterns of omission and addition in the McQueen version and consider their impact. As Stephanie Li has noted, "film adaptations of historical texts inevitably raise questions about how true they are to their original sources."[9] My objective, however, is not to find fault with McQueen's version for any lack of fidelity to the original source material. Northup's narrative is, after all, itself a mediated text: it was transcribed and edited by David Wilson, a New York lawyer, writer, and politician to whom Northup told his story. The text is not without its own inconsistencies and tensions, and it cannot be treated uncritically as authentic testimony to Northup's lived experience of slavery. For example, while some critics have noted the veracity of many elements of Northup's narrative, others have drawn attention to its striking similarities to Harriet Beecher Stowe's 1852 antislavery sensation *Uncle Tom's Cabin*, which was published one year before Northup's text.[10] Hence, faithfulness to Northup's original should not automatically be considered a positive, nor is any lack of it necessarily detrimental. Instead, I seek to answer Li's question, "What has been lost or gained in the translation to the big screen?" and address the implications of this translation.[11]

Second, I will also address, in the context of debates over the representability of slavery, the impact of McQueen's signature filmic language, which frequently blurs the boundary between narrative and nonnarrative form. Questions centered on the ethics and aesthetics of configuring slavery take on a new pertinence given McQueen's gift for sumptuous cinematography, an art perfected over many years' collaboration with cinematographer Sean Bobbitt, and his penchant for giving primacy to the suffering body in his work. The other chapters in this study argue that it is possible to construct an ethical filmic aesthetic out of the horrors of slavery. However, I suggest here that McQueen was unable to negotiate this minefield of ethics and representation while working within Hollywood. Furthermore, I suggest that the film's extremely moving visual and aural poetics ironically only deepen its problematic occlusion of slavery's systematicity.

Solomon Northup and Steve McQueen

In comparing McQueen's 2013 adaptation to Northup's 1853 narrative, it is necessary to recognize the challenges inherent in adapting a work for a very different sociopolitical milieu. In 1853, Northup was writing for a US audience preoccupied with debates surrounding slavery. Northup's narrative was published amid a maelstrom of heated discussion surrounding *Uncle Tom's Cabin* and three years after the notorious Fugitive Slave Act of 1850, a piece of draconian proslavery legislation that deprived runaway slaves of habeas corpus, the right to a jury trial, and the right to testify on their own behalf. As Daniel Sharfstein has explained, this act placed "the federal government in the service of slaveowners pursuing their runaways" and "allowed slaveowners and their authorized agents to 'pursue and reclaim' escapees on free soil," hence encouraging the kidnapping of free Blacks.[12] Moreover, the passage of the Kansas-Nebraska Act in 1854, "which allowed settlers to vote to determine whether Kansas [would join the Union as] a slave or free state," was just months away.[13] Although the secession of the slave states and the outbreak of the Civil War were still more than seven years away, Northup's narrative constituted an intervention into what Sharfstein describes as an "escalating national crisis over slavery" and a political and public discourse dominated by fiercely contested and polarized debates over bondage and freedom.[14]

In contrast, McQueen was operating within a contemporary context in which, as Paul Gilroy has noted, "slavery has been written off as part of the pre-history of our world" and racism itself is commonly "presented as anachronistic."[15] This changed context of reception informs Thomas Doherty's contention that in the twenty-first century, "the didactic purpose of the slave narrative—to rebuke the institution of slavery and the racist ideology that sustained it—is a dead letter."[16] However, Doherty's assessment overlooks the potential role of the slave narrative in promoting a robust conception of the significance of slavery to global capitalism. This point was certainly not lost on McQueen. In many publicity events pertaining to the release of his adaptation, McQueen took pains to make the case that he viewed his *12 Years a Slave* project as serving a myriad of progressive political purposes, including the highlighting of the persistence of socially entrenched, pernicious racial iniquities.[17] For example, in many interviews about his adaptation, McQueen spoke eloquently of the fact that "new" forms of slavery (including human trafficking, bonded and forced labor, and child slavery) are endemic globally, while chattel slavery persists in such Saharan nations as Niger, Mauritania, Chad, and Sudan. McQueen's advocacy on this issue resulted in his adaptation of *12 Years a Slave* receiving a special screening at the United Nations' New York headquarters whereupon the UN secretary-general of the time, Ban

The Slave Narrative in Hollywood | 153

Ki-Moon, praised McQueen's adaptation as "a wonderful work of art" and expressed his hope that *12 Years a Slave* would inspire the action necessary "to end all forms of slavery for good."[18]

Additionally, radical political perspectives were a prominent theme in McQueen's earlier video-installation work. Consider, for example, *Caribs' Leap* (2002) (figs. 4.1 and 4.2), *Western Deep* (2002) (fig. 4.3), and *Gravesend* (2007) (figs. 4.4 and 4.5), each of which uses techniques of historical and geographic juxtaposition to communicate a concern with the racialized and systemic character of capitalist exploitation and the connections between slavery, imperialism, and extractive capitalism.[19] *Caribs' Leap* evokes a collective act of sacrifice that occurred in 1651 on the eastern Caribbean island of Grenada. Rather than surrender to French soldiers, an unknown number of Caribs threw themselves over the cliffs

Figure 4.1. Steve McQueen, *Caribs' Leap* (2002). Super 8mm color film, transferred to video, sound, 28 min 53 sec, continuous play; 35 mm color film, transferred to video, no sound, 12 min 6 sec, continuous play. *Source:* © Steve McQueen. Courtesy of the artist, Thomas Dane Gallery, and Marian Goodman Gallery.

Figure 4.2. Steve McQueen, *Caribs' Leap*, 2002. Super 8mm color film, transferred to video, sound, 28 min 53 sec, continuous play; 35 mm color film, transferred to video, no sound, 12 min 6 sec, continuous play. *Source:* © Steve McQueen. Courtesy of the artist, Thomas Dane Gallery, and Marian Goodman Gallery.

Figure 4.3. Steve McQueen, *Western Deep*, super 8mm color film transferred to video, sound, 24 min 12 sec, continuous play. *Source:* © Steve McQueen. Courtesy of the artist, Thomas Dane Gallery, and Marian Goodman Gallery.

Figure 4.4. Steve McQueen, *Gravesend* (2007). 2 parts: high definition with 5.1 surround sound, 18 mins 04 secs, looped; silent 8mm, 54 secs, 06 frames. *Source:* © Steve McQueen. Courtesy of the artist, Thomas Dane Gallery, and Marian Goodman Gallery.

Figure 4.5. Steve McQueen, *Gravesend*, 2007. 2 parts: high definition with 5.1 surround sound, 18 mins 04 secs, looped; silent 8mm, 54 secs, 06 frames. *Source:* © Steve McQueen. Courtesy of the artist, Thomas Dane Gallery, and Marian Goodman Gallery.

to their deaths on the rocks below. Then, on a second screen, the film implicitly connects its depiction of colonial genocide in the seventeenth century to poverty and underdevelopment in present-day Grenada.

Western Deep journeys into the physical interior of the deepest gold mine in the world, the Tau Tona mines in South Africa, to address labor exploitation under neoliberal capitalism in postapartheid South Africa. The visual language of the two films, which were exhibited worldwide as a single video-installation artwork and as separate exhibits between 2002 and 2011, also links Grenada and South Africa to one another. Both films depict descent: the controlled descent down the lift shaft to the rock face in *Western Deep* serves as a counterpoint to the free-falling figure in *Caribs' Leap*. Further, while *Caribs' Leap* depicts a descent through light, *Western Deep* depicts a descent into darkness. This elegant aesthetic interplay of visual language connects Amerindian and Black African labor, resistance, and suffering and communicates the long history of racialized global capitalism.

Similarly, if more obliquely, *Gravesend* evokes an understanding of a radically uneven world-system that emphasizes the way in which the "high-tech" depends upon the "low-tech" by depicting coltan mining in the Congo and its final processing in Britain for use in electronic devices.[20] This, I suggest, is McQueen's work at its most incisive and imaginative, in which McQueen's aesthetic eye is in the service of what James Rondeau calls "a potent, [if] at times oblique, political unconscious."[21] In contrast, and despite McQueen's assertions of its contemporary political relevance, *12 Years a Slave* does not succeed as a vehicle for a radical politics.

We observed earlier the pressures that Gillo Pontecorvo faced when working within a Hollywood studio environment, and these pressures should not be underestimated in seeking to understand this discrepancy in McQueen's work. However, an additional explanation for this discrepancy can be identified by considering the attempt of *12 Years a Slave* to capture the universality of Northup's narrative without sufficient attention to its particularity. Of course, revisionist depictions of slavery in popular culture from D. W. Griffith's *The Birth of a Nation* to the present have tended to dramatically overemphasize slavery's particularity while also sustaining the potent fantasy that slavery was essentially benign and paternalistic. In this discourse, the so-called peculiar institution has long been mistakenly considered a relic of an outmoded society that bears little relation to our own. This perspective—which denies the centrality of slavery to capitalist modernity—has also proven an effective means of disavowing the slave experience as a potential source for an emancipatory politics. Translating Northup's narrative to the big screen and emphasizing its universal dimensions might have implicitly contested this pernicious mythology, but McQueen's adaptation instead manufactures a platitudinous universality based on sentiment rather than historical specificity. For example, the film's musical score—a repeated four-note theme written for cello and violin—has been described by Hans Zimmer, the composer, as a deliberately conceived strategy for communicating the "timelessness" of

Northup's story.[22] The unfortunate effect of this gesture to timelessness is the reduction of slavery in antebellum America to a simplified story of human greed, cruelty, and pathos.

The prolific character of the slave-narrative genre elaborates a further point of contrast between Northup's text and McQueen's adaptation. Solomon Northup's *Twelve Years a Slave* is one of 204 published North American slave narratives.[23] This genre, considered to have limited literary value until the institutionalization of Black Studies in American universities in the 1960s and 1970s, had been a key propaganda weapon in the hands of antislavery activists and abolitionists in the United States before the Civil War. The most well-known examples of the genre include Frederick Douglass's autobiographies (the first of which was a bestseller and is widely regarded as being the best-written example of the genre), Harriet Jacobs's *Incidents in the Life of a Slave Girl* (1861), and *The Interesting Narrative of the Life of Olaudah Equiano* (1789).[24] However, Solomon Northup's *Twelve Years a Slave*, also a bestseller, was an unusual example of the genre for several reasons. First, the arc of Northup's narrative is unique within the tradition of the antebellum slave narrative since the movement is initially from liberty to bondage. Second, as Sue Eakin and Joseph Lodgson note in the introduction to their 1968 edition, "no other slave has left such a detailed picture of life in the Gulf South."[25] In fact, Northup's narrative is our only firsthand account of slavery in the Deep South from the perspective of a former slave. Third, no other slave narrative contained such dramatic material, which was heralded by the full nineteenth-century title: *Twelve Years a Slave, Narrative of Solomon Northup, A Citizen of New York, Kidnapped in Washington City in 1841, and Rescued in 1853, From a Cotton Plantation Near the Red River in Louisiana*.[26] This was particularly important to McQueen, since he considered that Northup's experience of freedom in the North before his illegal enslavement made his narrative more accessible and his character more identifiable for a twenty-first-century audience.[27]

Solomon Northup's text, like many slave narratives, was written with the assistance of a white amanuensis, in this case a small-town northern lawyer, a minor author, and a former school superintendent by the name of David Wilson. Surprisingly, and unlike other collaborators in the writing of slave narratives, there is no evidence that Wilson was an abolitionist or that he "ever became a convert to antislavery ranks."[28] Significantly, Wilson's Preface reveals a further tension between Northup's original narrative and McQueen's 2013 adaptation. While McQueen has emphasized what he regards as the universality of Northup's story, stating that in his opinion *Twelve Years a Slave* is "a narrative about today. . . . It's a narrative about human respect, more than anything,"[29] in his editor's preface Wilson noted the narrative's local specificity: "It is believed that the following account of [Northup's] experience on Bayou Boeuf presents a correct picture of Slavery, in all its lights and shadows, as it now exists in that locality."[30] And on the very first page of his narrative, Northup emphasizes this, making clear the limitations of his purview: "I can speak of Slavery only so far as it came under my own observation—only so far as I have known and experienced it in my own person."[31]

The narrative begins with Northup's variation on the slave narrative's opening convention "I was born," instead announcing, "having been born a freeman." He then provides the reader with a brief outline of his family history in which he explains his status as a free Black in the North. Northup's ancestors on his paternal side, as far back as he could ascertain, "were slaves in Rhode Island" and belonged "to a family by the name of Northup."[32] Northup's father, Mintus Northup, was "emancipated by a direction in his [master's] will," and Solomon goes on to note that he received an education "surpassing that ordinarily bestowed on" children of his status. Significantly, Northup comments that even in the North, slavery was far from a benign institution and that although his father held "the warmest emotions of kindness, and even of affection towards the family in whose house he had been a bondsman," he nevertheless "comprehended the system of Slavery, and dwelt with sorrow on the degradation of his race."[33] This perspective on the condition of enslaved Blacks north of the Mason-Dixon line, as well as the view that slavery could not be ameliorated by the kindness of individuals, is not communicated in the film. Indeed, it is the first in a series of omissions that obscure slavery's systematicity, elevate Northup's status to high bourgeois, and undermine his accounts of resistance.

McQueen's version transforms Northup's linear memoir into a narrative structured by flashbacks, memories, and emotions—a change apparent from the outset. The film begins in media res with a white overseer issuing instructions to a sugar cane–cutting gang that includes the already-enslaved Northup. The camera is immersed in the foliage of green cane leaves before entering a clearing in which the cutting gang is at work. The toil of cane-cutting and the sound of machetes striking plant stalks merge with the singing of a work song. The camera then leads us back through the cane leaves before darkening and fading to a view from above a bedroom in which we can make out perhaps ten enslaved men and women turning in for the night. Next, in a brief scene of communal eating in silence, we see Northup come upon the idea of using blackberry juice, running on his supper plate, as pen ink, followed by him fashioning a rudimentary pen by candlelight and attempting to write. Although he is unsuccessful—the blackberry ink is too watery—the sequence pays an oblique tribute to Northup as an author and to the literary genre of the slave narrative. It conveys the determination of the enslaved and formerly enslaved to record their experiences and affirms their dignity and humanity.

This elegant opening sequence that powerfully bestows a somber decorum and dignity to slave life is then broken with an invented scene. Once again, the screen fades into darkness before the camera intrudes on perhaps a dozen enslaved men and women sleeping communally on the floor, followed by a brief sexual encounter between Northup and an enslaved female, whose name we never learn and who never reappears in the film. Although the encounter evokes feelings of betrayal and indignity—the enslaved woman turns away from Northup in tears while Northup recalls lying in his marital bed with his wife before his enslavement—McQueen has spoken of this scene as intended to demonstrate how enslaved people were owned yet could, in certain moments, take control of their own bodies.

In the 1853 text, Northup discusses meaningful romantic liaisons between enslaved people very differently. Following a description of how the enslaved community in the Bayou Boeuf region celebrated Christmas, "the only respite from constant labor the slave has through the whole year," Northup writes: "Cupid disdains not to hurl his arrows into the simple hearts of slaves."[34] He notes that Christmas presented an opportunity for slave couples to make a public show of "an exchange of tenderness" by sitting opposite each other during the "fun and merriment" of a rare social gathering that involved food, music, and dance long into the night.[35] Thus, while Northup discussed relationships among slaves with reticence and with an emphasis on their nourishing qualities, McQueen depicts enslaved sexual desire as eliciting shame and guilt. While neither of these dichotomous representations may in fact reflect the actual and more-complicated sexual lives of enslaved people, the distinct ideological thrust of each representation remains telling.

Another significant departure in McQueen's version is the representation of Northup and his family before his kidnapping. They are shown to be living a comfortable bourgeois life, complete with fine clothing and a

160 | From Havana to Hollywood

finely furnished house in a glamorized Saratoga Springs. Perhaps alluding to a flashback in which the Northups are out shopping and encounter impeccable manners and conduct (fig. 4.6), Doherty notes that McQueen's Saratoga in 1841 "might just as well be Cambridge, Massachusetts in 2013."[36] The danger of this resemblance is that McQueen's representation augments a familiar and insufficiently nuanced narrative of the antebellum United States in which the genteel North's mirror image is the barbarous and slaveholding South. Although Walter Johnson has noted that elements of Northup's narrative "may reflect [his] pride in his Northern origins and legal freedom," it certainly registers both a less-sanguine picture of the North and the family's humbler social status.[37]

Through descriptions of his occupations in the 1853 text, we learn that Northup scraped together a living by various means. These included laboring as a hired hand on canal construction, woodcutting, small-scale farming, and playing his violin at local dances. In 1834, Northup moved with his family to Saratoga Springs, New York, in pursuit of better prospects. These, however, failed to materialize, and he found himself laboring

Figure 4.6. The Northups shopping in a highly glamorized Saratoga Springs, *12 Years a Slave*. *Source:* Steve McQueen, dir., *12 Years a Slave* (2013), UK / USA. New Regency Productions / River Road / Plan B.

on the railroad before securing employment in the tourist season driving a hack; in the winter season he once more relied on his violin. By 1841, the year of his kidnapping, Northup writes of his disappointment: "The flattering anticipations which, seven years before, had seduced us from the quiet farmhouse, on the east side of the Hudson, had not been realized. Though always in comfortable circumstances, we had not prospered."[38] It is striking that the visual representation in McQueen's adaptation does not accord with Northup's description of his family's social situation. As a freeman in Saratoga Springs, McQueen's Northup looks like a well-to-do country gent in a fine three-piece suit, and when Northup is seduced by his kidnappers' promise of a good salary for playing his fiddle in their circus troupe, his eager acceptance appears guileless. The temptation of a decent wage—"one dollar for each day's services," plus three dollars for each evening's performance—is much more convincing in the original.[39] Moreover, McQueen's decision to portray the Northups in Saratoga Springs as possessing impeccable bourgeois tastes, and the inclusion of scenes in which the Northups are greeted with great deference and cordiality by white shopkeepers and strangers, dramatically embellishes the lives of free Blacks in the North, where freedom was legally and socially restricted and racism remained rife.[40] Thus, McQueen's representation of the North is one of the means by which the film obscures Northup's descriptions of slavery's systemic character. This is something that Northup recalls his father also understanding when he observes the inadequacy of seeking to explain the evil of slavery by leveling blame at individuals. Indeed, midway through his narrative, Northup writes that "it is not the fault of the slaveholder that he is cruel, so much as it is the fault of the system under which he lives."[41]

In addition, Northup's narrative is notable for its detailed descriptions of the processes of cotton and sugar cultivation and production as they were practiced under the system of slavery.[42] Critics have noted that these descriptions "are recognized classics" within the literature of slavery.[43] Although his perspective as an enslaved field hand did not enable him to perceive slavery's global dimensions, Northup's descriptions indicate an understanding of the role of slave labor in the production of valued market commodities and the stringency of consumers' requirements for such commodities. Hence, Northup describes the importance of precision when cutting cane—the need "to sever all the green from the ripe part"— to avoid souring the molasses that would render the product "unsalable." Furthermore, he describes processed "white or loaf sugar" as "clear, clean, and white as snow" when packed in hogsheads, "ready for market."⁴⁴ This emphasis on the production of a commodity for the market as a mode of explanation for plantation slavery is absent in the McQueen version, which instead conceives of slavery as either paternalistic or barbarous based merely on the contrasting personalities of individual slave owners. For example, in McQueen's version, Northup's first master, the aristocratically mannered William Ford, is recognizably the man Northup described as being "kind, noble, candid, [and] Christian." However, Northup described not just the individual but also the impact of his circumstances on his perspective: "The influences and associations that had always surrounded him, blinded him to the inherent wrong at the bottom of the system of Slavery."⁴⁵ Thus, Northup makes explicit that the institution of slavery could not be comprehended at the level of the individual.

Later in the narrative, reflecting on his period of enslavement under Epps—a violent, psychotic, and lusty slave owner who anticipates William Faulkner's Sutpen in *Absalom, Absalom!* (1936)⁴⁶—Northup expands on his analysis of the relationship between the individual and society as a mode of historical explanation. He writes: "There may be humane masters, as there certainly are inhumane ones—there may be slaves well-clothed, well-fed, and happy, as there surely are those half-clad, half-starved and miserable; nevertheless, the institution that tolerates such wrong and inhumanity as I have witnessed, is a cruel, unjust, and barbarous one."⁴⁷ C. L. R. James's evaluation some eighty years later, in his history of the Haitian Revolution, *The Black Jacobins*, offers a compelling comparison: "There were good and bad Governors, good and bad Intendants, as there were good and bad slave-owners. But this was a matter of pure chance. It was the system that was bad."⁴⁸ Such analysis is lost in McQueen's adaptation. The impact of the excellent performances of Benedict Cumberbatch and, especially, Michael Fassbender, who play the contrasting slave owners—the saintly Ford and the monstrous Epps—compounds this problem. While McQueen has insisted that "Epps is a human being" and that "as much as we want to think of him as a monster [or] as a devil, he's not," it is hard to witness Fassbender's virtuoso performance of Epps as psychotic and borderline deranged, ravaged with drink and lust, and not be persuaded otherwise.⁴⁹ The dichotomous presentation of saintly or monstrous individual slave owners was of course present in Northup's original, but it was tempered by an emphasis that in slave society, where everything was infected and debased, the psychological analysis of individuals had limited explanatory power.

More extraordinary still than the omission of Northup's perspective on slavery as a system, however, is that his accounts of slave resistance are either eliminated or distorted in the McQueen version. In his narrative, Northup asserted that the temptation of flight and rebellion among enslaved populations was ever present. For example, Northup described the plans he claimed to have made with two of his fellow captives, Arthur (also a kidnapped freeman) and Robert, to attempt a mutiny on the Orleans, a paddle steamer that was transporting them to the New Orleans slave market. Northup describes how their planned attempt to take possession of the brig and sail the vessel to New York was meticulously thought through over a period of days and how various components of the plan were carefully tested for feasibility (such as how they might reach the deck from the hold in the dead of night). Ultimately, we learn that Northup and his fellow conspirators never had an opportunity to put their plans into action—the designs were derailed by Robert's death from smallpox four days before they were to arrive in New Orleans. Although Northup's account of these plans also reveals his disdain for what he perceives as the limited revolutionary capacity of many of his fellow enslaved men and women, the way in which the episode has been transposed into the McQueen version supplants resistance with abject hopelessness. All the careful planning is absent, and Northup's unwillingness to trust his fellow slaves, whom he considers servile, is distorted in the speech of Arthur, who in the film is renamed "Clemens Ray": "Three can't stand against the whole crew. The rest here are niggers, born and bred slaves. Niggers ain't got no stomach for a fight, not a damn one." As Marc Norton observes, these lines signal the end of the planned insurgency in the McQueen version. Furthermore, Robert does not die from smallpox. Instead, he is slain by a white sailor in the dead of night for attempting to prevent the rape of Eliza, an enslaved woman who had been sold downriver to William Ford by her former enslaver's heirs. The insertion of Robert's murder is troubling for several reasons. First, as Stephanie Li notes, "the scene is historically suspect. The sailor does not own the slave [whom he murders] and [he] would certainly be punished for the loss of such a valuable commodity." Moreover, Li explains, "McQueen's version of Robert's death" serves "to contextualize the passivity that defines much of Northup's response to the horrors he witnesses throughout the film."[50] While in his narrative Northup was never naïvely optimistic about the prospect of successful resistance, in McQueen's version Northup's powerlessness is profoundly exacerbated.

McQueen's exposition of passivity, impotence, and relentless suffering endured by enslaved Blacks thus fails to capture the nuances of Northup's original narrative. For example, entirely absent from the film are the ideas Northup narrates in the final section of chapter seventeen, which is titled "The Idea of Insurrection." Here, Northup tells the history of an attempted slave uprising in the Bayou Boeuf region led by the slave Lew Cheney, with whom Northup had become personally acquainted. Northup explains that Cheney traveled from plantation to plantation preaching the idea of "fighting a crusade" all the way to the free land of Mexico, but that, at the last moment, the would-be slave rebels were discovered, and Cheney, "in order to curry favor with his master . . . determined to sacrifice all his companions."[51] However, notwithstanding Cheney's treachery and the ultimate failure of the rebels' plan (as well as the brutal response from the plantocracy), Northup writes eloquently of the ever-present and empowering allure of contemplating violent resistance to enslavement:

> Such an idea as insurrection, however, is not new among the enslaved population of Bayou Boeuf. . . . They are deceived who flatter themselves that the ignorant and debased slave has no conception of the magnitude of his wrongs. They are deceived who imagine that he arises from his knees, with his back lacerated and bleeding, cherishing only a spirit of meekness and forgiveness. A day may come—it will come, if his prayer is heard—a terrible day of vengeance, when the master in his turn will cry in vain for mercy.[52]

It is instructive to note that a version of Northup's narrative, stripped of its accounts of Black agency and rebellion, has become a successful and critically applauded feature film, while films that would represent Black resistance prominently, such as Danny Glover's long-planned biopic of Toussaint Louverture, remain in limbo, unable to secure sufficient funding for a "lack of white heroes."[53] This constitutes further evidence that, as was argued in the introduction, the most radical event of the Atlantic World's age of revolutions still presents a narrative deemed too dangerous for the mainstream, while even projects focused on "lesser" Black slave rebellions and resistance have remained almost entirely beyond the pale for Hollywood.

Ethics and Aesthetics

Having considered McQueen's adaptation alongside Northup's original narrative, I now turn to the impact of McQueen's filmic language on the ideological thrust of *12 Years a Slave*. Melissa Anderson poses the following question to highlight what she sees as the central dilemma of McQueen's adaptation: Is it "even conceivable to graphically represent the unimaginable without further cheapening the lives one sets out to honor or diminishing the horrors of a monstrous epoch?"[54] Anderson's question suggests that the ethical-aesthetic tightrope that must be walked in any artistic recuperation of historical trauma is especially treacherous when it comes to visual representations, which lend themselves to voyeurism more readily than do other cultural forms.

The danger of visual aestheticism diminishing historical trauma is especially real for a director such as McQueen, whose work, his critics have suggested, tends to give "primacy to the fastidiously composed image over human emotion."[55] While the mere act of filmic aesthetic construction inevitably prettifies reality, McQueen's eye for stunning visual harmonies and his cinematographic skill ensure that *12 Years a Slave* is, despite its horrors, a visually striking film. This prompts a question that dovetails with Nick Nesbitt's work on the Haitian writer Edwidge Danticat: How does one "turn the partial guilt of artistic representation" back on the total guilt of slavery?[56] In an attempt to address this problem, I consider the effect of McQueen's technique—manifest most prominently in exquisite representations of the natural world and his penchant for nonnarrative filmic grammar—on the treatment of violence and torture.

The tension in McQueen's *12 Years a Slave* between representing the horrors of slavery and displaying the splendor of the natural world of the South has drawn considerable comment.[57] McQueen's longtime cinematographer and collaborator Sean Bobbitt has stated that it was an intended goal to "embrace and use for a number of different effects" the "inherent natural beauty" of Louisiana.[58] In several interviews, McQueen has attempted to defend this approach as a mode of artistic truthfulness. For McQueen, the coexistence of beauty and horror is to be explained as part of "the perversity of the world," and he suggests that his filmic representation of this depravity belongs to an artistic tradition stretching back to Goya:

> In terms of art, it goes back to Goya, the Spanish painter who was creating some of the most horrific images of torture and devastation and war—and yet they're beautiful paintings. . . . Reality is perverse. . . . That's the haunting thing—and the difficult thing. It's like when a child asks you, "Why is the world so unfair?" The only answer is that it just is. The world is

unfair. That's reality. So rather than fighting against the reality, you embrace it—which in turn makes it even more horrific.[59]

Whether McQueen's embrace of Louisiana's magnificent scenery succeeds in exacerbating the horror of Northup's narrative is arguable, but beyond dispute is the visual beauty of McQueen's *12 Years a Slave*. McQueen's resplendent and sumptuous cinematic chiaroscuro depicts the natural world of Louisiana in all its splendor (fig. 4.7). The beauty of its flora and its numerous waterways—lagoons, bayous, and inlets—is exquisitely enhanced by a kaleidoscopic array of subtle variations of light and shade; dappled sunlight plays on majestic live oaks and cypress trees adorned with creepers and Spanish moss; and even the cane and cotton fields, sites of intense suffering, are evoked as intensely beautiful. Such stunning filmic artwork confirms McQueen's standing as a visual artist of extraordinary talents.

Yet these sensual visuals of the Gulf South undercut the representation of daily miseries endured under slavery, existing uneasily with Northup's descriptions in the 1853 text of the natural world around him as a source of terror and a barrier to escape: "The nature of the country is such as renders it impossible to pass through it with any safety."[60] While Northup narrates in considerable detail the dangers posed by a wilderness teeming with wild animals, snakes, and alligators, McQueen's version evokes an intensely hospitable natural environment. It thus becomes necessary to ask whether McQueen and Bobbitt's gorgeous cinematography reproduces the

Figure 4.7. Sunlight and flora on the bayou, *12 Years a Slave*. *Source:* Steve McQueen, dir., *12 Years a Slave* (2013), UK / USA. New Regency Productions / River Road / Plan B.

colonial gaze of the tropics as paradisiacal. This question assumes even greater analytic and probative value when we recall that this colonial gaze was also paradoxically charged with apprehensions of unseen evil and forbidden sensuality. McQueen is hardly alone among filmmakers who have been visually seduced by the aesthetics of the plantation's southern setting—and even of the plantation itself. Indeed, it is a characteristic trait of "plantation movies"—from D. W. Griffith's *The Birth of a Nation* of 1915 to Victor Fleming's *Gone with the Wind* of 1939 to Quentin Tarantino's *Django Unchained* of 2012—that what the camera perceives as beautiful was a source of terror and despair for enslaved populations.[61] In this respect, then, the visual aestheticism of McQueen's *12 Years a Slave* allows us to position the film firmly within the lineage of the mythmaking plantation genre.

An additional effect of the film's aesthetic is that, far from intensifying perceptions of slavery's extremities, the ordinary brutality of slavery is lost. In fact, still shots that afford pleasure are deployed immediately following scenes of distressing suffering, as if to comfort the audience. While McQueen does depict harrowing scenes of brutal violence and torture, the daily miseries and hardships of slavery—evoked very clearly in the 1853 text—are diminished. While McQueen's version shows some scenes of enslaved work, they fail to register the impact of hard labor on enslaved bodies. This is especially ironic given his emphasis on the body as a site of suffering elsewhere in the film and throughout his other works. For example, in *Western Deep* McQueen takes us into the darkness and claustrophobia of the lift and mine shafts, showing us the hot, dusty, and dangerous conditions of labor and the faces and bodies of the miners. Thomas McEvilley notes that the message of *Western Deep* is unequivocally that "labor in a capitalist society is a hell of exploitation and humiliation."[62] This is especially apparent in an extended sequence in which we observe Black miners carrying out mandatory, supervised physical exercises in unison, stepping up and down as buzzers sound and red lights flash above their heads, before having their body temperatures monitored. This sequence evokes chain-gang and plantation labor, as well as the institutional repression of prison regimes, but it also emphasizes the strength and stoicism of the miners by depicting their capacity to survive in an extreme environment. There are no comparable sequences in *12 Years a Slave*. Instead, attention to the conditions of slave labor is supplanted by prolonged and graphic torture scenes: Patsey's whipping (the most horrific episode of torture) and Northup's near death by lynching are drawn out for over four minutes each. The film thus gives primacy to the traditional focus on slavery as punishment, physical torture, and sexual exploitation. "Slow," or structural, violence is usurped by spectacular, or superstructural, violence.[63] The problems with this approach are manifold but are encapsulated in the words of Joanne Laurier: "Slavery was not simply the sum total of beatings and whippings—as real as they were and as much as they were an integral part of the institution."[64] McQueen's representation thus misconceives slavery as an aberration rather than identifies it as a system of capitalist labor fundamental to the making of the modern world and the modern self.[65]

Moreover, slave labor is usurped by McQueen's fondness for what Dana Stevens has described as "contemplative insert shots," which often focus on a detail from nature, such as "cypress trees reflected in peach-colored bayous at sunset, [or] caterpillars crawling over cotton bolls."[66] Moreover, such insert shots are also on occasion sexualized, as in the example of the caterpillar and cotton plant that can be read as a metaphorical representation of female genitalia in the manner of Georgia O'Keefe's flower paintings (fig. 4.8). Such visually commanding shots stand at the threshold of narrative and nonnarrative cinema; yet, while McQueen shows us close-ups of cotton plants, he refrains from focusing on what cotton-picking does to the pickers' hands. McQueen misses an opportunity here to inform his audience of one aspect of the mundane suffering of cotton pickers. Instead, when representing slave suffering, McQueen stages highly theatrical and harrowing incidents of torture.

Figure 4.8. Caterpillar and cotton plant, *12 Years a Slave*. *Source:* Steve McQueen, dir., *12 Years a Slave* (2013), UK / USA. New Regency Productions / River Road / Plan B.

Northup's Lynching and Patsey's Whipping

The scene in which Northup is lynched by Tibeats and two of his companions is one of the film's most harrowing. The representation of the lynched or hanged slave—suspended either from ropes, hooks, or chains—is, as the work of Marcus Wood reminds us, one of the most iconic and notorious cultural symbols of the atrocity of slavery.[67] The lynching scene in *12 Years a Slave* seeks to evoke this cultural history by using a long take—an uninterrupted shot that disrupts the film's narrative rhythm—during which the camera remains unwaveringly focused on Northup's torture. In interviews subsequent to the making of the film, McQueen stated that there was a twofold purpose in lingering on Northup's lynching: first, McQueen explained that he wanted to force the audience to watch long after they wanted to turn away; and second, McQueen spoke of his wish to commemorate not only the untold numbers of slaves murdered by lynching but also the many thousands of post-slavery Jim Crow lynchings.[68] Thus, the visual medium of film breaks the temporal bounds of Northup's original memoir.

Although McQueen's representation of Northup's lynching is disturbing, it fails to communicate that Northup's prolonged torment is to be explained by the white legal property codes of antebellum Louisiana. It is the chattel mortgage that Ford has taken out on Northup that ensures his agony must last until his owner returns to cut him down. In the absence of historical analysis, this enactment of depravity becomes merely a horror show that, as Laurier observes, inflicts suffering on the audience while failing "to arrive at its truth."[69] Thus, contrary to the view of some of the film's more enthusiastic critics, McQueen's strategy cannot accurately be dubbed "didactic."[70] Moreover, his strategy of dramatically emphasizing the horror of the torture and sexual abuse of enslaved bodies might be considered especially fraught in the twenty-first century. This is because audiences have become so accustomed to cinematic, televisual, and internet images of grotesque violence that shock tactics may no longer be effective. While it was essential in 1853, to further the abolitionist cause, for Northup to narrate the facts of the sexual abuse he had witnessed and the viciousness to which he was victim in visceral detail, transposing these elements to the big screen in the twenty-first century runs the risk of unwittingly pornographizing historic sexual atrocity and violence. Consider, for example, the film's emotional crescendo, a scene in which Patsey endures a sadistic whipping that Joanne Laurier considers "an interminable, lurid sequence" and that Melvyn Stokes notes "is prolonged to the point that it seems inspired by McQueen's previous film about sexual fantasies, *Shame*."[71]

While this critique illuminates the problematic question of how one depicts the true nature of plantation violence without driving one's audience away, it also constitutes another example of how McQueen attributes suffering under slavery to the evil of individual "mad masters" rather than systemic issues. In this schema, Epps becomes an exemplar of utter evil, as shown by his savage torture of Patsey. Patsey's torment is compounded further by the fact that Epps's infatuation with her disgusts his wife, who is then driven by extreme sexual jealousy to abuse Patsey herself. Yet this representation is also problematic since, as Jasmine Nichole Cobb has argued, it encourages the audience to "observe Mistress Epps . . . as sadistic and jealous" without appreciation for her entrapment within a domestic sphere dictated by nineteenth-century gender politics.[72] Further, the critic Melvyn Stokes has noted that this distorts Northup's original account: "while conceding Mistress Epps was of a jealous disposition, [Northup] also observed that 'there was much in her character to admire.'"[73] Similarly, Cobb notes, McQueen's representation of Tibeats, "the 'poor white trash' overseer," emphasizes his status as an ignorant, racist scoundrel but does not offer the audience "a broad enough view of slavery as a system to understand labor competition as a counterpart to the racism we see in his character."[74] We cannot overlook that Tibeats forms a sharp contrast with Northup's first master, William Ford, who is the epitome of the "gentlemanly master" in McQueen's version. With this portrayal, McQueen appears to have inadvertently given new credence to the archetype of the honorable, aristocratic Southern gentleman. It should also be noted that Ford's demeanor contrasts starkly with that of Tibeats and Epps, whose viciousness correlates to their class positions, one a poor white and the other an upstart member of the planter elite. The problems caused by McQueen's demonic Epps, played by Michael Fassbender, were noted by Michael Wood in the *London Review of Books*. Wood writes:

> Fassbender is terrific in this role, but the result is similar to Hannibal Lecter's running away with *The Silence of the Lambs*. . . . The larger question of slavery is already edged away by the theme of the time-bound enslavement of a free man [and] even the question of Northup's rights is usurped by the new/old show of the exotic evil of the mad master. So that was the problem: a few crazy sadists like Epps. Remove

the bad apples, and the crop will be as good as it ever was. This is not where the film has any intention of going, but it is where it gets.⁷⁵

Similarly, in *Cinema Scope*, Julian Carrington argued that "by characterizing Northup's oppressors as semi-demonic sadists, McQueen and [screenwriter John] Ridley invite viewers to overlook the reality of American slavery as a system of economic exploitation that was practiced not by some intrinsically malevolent historical 'other,' but by individuals not fundamentally dissimilar to themselves, and which remains evident in contemporary systemic disparities of power and privilege."⁷⁶ Thus, *12 Years a Slave* fails to contextualize the agency and suffering of its dramatis personae and reduces the institution of slavery to little more than the backdrop to a sensational and gory costume melodrama.

An Adaptation Mishandled

While McQueen's adaptation of Northup's narrative is polished and cinematographically accomplished, it fails to capture the fundamental fact that, as Greg Grandin has put it, "slavery created the modern world, and the modern world's divisions (both abstract and concrete) are the product of slavery."⁷⁷ Instead, McQueen's *12 Years a Slave* elects to explain away the horrors of slavery by focusing on individual "evil doers." However, Northup's original memoir conspicuously denies the accuracy of this explanatory mode. Furthermore, the aestheticized filmic language of *12 Years a Slave* diminishes the attempted representation of the human devastation wrought by slavery. Additionally, whereas the abstract and fractured aesthetics of three of McQueen's art films and video-installation works—namely, *Caribs' Leap*, *Western Deep*, and *Gravesend*—conjure race as a vector of oppression under capitalism across space and time, *12 Years a Slave* forecloses any such analysis. Moreover, our earlier analysis of Gillo Pontecorvo's *Burn!* as a successful fusion of "First," "Second," and "Third" cinematic practices refutes any suggestion that McQueen's art-house techniques could not have been adapted to the Hollywood feature film. But since more than forty years separate *Burn!* and *12 Years a Slave*, it is worth considering two other popular examples focused on the subject of the Black diaspora that demonstrate that a focus on individuals need not result in the occlusion of systemic explanation.

David Simon and Eric Overmyer's HBO series *Tremé* (2010–2013) and Lars von Trier's *Manderlay* (2005) are examples of successful televisual and cinematic forms that have succeeded at the level of systemic explanation.[78] While the production and circulation histories of these two examples differ from McQueen's *12 Years a Slave*, they are nevertheless roughly contemporaneous with McQueen's adaption and serve as useful comparators. In *Tremé*, which tracks the lives of several individuals living through the aftermath of Hurricane Katrina in New Orleans, the creative use of "lens language" locates individual narratives within a larger, systemic tragedy. For example, Stephen Shapiro reads the moment in which one of the central characters, the downtrodden La Donna, finally tracks down her brother's body in a makeshift mobile morgue comprised of refrigerated white trucks. The camera rotates around La Donna clockwise before spinning counterclockwise, as the viewer and La Donna both take in the dizzying number of trucks, all of which contain other victims of Katrina's longue dureé. Shapiro notes that the uniformly white trucks recall New Orleans's levees but also the slave ship. Via such simple but effective lens language, the viewer is reminded not to lose sight of the systemic tragedy while focusing on the story of an individual.[79]

A sensitivity to transhistorical, underlying systemic connections can also be found in Lars von Trier's *Manderlay*. Trier emphasizes that the abolition of slavery in the United States did not usher in a new age of racial equality and happiness by setting the story in an Alabama community that was ignorant of the fact that slavery had been abolished. Although repugnant in many ways—the film is both misogynistic and deeply problematic in its portrayal of Blacks as complicit in their own enslavement—*Manderlay* refuses to overlook the horrors of continuing and systemic Black immiseration. As the end credits roll, we see a montage of American racial atrocities and ironies from the nineteenth to the twenty-first centuries, including iconic images of the Ku Klux Klan, anti-desegregation protests, police brutality, African Americans serving in Vietnam and Iraq, and the Black Power movement. The radicalism of this approach—which juxtaposes disparate images of oppression, violence, and resistance, thereby suggesting a deep causal explanation—is arguably more faithful to the spirit of Northup's narrative than is McQueen's adaptation.

Moreover, we have observed that McQueen's own work includes powerful examples of the explanatory potential of the technique of juxtaposition. In *Gravesend*, McQueen uses the technique to vividly convey the dependence of advanced technological society on resource extraction in the deprived peripheral location of the Congo. The dynamic of this relation is also recalled by the title, the point of departure in Joseph Conrad's *Heart of Darkness*. Such techniques could also have been deployed in *12 Years a Slave*. McQueen could have interspersed, among the many beautiful shots of Southern landscapes, images of cotton mills in Lancashire, of middlemen in the northern United States profiting from slavery, or of the cotton trading markets in London. Notably, Gillo Pontecorvo, Tomás Gutiérrez Alea, and Sergio Giral, whose slavery films were discussed earlier in this study, adopted such strategies. For example, in *Burn!* the existence of a colonial global network of capitalist exploitation is evoked throughout the film, including in a scene in which traders at the London Stock Exchange react with excitement to the rising share prices of the world's leading sugar companies. Pontecorvo's representational strategy ensures that slavery is not portrayed as an evil hermetically sealed on the plantations of the Americas. Like the montage in *Manderlay*, it also makes clear that the abolition of slavery did not herald a new chapter of civilized humanity. On the contrary, as recent scholarship has made clear, the end of cotton slavery in the southern United States, for example, was the catalyst for the massive expansion of cotton production in India, Egypt, and Brazil—and concomitant new forms of labor exploitation in those territories.[80]

Coming hot on the heels of a series of Hollywood feature films about Black diasporic experience—for example, *The Help* (2011), *Django Unchained* (2012), *Belle* (2013), *The Butler* (2013), and *Selma* (2014)—the success of *12 Years a Slave* prompts us to wonder whether having long overlooked slavery and its legacies, Hollywood is now cashing in on Black history and engaged in the manufacture of new fantasies and denials about slavery, Black lives, and Black suffering.[81] Although *12 Years a Slave* is powerful and assured filmmaking that retains the emotional and personal drama of Northup's memoir, it also lacks the dynamics of historical change and drains Northup's narrative of its accounts of slave resistance, its politics, and its specificity. This is regrettable since the film looks set to become a cultural touchstone about slavery for many years to come.

Conclusion

Despite a deep and recurring interest in slavery and the struggle for abolition, in North America and Europe there has been an equally strong reluctance to depict Black resistance in ways that acknowledge the agency of enslaved men and women. Acts of slave resistance went unacknowledged, disparaged, and denigrated within slave societies. The overwhelming absence of Black resistance within the treatment of slavery in American cinema testifies to the fact that slave self-liberation remains a troubling and uncomfortable subject for the silver screen. However, *From Havana to Hollywood: Slave Resistance in the Cinematic Imaginary* has argued that Gillo Pontecorvo's *Burn!*, Tomás Gutiérrez Alea's *La última cena*, and Sergio Giral's trilogy of *"negrometrajes"* constitute bold challenges to this pattern of silencing and disavowing Black resistance to slavery. These five neglected feature films imagine and re-create the past to fuel visions of a liberated future, and their narratives are driven by diverse forms of Black agency. Contrastingly, I have also argued that, despite its aspirations to challenge the manner of slavery's traditional treatment in Hollywood, the effacement of Black resistance in Steve McQueen's *12 Years a Slave* is an indication that the representation of Black agency in Hollywood remains taboo. Indeed, I have argued that *12 Years a Slave* merits reexamination to see the flaws in its assumptions as well as the flaws in its representation of who has agency and to what effect.

The virtues of Pontecorvo's, Gutiérrez Alea's, and Giral's slavery films are manifold. They celebrate Black power, they draw attention to slavery's function within the history of global capitalism and imperialism, they show how film art can break the bounds of nationalism to understand resistance to slavery on transnational terms, and they insist upon revolutionary politics as a necessary path for the realization of progressive social transformation. Their mode of representing slavery has a strikingly Marcusean thrust: boldly envisioning radical futures, they imagine possibilities for the achievement of social justice, assert that "the horizon of history is still open," and project a conviction that "if the remembrance of things past would become a motive power in the struggle for changing the world, the struggle would be waged for a revolution hitherto suppressed in the previous historical revolutions."[1] Moreover, their stylistic achievements and innovations are remarkable and stand as testimony to the aesthetic and communicative power of cinema. However, regrettably, the ideological thrust of Pontecorvo's, Gutiérrez Alea's, and Giral's slavery films has not been absorbed into the mainstreams of public knowledge and consciousness in North America and Europe. Consequently, recuperating these films such that they will enjoy a greater degree of critical visibility and attention has been the major element of this project's raison d'être. Therefore, Edward Said's notion of *worldliness* has been employed as a generative and animating principle in the pursuit of this goal. Linking the works of Pontecorvo, Gutiérrez Alea, and Giral to Steve McQueen's *12 Years a Slave* has also served to demonstrate the ideological gulf that separates slavery films produced in the traditions of Third Cinema from those produced in Hollywood.

In 1938, in the preface to the first edition of *The Black Jacobins*, C. L. R. James wrote these scintillating words: "Tranquility today is either innate (the philistine) or to be acquired only by a deliberate doping of the personality."[2] While the 2020s can and should be distinguished from the 1930s, I believe that James's words remain instructive and that the global crises of our contemporary moment are no less existential than were those of the 1930s. In the face of the seemingly overwhelming challenges we face today, this book has argued that a selected corpus of slavery films offers perspectives that might yet help us to theorize and envision alternative modes of being in the world. Pontecorvo's, Gutiérrez Alea's, and Giral's slavery films give us reason to believe that with collective action, resistance, and human agency, alternatives that might seem impossible are in fact realizable. The extraordinary and ceaseless effort of countless men and women throughout the history of Atlantic slavery to resist their enslavement is evidence that another world was perceived to be not only possible but an urgent, moral-political imperative. In a reprehensible world, the legacy of Black resistance to slavery is a gift to all humankind.

Notes

Introduction

1. Langston Hughes, "Moscow and Me," [July 1933], *The Collected Works of Langston Hughes: Vol. 9: Essays on Art, Race, Politics, and World Affairs*, ed. Christopher C. De Santis (Columbia: University of Missouri Press, 2002), 59.

2. For an overview of this troubled history see, Donald Bogle, *Toms, Coons, Mulattoes, Mammies, and Bucks* [1973], 5th ed. (updated and expanded) (New York: Bloomsbury, 2016); Brenda Stevenson, "Filming Black Voices and Stories: Slavery on Americas Screens," *Journal of the Civil War Era* 8, no. 3 (2018), 488–520; and Melvyn Stokes, "From Uncle Tom to Nat Turner: An Overview of Slavery in American Film, 1903–2016," *Transatlantica*, no. 1 (2018): https://doi.org/10.4000/transatlantica.12814.

3. Raymond Williams, "Base and Superstructure in Marxist Cultural Theory," *New Left Review*, no. 82 (1973): 8–10.

4. Stanley Kubrik, dir., *Spartacus* (Bryna Productions, 1960); Howard Fast, *Spartacus* (1951; repr., London: Routledge, 1996). For analysis of Kubrik's *Spartacus*, see Natalie Zemon Davies, *Slaves on Screen: Films and Historical Vision* (Cambridge, MA: Harvard University Press, 2000), 17–40.

5. W. E. B. Du Bois, *The Suppression of the African Slave Trade to the United States of America* (1896; repr., New York: Oxford University Press, 2014); C. L. R. James, *The Black Jacobins*, 2nd ed. rev. (1938, 1963; repr., New York: Vintage, 1989); C. L. R. James, *A History of Negro Revolt* (London: Fact,1938); Eugene Genovese, *Roll, Jordan, Roll: The World the Slaves Made* (1974; repr., New York: Vintage, 2008). Also see Herbert Aptheker's landmark *American Negro Slave Revolts* (New York: Columbia University Press, 1943) and the preceding journal article: Herbert Aptheker, "American Negro Slave Revolts," *Science & Society* 1, no. 4 (1937): 512–38. The sheer quantity of scholarship on slave resistance in the Atlantic World has grown enormously in recent years. For a bibliography, see Amy Marie Johnson, "Slave Resistance in the Atlantic World," *Oxford Bibliographies*, January 15, 2019, https://doi.org/10.1093/OBO/9780199730414-0310.

6. James Walvin, introduction to C. L. R. James, *The Black Jacobins*, 2nd ed. rev. [1938, 1963, foreword added 1980] (London: Penguin, 2001), vii.

7. On "silencing" and "disavowal," see Michel-Rolph Trouillot, *Silencing the Past: Power and the Production of History* (Boston: Beacon Press, 1995); and Sibylle Fischer, *Modernity Disavowed: Haiti and the Cultures of Slavery in the Age of Revolution* (Durham, NC: Duke University Press, 2004).

8. Charles Forsdick, "Interpreting 2004: Politics, Memory, Scholarship," *Small Axe*, no. 27 (October 2008): 6. For further analysis of *Amazing Grace* that identifies the film's effacement of Black agency, see Peter Linebaugh, "Amazing Disgrace," *Counterpunch*, February 28, 2007, http://www.counterpunch.org/2007/02/28/an-amazing-disgrace/; and Marcus Wood, *The Horrible Gift of Freedom: Atlantic Slavery and the Representation of Emancipation* (Athens: University of Georgia Press, 2010), 344–53. Both Linebaugh and Wood dub the film an "*Amazing Disgrace.*"

9. Kenneth Mohammed, "Sorrow and Regret Are Not Enough. Britain Must Finally Pay Reparations for Slavery," *Guardian*, March 29, 2022, https://www.theguardian.com/global-development/2022/mar/29/sorrow-and-regret-are-not-enough-britain-must-finally-pay-reparations-for-slavery; Report of the United Nations High Commissioner for Human Rights [Michelle Bachelet], "Racism, Racial Discrimination, Xenophobia and Related Forms of Intolerance, Follow-Up to and Implementation of the Durban Declaration and Programme of Action," A/HRC/47/53, June 21–July 9, 2021, 20, https://www.ohchr.org/en/documents/reports/ahrc4753-promotion-and-protection-human-rights-and-fundamental-freedoms-africans.

10. Massimiliano Tomba, *Insurgent Universality: An Alternative Legacy of Modernity* (New York: Oxford University Press, 2019).

11. Danny Peary, "*Burn!*" *Criterion Collection*, December 10, 1991, https://www.criterion.com/current/posts/947-burn.

12. Julianne Burton, "Part I: Revolutionary Cuban cinema," *Jump Cut*, no. 19 (December 1978): 17–20, https://www.ejumpcut.org/archive/onlinessays/JC19folder/CubanFilmIntro.html.

13. Edward W. Said, "Politics of Knowledge," *Raritan: A Quarterly Review* 11, no. 1 (1991); repr., Edward W. Said, *Reflections on Exile and Other Literary and Cultural Essays* (London: Granta, 2000), 382.

14. Neil Lazarus, *The Postcolonial Unconscious* (Cambridge: Cambridge University Press, 2011), 183.

15. Edward W. Said, *The World, the Text, and the Critic* (Cambridge, MA: Harvard University Press, 1983), 151–52.

16. Said, *The World*, 234.

17. Edward W. Said, *Culture and Imperialism* (New York: Alfred A. Knopf, 1993), 13.

18. Said, *Culture and Imperialism*, 96.

19. Said, *Culture and Imperialism*, 320.

20. Said, *Culture and Imperialism*, 319, 298.
21. Said, "Politics of Knowledge," 372–85.
22. Timothy Brennan, *Places of Mind: A Life of Edward Said* (New York: Farrar, Straus, and Giroux, 2021), 299.
23. Said, "Politics of Knowledge," 379.
24. Said, "Politics of Knowledge," 374.
25. Said, "Politics of Knowledge," 373–74, 385.
26. Brennan, *Places of Mind*, 299.
27. Said, "Politics of Knowledge," 381.
28. Said, "Politics of Knowledge," 381.
29. Said, "Politics of Knowledge," 375, 379.
30. Said, "Politics of Knowledge," 382; italics in original.
31. The classic manifesto for a project of "Third Cinema" is: Fernando Solanas and Octavio Getino, "Towards a Third Cinema: Notes and Experiences for the Development of a Cinema of Liberation in the Third World" (1969). First published in Spanish as "Hacia un tercer cine," in *Tricontinental* (Cuba), no. 13 (1969); repr. in Michael Chanan, ed., *Twenty-Five Years of the New Latin American Cinema* (London: BFI, 1983), 17–27.
32. Lazarus, *The Postcolonial Unconscious*, 9.
33. For an account of the transition from embedded liberalism to disembedded neoliberalism, see David Harvey, *A Brief History of Neoliberalism* (Oxford: Oxford University Press, 2005).
34. David Scott, *Conscripts of Modernity: The Tragedy of Colonial Enlightenment* (Durham, NC: Duke University Press, 2004), 29.
35. The subsumption or supplanting of "Third Cinema" by "World Cinema" is evident not only from the marketization of World Cinema but also from any number of film studies readers which pay scant regard to Third Cinema but allocate considerable space to the discussion of World Cinema. See, for an example, John Hill and Pamela Church Gibson, eds., *The Oxford Guide to Film Studies* (Oxford: Oxford University Press, 1998).
36. Fredric Jameson, *The Geopolitical Aesthetic: Cinema and Space in the World-System* (Bloomington: Indiana University Press, 1992; repr., 1995), 186–87.
37. Jameson, *The Geopolitical Aesthetic*, 188.
38. This aspect of my argument is indebted to Marshall Berman's magisterial theorization of modernity. Marshall Berman, *All That Is Solid Melts Into Air: The Experience of Modernity* (1982; repr., New York: Penguin, 1988), esp. 34–36.
39. Bertolt Brecht, qtd. in: Jameson, *The Geopolitical Aesthetic*, 213.
40. Bogle, *Toms, Coons, Mulattoes*, xxiv.
41. Natalie Zemon Davis, *Slaves on Screen: Film and Historical Vision* (Cambridge, MA: Harvard University Press, 2000); Alyssa Goldstein Sepinwall, *Slave Revolt on Screen: The Haitian Revolution in Film and Video Games* (Jackson: University Press of Mississippi, 2021).

180 | Notes to Introduction

42. Davis, *Slaves on Screen*, 4, 5.
43. Sepinwall, *Slave Revolt on Screen*, 11.
44. Sepinwall, *Slave Revolt on Screen*, 30.
45. "*El Siglo* and *The Last Supper* thus show how Cuban filmmakers have invoked Haiti's revolution to comment on their country's history, even while downplaying the agency of enslaved people." Sepinwall, *Slave Revolt on Screen*, 48. For an English translation of *El siglo de las luces*, see Alejo Carpentier, *Explosion in a Cathedral*, trans. John Sturrock (Minneapolis: University of Minnesota Press, 2001). The adaptation of Carpentier's novel appeared in France as a four-hour-plus TV miniseries titled *La siècle des lumières*. A two-hour version screened at Latin American film festivals. Humberto Solás, dir., *El siglo de las luces* (Ekran / France 3 / ICAIC, 1992).
46. As part of their mobilization of the Marxist theory of combined and uneven development for the analysis of world literature as the literature of the modern capitalist world-system, the Warwick Research Collective has argued that "the dialectics of core and periphery . . . underpin all cultural production in the modern era." WReC: Warwick Research Collective, *Combined and Uneven Development: Towards a New Theory of World-Literature* (Liverpool: Liverpool University Press, 2015), 51.
47. Edward W. Said, *Orientalism: Western Conceptions of the Orient* [1978] (London: Penguin, 1995), 20.
48. Brennan, *Places of Mind*, 180.
49. The Edison-Porter film, along with many other film adaptations of *Uncle Tom's Cabin*, is available to view at: *Uncle Tom's Cabin and American Culture: A Multi-Media Archive* maintained by Stephen Railton, http://utc.iath.virginia.edu. *The Great Train Robbery*, which was also made by Porter for Edison's company, is usually cited as the first American feature film, but it was not released until December 1903.
50. Stephen Railton, "Uncle Tom's Cabin on Film," *Uncle Tom's Cabin and American Culture: A Multi-Media Archive*, http://utc.iath.virginia.edu/onstage/films/fihp.html.
51. Stephen Railton, "Readapting *Uncle Tom's Cabin*," in *Nineteenth Century American Fiction on Screen*, ed. by R. Barton Palmer (Cambridge: Cambridge University Press, 2007), 67, 68.
52. Stevenson, "Filming Black Voices and Stories," 488.
53. David W. Griffith, dir., *The Birth of a Nation* (Hollywood: David W. Griffith Corporation, 1915); Thomas Dixon Jr., *The Clansman: An Historical Romance of the Ku Klux Klan*,(1905; repr., Lexington: University Press of Kentucky, 1970).
54. Woodrow Wilson, qtd. in "*The Birth of a Nation*," American Film Institute Catalog, https://catalog.afi.com/Film/1826-THE-BIRTHOFANATION?sid=175416d2-788a-4066-b7fc-cca3c67c165d&sr=11.512245&cp=1&pos=0.

55. Melvyn Stokes, *D. W. Griffith's* The Birth of a Nation: *A History of the Most Controversial Motion Picture of All Time* (Oxford: Oxford University Press, 2007), 3.

56. Stevenson, "Filming Black Voices and Stories," 492; Stokes, *D. W. Griffith's* The Birth of a Nation, 6.

57. Stevenson, "Filming Black Voices and Stories," 492, 493.

58. Michel Paradis, "The Lost Cause's Long Legacy," *Atlantic*, June 26, 2020, https://www.theatlantic.com/ideas/archive/2020/06/the-lost-causes-long-legacy/613288/.

59. Thomas L. Connelly and Barbara L. Bellows, *God and General Longstreet: The Lost Cause and the Southern Mind* (Baton Rouge: Louisiana State University Press, 1982), 1.

60. David Blight, *Race and Reunion: The Civil War in American Memory* (Cambridge, MA: Harvard University Press, 2001), 257.

61. Blight, *Race and Reunion*, 266.

62. For an examination of British sympathy for the Confederacy during and after the Civil War, see Michael J. Turner, *Stonewall Jackson, Beresford Hope, and the Meaning of the American Civil War in Britain* (Baton Rouge: Louisiana State University Press, 2020). Also see Amanda Foreman, *A World on Fire: An Epic History of Two Nations Divided* (London: Allen Lane, 2010), which narrates the history of British-American relations from 1812 to 1872.

63. Melvyn Stokes, "From Uncle Tom to Nat Turner: An Overview of Slavery in American Film, 1903–2016," *Transatlantica*, no. 1 (2018); 2, https://doi.org/10.4000/transatlantica.12814, 2.

64. Stokes, "From Uncle Tom to Nat Turner," 3.

65. J. Ronald Green, *Straight Lick: The Cinema of Oscar Micheaux* (Bloomington: Indiana University Press, 2000), 2, 4.

66. Green, *Straight Lick*, 4.

67. Stokes, "From Uncle Tom to Nat Turner," 4.

68. Stevenson, "Filming Black Voices and Stories," 493–94.

69. Victor Fleming, dir., *Gone with the Wind* (Selznick International Pictures/MGM, 1939).

70. Bogle, *Toms, Coons, Mulattoes*, 78.

71. Stevenson, "Filming Black Voices and Stories," 495.

72. Perhaps the most well-known parody of the those spawned by the movie poster is Bob Light and John Houston's poster that places Ronald Reagan and Margaret Thatcher in roles of Butler and O'Hara. See "Gone with the Wind (Ronald Reagan; Margaret Thatcher)," by Bob Light and John Houston, printed by East End Offset Ltd, published by Socialist Workers Party, offset lithograph printed in blue and red, 1981 or after, https://www.npg.org.uk/collections/search/portrait/mw251471/Gone-with-the-Wind-Ronald-Reagan-Margaret-Thatcher.

73. Judith Bettelheim, *AfroCuba: Works on Paper, 1968–2003* (San Francisco: San Francisco State University, 2005), 64. The potent visual satire of "Gone with the Macho" was also directed at a contemporaneous, local Cuban debate over the relationship between tropicality and eroticism. This debate was a particularly charged one in the context of the re-emergence of sex tourism in the post-1993 Cuban tourist economy. See: Ariel Ribeaux quoted in Bettelheim, *AfroCuba*, 64.

74. For a recent scholarly discussion of *Gone with the Wind*'s enduring cultural afterlife, see the collection of essays in the special section of *Gone with the Wind after Gone With the Wind* in *Transatlantica*, no. 1 (2019), https://doi.org/10.4000/transatlantica.13801.

75. See, for example, John M. Stahl, dir., *The Foxes of Harrow* (20th Century Fox, 1947); Raoul Walsh, dir., *Band of Angels* (Warner Bros., 1957).

76. Stevenson, "Filming Black Voices and Stories," 501.

77. Said, "Politics of Knowledge," 376.

78. Sepinwall, *Slave Revolt on Screen*, 79.

79. Sepinwall, *Slave Revolt on Screen*, 85–86.

80. Herbert Biberman, dir., *Slaves* (Slaves Company / Theatre Guild, 1969).

81. Stevenson, "Filming Black Voices and Stories," 501.

82. Also consider the portrayal of white plantation women in Richard Fleischer's *Mandingo* (Paramount Pictures, 1975).

83. Stokes, "From Uncle Tom to Nat Turner," 6.

84. Marcus Wood, *Slavery, Empathy, Pornography* (Oxford: Oxford University Press, 2002), 87–90.

85. Richard Fleischer, dir., *Mandingo* (Paramount Pictures, 1975).

86. Andrew de Vos, "'Expect the Truth': Exploiting History with *Mandingo*," *American Studies* 52, no. 2 (2013): 17.

87. de Vos, "Expect the Truth," 17.

88. Robin Wood, *Sexual Politics and Narrative Film: Hollywood and Beyond* (New York: Columbia University Press, 1998), 267. See also Linda Williams, "Skin Flicks on the Racial Border: Pornography, Exploitation, and Interracial Lust," in *Porn Studies*, ed. Linda Williams (Durham, NC: Duke University Press, 2004), 271–308.

89. Steve Carver, dir., *Drum* (United Artists, 1976).

90. Stokes, "From Uncle Tom to Nat Turner," 7.

91. Stevenson, "Filming Black Voices and Stories," 504.

92. Stokes, "From Uncle Tom to Nat Turner," 7–8.

93. Stokes, "From Uncle Tom to Nat Turner," 8.

94. Berman, *All That Is Solid Melts Into Air*, 333–34.

95. Stokes, "From Uncle Tom to Nat Turner," 8.

96. Steven Spielberg, dir., *Amistad* (DreamWorks Pictures, 1997).

97. Figures available at: "*Amistad*," Internet Movie Database (IMDb), https://www.imdb.com/title/tt0118607/.

98. *United States v. The Amistad*, 40 U.S. 15 Pet. 518 518 (1841).
99. Wood, *The Horrible Gift of Freedom*, 166.
100. *Scott v. Sandford* 60 U.S. 393 (1856); *Plessy v. Ferguson* 163 U.S. 537 (1896).
101. Wood, *The Horrible Gift of Freedom*, 16.
102. Wood, *The Horrible Gift of Freedom*, 16.
103. For a discussion of *Amazing Grace* in the context of the cultural memory of the bicentenary of the abolition of the slave trade in Britain, see Emma Waterton et al., "Forgetting to Heal: Remembering the Abolition Act of 1807," *European Journal of English Studies* 14, no. 1 (2010): 23–36, https://doi.org/10.1080/13825571003588403.
104. Wood, *The Horrible Gift of Freedom*, 14.
105. Steven Spielberg, dir., *Lincoln* (DreamWorks Pictures, 2012).
106. Peter Bradshaw, "*Django Unchained*: First Look Review," *Guardian*, December 12, 2012, https://www.theguardian.com/film/2012/dec/12/django-unchained-first-look-review.
107. Reynaldo Anderson, D. L. Stephenson, and Chante Anderson, "Crowdsourcing" "The Bad-Ass Slave": A Critique of Quentin Tarantino's *Django Unchained*, in *Quentin Tarantino's Django Unchained: The Continuation of Metacinema*, ed. Oliver C. Speck (New York: Bloomsbury Academic, 2014), 227–42.
108. Ian Jack, "All That Bloody Mayhem and We're Still Supposed to Take *Django Unchained* Seriously?" *Guardian*, January 25, 2013, https://www.theguardian.com/commentisfree/2013/jan/25/bloody-mayhem-tarantino-django-seriously.
109. Ta-Nehisi Coates, "The Case for Reparations," *Atlantic*, June 2014, https://www.theatlantic.com/magazine/archive/2014/06/the-case-for-reparations/361631/.
110. Stokes, "From Uncle Tom to Nat Turner," 14.
111. In some cases, the sudden critical souring was inextricably bound up with the resurfacing of Parker's long-forgotten acquittal on rape charges seventeen years before the movie's release.
112. See, for example, Wendy Ide, "*The Birth of a Nation* Review—Hardly Revolutionary," *Guardian*, December 11, 2016, https://www.theguardian.com/film/2016/dec/11/the-birth-of-a-nation-review-ridden-cliches-nate-parker-nat-turner; Peter Bradshaw, "*The Birth of a Nation* Review—Biblical Passion and Cheesy Emotion," *Guardian*, December 8, 2016, https://www.theguardian.com/film/2016/dec/08/the-birth-of-a-nation-review-nat-turner-nate-parker; Christopher Orr, "Grappling With *The Birth of a Nation*," *Atlantic*, October 6, 2016, https://www.theatlantic.com/entertainment/archive/2016/10/grappling-with-the-birth-of-a-nation/503246/; and Richard Brody, "The Cinematic Merits and Flaws of Nate Parker's *The Birth of a Nation*," *New Yorker*, October 9, 2016, https://www.newyorker.com/culture/richard-brody/the-cinematic-merits-and-flaws-of-nate-parkers-the-birth-of-a-nation. For a scholarly roundtable discission of the film see: Vernon Burton et al., "*The Birth of a Nation*: A Roundtable," *Civil War History* 64, no. 1 (2018): 56–91.

113. Charles Forsdick and Christian Høgsbjerg, "Sergei Eisenstein and the Haitian Revolution: 'The Confrontation Between Black and White Explodes Into Red,'" *History Workshop Journal* 78, no. 1 (2014): 157–85; Hazel Rowley, *Richard Wright: The Life and Times* (New York: Henry Holt and Company, 2001), 387; Philip Kaisary, *The Haitian Revolution in the Literary Imagination: Radical Horizons, Conservative Constraints* (Charlottesville: University of Virginia Press, 2014), 8.

114. Chris Rock, dir., *Top Five* (Paramount Pictures, 2014).

115. Sepinwall, *Slave Revolt on Screen*, 3. For a detailed analysis, see Sepinwall, *Slave Revolt on Screen*, 101–12.

116. Sepinwall, *Slave Revolt on Screen*, 3.

117. Victor Halperin, dir., *White Zombie* (United Artists, 1932); William Seabrook, *The Magic Island* (1929; repr., London: George G. Harrap, 1931); Wes Craven, dir., *The Serpent and the Rainbow* (MCA/Universal Pictures, 1987); Wade Davis, *The Serpent and the Rainbow: A Harvard Scientist's Astonishing Journey into the Secret Societies of Haitian Voodoo, Zombis, and Magic* (1985; repr., New York: Simon & Schuster, 2010).

118. Kasi Lemmons, dir., *Harriet* (Focus Features, 2019).

119. Alissa Wilkinson, "Why 'the Whole Environment in Hollywood Had to Change' for *Harriet* to Get Made," *Vox*, November 4, 2019, https://www.vox.com/culture/2019/11/4/20940561/harriet-interview-gregory-allen-howard.

120. Barry Jenkins, dir., *The Underground Railroad* (Amazon Studios, 2021).

121. Joanne Laurier, "Barry Jenkins' *The Underground Railroad*: 'Freed' from Important Realities of History," *World Socialist Web Site*, May 31, 2021. https://www.wsws.org/en/articles/2021/06/01/unde-j01.html.

122. David R. Shumway, *John Sayles* (Urbana: University of Illinois Press, 2012), 35.

123. Jonathan Rosenbaum, "Chains of Ignorance: Charles Burnett's *Nightjohn*," in *Essential Cinema: On the Necessity of Film Canons* (Baltimore: Johns Hopkins University Press, 2004), 285.

124. James Naremore, *Charles Burnett: A Cinema of Symbolic Knowledge* (Oakland: University of California Press, 2017), 124.

125. Rosenbaum, "Chains of Ignorance," 287.

126. Sophie Saint-Just, "Creolization on Screen: Guy Deslauriers's *The Middle Passage* as Afro-Diasporic Discourse [*Le passage du milieu*]," *African and Black Diaspora: An International Journal* 12, no. 3 (2019): 298.

127. William Hazlitt, qtd. in: Marcus Wood, *Blind Memory: Visual Representations of Slavery in England and America 1780–1865* (Manchester: Manchester University Press, 2000), 16.

128. Paul Gilroy, *The Black Atlantic: Modernity and Double Consciousness* (London: Verso, 1993).

129. Haile Gerima, dir., *Sankofa* (Mypheduh Films, 1993). Notably, the narrative device of temporal displacement to the antebellum South has reappeared in subsequent slavery films, most recently in the low-budget, slavery horror film *Antebellum*, starring Janelle Monáe. Gerard Bush and Christopher Renz, dirs., *Antebellum* (Lionsgate / QC Entertainment, 2020).

130. Robert Stam, *Tropical Multiculturalism: A Comparative History of Race in Brazilian Cinema and Culture* (Durham: Duke University Press, 1997), 228.

131. Haitian cinematic perspectives on the Haitian Revolution constitute an important and severely overlooked contribution. For examples and analysis, see Sepinwall, *Slave Revolt on Screen*, 135–78.

132. Gillo Pontecorvo, dir., *Quemada (Burn!)* (Produzioni Europee Associati, 1969).

133. Tomás Gutiérrez Alea, dir., *La última cena* (ICAIC, 1976); and *El otro Francisco* (ICAIC, 1974), *Rancheador* (ICAIC, 1976), and *Maluala* (ICAIC, 1979), all dir. Sergio Giral.

134. Steve McQueen, dir., *12 Years a Slave* (Fox Searchlight, 2013).

Chapter 1

1. Screenplay authored by Franco Solinas (credited), Giorgio Arlorio (credited), and Gillo Pontecorvo (uncredited).

2. Edward Said, "The Quest for Gillo Pontecorvo" [1988] rpt. *Reflections on Exile and Other Literary and Cultural Essays* (London: Granta, 2001), 283. Said's biographer Timothy Brennan writes that while Said was passionate about Pontecorvo's early work, he was disenchanted by Pontecorvo's late work in pursuit of artistic autonomy. Brennan, *Places of Mind*, 285.

3. The much-commented-on grainy black-and-white newsreel effect was obtained by the use of a particular film stock (Dupont 4) and the meticulous adoption of a labor-intensive technique known as *controtipare*. Carlo Celli explains: "The final print is made from a copy of the original negative, which is reexposed, causing a decrease in the quality of the film and resulting in a grainy newsreel hue." In the making of *The Battle of Algiers*, this technique was repeated twice. Carlo Celli, *Gillo Pontecorvo: From Resistance to Terrorism* (Lanham, MD: Scarecrow Press, 2005), 32.

4. Madeleine Dobie, "*The Battle of Algiers* at 50: From 1960s Radicalism to the Classrooms of West Point," *Los Angeles Review of Books*, September 25, 2016, https://www.lareviewofbooks.org/article/battle-algiers-50-1960s-radicalism-classrooms-west-point/.

5. Toussaint Louverture: "In overthrowing me, you have cut down in San Domingo only the trunk of the tree of liberty. It will spring up again by the

roots for they are numerous and deep." Cited in James, *The Black Jacobins*, 334. *The Black Jacobins* was available in French and Italian translations by the time of *Burn*'s release: *Les Jacobins Noirs* (Paris: Gallimard, 1948) and *I Jacobini Neri* (Milan: Feltrinelli, 1968).

    6. Stephen Hunter, "*Queimada*: Revolution in Perpetual Motion," *Washington Post*, October 15, 2004, https://www.washingtonpost.com/wp-dyn/content/article/2004/10/15/AR2005033114801.html.

    7. Vincent Canby, "The Screen: Marlon Brando and Black Revolution," *New York Times*, October 22, 1970, https://www.nytimes.com/1970/10/22/archives/the-screen-marlon-brando-and-Black-revolution.html.

    8. "It is not enough to have taken away Toussaint [Louverture], there are 2,000 leaders." Charles Leclerc to Napoleon, August 25, 1802, qtd. in: James, *The Black Jacobins*, 346.

    9. Said, "The Quest for Gillo Pontecorvo," 291.

    10. Davis, *Slaves on Screen*, 44.

    11. Eric Williams, *Capitalism and Slavery* (Chapel Hill: University of North Carolina Press, 1944, 1994).

    12. Other sympathetic readings include: Davis, *Slaves on Screen*, 41–55; Forsdick and Høgsbjerg, "Sergei Eisenstein and the Haitian Revolution," 157–85; Michael T. Martin, "Podium for the Truth? Reading Slavery and the Neocolonial Project in the Historical Film: *Queimada! (Burn!)* and *Sankofa* in Counterpoint," *Third Text* 23, no. 6 (2009): 717–31; Michael T. Martin and David C. Wall, "The Politics of Cine-Memory: Signifying Slavery in the Historical Film," in *A Companion to the Historical Film*, eds. Robert A. Rosenstone and Constantin Parvulescu (Hoboken: Wiley-Blackwell, 2013), 445–67; Mike Wayne, *Political Film: The Dialectics of Third Cinema* (London: Pluto Press, 2001), 44–45; and Marcus Wood, *The Horrible Gift of Freedom*, 30–32.

    13. Fredric Jameson, *The Political Unconscious: Narrative as a Socially Symbolic Act* (Ithaca, NY: Cornell University Press, 1981), 206–81.

    14. Following Fernando Solanas and Octavio Getino in their profoundly influential 1969 manifesto, "Towards a Third Cinema: Notes and Experiences for the Development of a Cinema of Liberation in the Third World," I define First Cinema as commercial cinema, and especially the cinema of Hollywood; Second Cinema as art or auteur cinema; and Third Cinema as the cinema of anti-imperialist struggle and decolonization. Fernando Solanas and Octavio Getino, "Towards a Third Cinema: Notes and Experiences for the Development of a Cinema of Liberation in the Third World" (1969). First published in Spanish as "Hacia un tercer cine," in *Tricontinental* (Cuba), no. 13 (1969). Repr. in Michael Chanan, ed., *Twenty-Five Years of the New Latin American Cinema* (London: BFI, 1983), 17–27.

    15. Sepinwall, *Slave Revolt on Screen*, 30.

    16. Celli, *Gillo Pontecorvo*, vii, 89.

17. Joan Mellen, "A Reassessment of Gillo Pontecorvo's *Burn!*" *Cinema*, no. 32 (1972): 38.

18. Pauline Kael, qtd. in Mellen, "Reassessment," 41.

19. "Using the Contradictions of the System: An Interview with Gillo Pontecorvo," (interview by Harold Kalishman and Gabriel Landau), *Cinéaste* 6, no. 2 (1974): 6.

20. In Italy in 1970, *Burn!* received David di Donatello and Golden Goblet awards; in Spain in 1972, a Fotogramas de Plata award; and in Turkey, despite being banned there when first released, *Burn!* was awarded the prize in the category of Best Foreign Film by the Turkish Film Critics Association on two occasions, 1972 and 1974.

21. Danny Peary, "*Burn!*" *Criterion Collection*, December 10, 1991, https://www.criterion.com/current/posts/947-burn. Viz., also: "*Burn!* should be regarded as a classic, but because most American critics compared it unfavourably to [*The Battle of Algiers*] and its distributor, United Artists, released the picture without publicity, relatively few people have seen it and it has been relegated to cult status." Danny Peary, *Cult Movies: The Classics, the Sleepers, the Weird, and the Wonderful* (New York: Delta, 1981), 41.

22. Geoff Andrew, "*Queimada! (Burn!)*, 865, in *Time Out Film Guide*, ed. John Pym (London: Time Out Guides Limited, 2011); Marlon Brando (with Robert Lindsey), *Brando: Songs My Mother Taught Me* (New York: Random House, 1994), 320.

23. Forsdick and Høgsbjerg, "Sergei Eisenstein and the Haitian Revolution," 157.

24. Davis, *Slaves on Screen*, 42.

25. Mellen, "Reassessment," 47.

26. Frantz Fanon, *The Wretched of the Earth* [1961], trans. Richard Philcox (New York: Grove Press, 2004), 54.

27. Wayne, *Political Film*, 44.

28. Fredric Jameson, "Third-World Literature in the Era of Multinational Capitalism," *Social Text*, no. 15 (1986): 68–69.

29. Stevenson, "Filming Black Voices and Stories: Slavery on Americas Screens," 508; Alan Stone, "Last Battle: Gillo Pontecorvo's *Burn!*" *Boston Review* 29, no. 2 (April/May 2004), https://bostonreview.net/articles/alan-stone-last-battle/.

30. Joan Mellen, "An Interview with Gillo Pontecorvo," *Film Quarterly* 26, no. 1 (1972): 9.

31. Davis, *Slaves on Screen*, 145n10.

32. Sepinwall, *Slave Revolt on Screen*, 34.

33. Ella Shohat and Robert Stam, *Unthinking Eurocentrism: Multiculturalism and the Media* (New York: Routledge, 2014), 188.

34. Peary, *Cult Movies*, 43.

35. Wayne, *Political Film*, 44–45.
36. Jameson, *The Political Unconscious*, 206–80.
37. Davis, *Slaves on Screen*, 44.
38. Edward Said, "Through Gringo Eyes: With Conrad in Latin America," *Harper's* (April 1988), repr. Edward Said, *Reflections on Exile and Other Literary and Cultural Essays* (London: Granta, 2001), 276.
39. Celli, *Gillo Pontecorvo*, 71.
40. Mellen, "Reassessment," 43.
41. "Contradictions of the System," 4.
42. Benita Parry, *Conrad and Imperialism: Ideological Boundaries and Visionary Frontiers* (London: Macmillan, 1983), 22; Said, "The Quest for Gillo Pontecorvo," 286; Stephen Hunter, "*Queimada*: Revolution In Perpetual Motion," *Washington Post*, October 15, 2004, https://www.washingtonpost.com/wp-dyn/content/article/2004/10/15/AR2005033114801.html.
43. Said, "The Quest for Gillo Pontecorvo," 286.
44. Jameson, *The Political Unconscious*, 206.
45. Gillo Pontecorvo, qtd. in Danny Peary, "*Burn!*" Criterion Collection, December 10, 1991, https://www.criterion.com/current/posts/947-burn. Pontecorvo himself claimed that his primary cinematic influences are "three-quarters Rossellini" and one-quarter Eisenstein among other montage-influenced Soviet directors. Celli, *Gillo Pontecorvo*, xxvi.
46. Jameson, *The Political Unconscious*, 208.
47. Celli, *Gillo Pontecorvo*, 71.
48. After *Kapò*, Pontecorvo received offers from around the world to direct various film projects. However, unable to compromise on his artistic and political vision, Pontecorvo became notorious for turning down, leaving unfinished, or withdrawing from projects. See Celli, *Gillo Pontecorvo*, 103–19.
49. Celli, *Gillo Pontecorvo*, vi.
50. After *Burn!*, Pontecorvo completed only one more feature film: *Ogro* (1979). The film, which Pontecorvo always regretted, tells the story of ETA's 1973 assassination of Carrerro Blanco, the Spanish prime minister under Franco. In 1988, Said speculated that Pontecorvo's later retreat into the realm of aesthetics blocked his creative consciousness. Celli argues that by later life Pontecorvo had lost the "certainty in his ideological convictions" that had sustained his early work. Said, "The Quest for Gillo Pontecorvo," 291; Celli, *Gillo Pontecorvo*, 108.
51. "Contradictions," 6.
52. "Contradictions," 6.
53. Gillo Pontecorvo, qtd. in John J. Michalczyk, *The Italian Political Filmmakers* (London: Associated University Presses, 1986), 182.
54. Ebert, "Pontecorvo: 'We Trust the Face of Brando.'"
55. Celli, *Gillo Pontecorvo*, 70.

56. Wayne, *Political Film*, 44.
57. Gillo Pontecorvo and Neelem Srivastava, "Interview with the Italian film director Gillo Pontecorvo," Rome, Italy, July 1, 2003, *Interventions: International Journal of Postcolonial Studies* 7, no. 1 (2005): 115.
58. Celli, *Gillo Pontecorvo*, 72.
59. Celli, *Gillo Pontecorvo*, 72–73.
60. Mellen, "An Interview with Gillo Pontecorvo," 10.
61. Ebert, "Pontecorvo: 'We Trust the Face of Brando.'"
62. Mellen, "An Interview with Gillo Pontecorvo," 10.
63. Gillo Pontecorvo, qtd. in Said, "The Quest for Gillo Pontecorvo," 287.
64. Marlon Brando, *Brando: Songs My Mother Taught Me*, 320; Celli, *Gillo Pontecorvo*, 73.
65. Celli, *Gillo Pontecorvo*, 74–76.
66. Brando, *Brando: Songs My Mother Taught Me*, 320.
67. Mellen, "An Interview with Gillo Pontecorvo," 9; Said, "The Quest for Gillo Pontecorvo," 286.
68. Mellen, "Reassessment," 42.
69. Wayne, *Political Film*, 45.
70. Stone, "Last Battle."
71. Stone, "Last Battle."
72. Mellen, "Reassessment," 41.
73. Michalczyk, *The Italian Political Filmmakers*, 280–81n27. See also Mellen, "A Reassessment," 41; and Stone, "Last Battle."
74. Mellen, "An Interview with Gillo Pontecorvo," 6, 7.
75. Said, "The Quest for Gillo Pontecorvo," 287.
76. Mellen, "An Interview with Gillo Pontecorvo," 6, 7.
77. Mellen, "An Interview with Gillo Pontecorvo," 8.
78. Mellen, "An Interview with Gillo Pontecorvo," 8.
79. Mellen, "An Interview with Gillo Pontecorvo," 6.
80. Mellen, "An Interview with Gillo Pontecorvo," 4; Said, "The Quest for Gillo Pontecorvo," 286.
81. Stone, "Last Battle."
82. Karl Marx, *Capital: Vol. 3: The Process of Capitalist Production as a Whole* (1894; repr., New York: International Publishers, 1977), 820.
83. Joseph R. Slaughter, *Human Rights, Inc.: The World Novel, Narrative Form, and International Law* (New York: Fordham University Press, 2007), 15. See also Philip Kaisary, "Socioeconomic Rights and the Haitian Revolution," in *Social Rights and the Politics of Obligation in History*, eds. Charles Walton and Steven Jenson (Cambridge: Cambridge University Press, 2022), 82–98.
84. Jameson, *The Geopolitical Aesthetic*, 4.
85. Kaisary, *The Haitian Revolution in the Literary Imagination*, 61, 71–72, 94–95. See also: Wood, *Blind Memory*, 269.

86. Fredric Jameson, "Reification and Utopia in Mass Culture" [1979], *Signatures of the Visible* (London: Routledge, 1992), 11–46.

87. Teshome H. Gabriel, *Third Cinema in the Third World: The Aesthetics of Liberation* (Ann Arbor, MI: UMI Research Press, 1982), 2.

88. An interview with Aimé Césaire conducted by René Depestre (1967), in Aimé Césaire, *Discourse on Colonialism*, trans. Joan Pinkham (New York: Monthly Review, 2000), 90; Frantz Fanon, "Address to the First Congress of Negro Writers and Artists" (Paris, 1956). Repr. "Racism and Culture" in *Toward the African Revolution* by Frantz Fanon, trans. Haakon Chevalier (New York: Grove Press, 1967), 43.

89. Celli, *Gillo Pontecorvo*, 54, 67, 71, 76, 81; Davis, *Slaves on Screen*, 52; and Massimo Ghirelli, *Gillo Pontecorvo*, Special Issue of *Il Castoro Cinema*, no. 60 (December 1978): 75.

90. Wood, *The Horrible Gift of Freedom*, 32.

91. For an elaboration of this interpretation of Lawrence's work, see Kaisary, *The Haitian Revolution in the Literary Imagination*, 79–84.

92. See François Cauvin, "Toussaint Louverture," (2009), https://cheurtelou.wixsite.com/fcauvin?pgid=j3v9reg1-afc82287-2063-4777-9ed8-3881f2708a82; and Edouard Duval Carrié, "Memory #1" (2017), http://duval-carrie.com/project/memory-1/. Lawrence's painting was itself based on a much earlier image of Louverture, François Séraphin Delpech's 1832 engraving of Nicolas-Eustache Maurin's Toussaint L'Ouverture. For analysis, see Kaisary, *The Haitian Revolution in the Literary Imagination*, 82–84.

93. Remeike Forbes, "The Black Jacobin: Our Visual Identity," *Jacobin*, March 3, 2012, https://jacobinmag.com/2012/03/the-Black-jacobin-2.

94. Jacob Lawrence, *The Life of Toussaint L'Ouverture*, no. 20 (1938). Tempera on paper, 19 × 11½ in. (Aaron Douglas Collection, Amistad Research Center, Tulane University, New Orleans, Louisiana); Anne-Louis Girodet, *Portrait of Citizen Belley*, 1797. Oil on canvas, 158 × 111 cm. (Châteaux de Versailles et de Trianon, Versailles); Kimathi Donkor, *Toussaint L'Ouverture at Bedourete*, 2004. Oil on linen, 136 × 183 cm. (Collection of the artist.)

95. Aimé Césaire, qtd. in Nick Nesbitt, "Négritude," in *Africana: The Encyclopedia of the African American Experience*, 2nd ed., vol. 4, eds. Kwame Anthony Appiah and Henry Louis Gates Jr. (Oxford: Oxford University Press: 2005), 193–99, esp. 198.

96. Aimé Césaire, *Notebook of a Return to My Native Land / Cahier d'un retour au pays natal*, trans. Mireille Rosello with Annie Pritchard (1939; repr., Newcastle upon Tyne: Bloodaxe, 1995).

97. Davis, *Slaves on Screen*, 48.

98. Fanon, *The Wretched of the Earth*, 51.

99. Acts, Chapter 16, Verses 35–40. Authorized King James Bible with Apocrypha.

100. Terry Eagleton, *The Gospels: Jesus Christ* (London: Verso, 2007), xvii. Texts selected and annotated by Giles Fraser.

101. Wood, *The Horrible Gift of Freedom*, 31.

102. Said, "The Quest for Gillo Pontecorvo," 286–87.

103. Mellen, "An Interview with Gillo Pontecorvo," 9.

104. Wood, *The Horrible Gift of Freedom*, 31.

105. Alea: "Criticism will never attain a high level of efficacy as long as the show itself embodies that [repressive] ideology in its external appearance, on its surface, in its immediacy." A footnote that immediately follows those words reads as follows: "The film *Burn* offers us an eloquent example of contrast between its explicit message—presented through oral language, through words which encompass concepts and ideas that are definitively revolutionary and specifically anticolonial—and its implicit *myth* about Europe's 'unshakeable' superiority—expressed not just through Marlon Brando's powerful and dynamic image and charismatic personality and the dramatic situations where he shows himself to be always *above* the people's drama, but also through the film's very 'style' which others would call its 'structural dynamics' (Althusser) perhaps with a more limited viewpoint but equally referring to the phenomenal, the immediate, the formal which, in this case, may be the result of the filmmakers' unconsciously paternalistic attitude." Tomás Gutiérrez Alea, *The Viewer's Dialectic*, trans. Julia Lesage (Havana: José Martí Publishing House, 1988), 47. Italics in the original.

106. Davis, *Slaves on Screen*, 52.

107. Amy Taubin, "Art and Industry," *Film Comment*, July/August 2007. http://filmlinccom.siteprotect.net/fcm/artandindustry/burn.htm.

108. Jameson, *The Geopolitical Aesthetic*, 186.

109. Fredric Jameson, "The Future City," *New Left Review*, no. 21 (2003): 76.

Chapter 2

1. Frantz Fanon, *Peau noire, masques blancs* (Paris: Éditions du Seuil, 1952), 178.

2. Screenplay authored by Tomás Gutiérrez Alea, Tomás González, and María Eugenia Haya.

3. See, for examples, Vincent Canby, "*The Last* Supper, A Parable From Cuba," *New York Times*, May 5, 1978, C5; Philip French, "Crucified in Cuba," *The Observer*, March 11, 1979, 14; and Penelope Gilliatt, "Last Supper in Havana," *New Yorker*, May 15, 1978, 120–24.

4. The Instituto Cubano del Arte e Industria Cinematográficos (Cuban Institute of Cinematographic Art and Industry), or ICAIC, absorbed *Cine Rebelde*, the revolutionary film organization that had been established early in January 1959 on the rebels' assumption of power. Two short documentary films were produced

under the auspices of *Cine Rebelde*, including one by Alea: *Esta Tierra Nuestra* ("This is Our Land"). In the March 24 decree, film was expressly recognized as an art form, freed from market constraints, and the ICAIC was tasked with the creation, production, distribution, and exhibition of films of an artistically and socially committed character. For a detailed history of the ICAIC, see Michael Chanan, *Cuban Cinema* (Minneapolis: University of Minnesota Press, 2004). See also Julianne Burton, "Film and Revolution in Cuba: The First Twenty-Five Years," in *Cuba: Twenty-Five Years of Revolution, 1959-1984*, eds. Sandor Halebsky and John M. Kirk (New York: Praegar, 1985), 134-53.

5. Burton, "Film and Revolution in Cuba," 142.

6. Susan Lord, "Introduction: New Women, Old Worlds," in *The Cinema of Sara Gómez: Reframing Revolution*, eds. Susan Lord and María Caridad Cumaná (Bloomington: Indiana University Press, 2021), 5.

7. *La última cena* was a prizewinner at the Huelva Latin American Film Festival (1976) and the São Paulo International Film Festival (1978). Schroeder notes the film's popularity in Brazil: Schroeder, *Tomás Gutierrrez Alea: The Dialectics of a Filmmaker*, 2. Chanan notes the film's success in London's West End: Chanan, "Enduring Memories," *New Statesman*, 40.

8. Celli, *Gillo Pontecorvo*, 89.

9. Tomás Gutiérrez Alea, *The Viewer's Dialectic*, trans. Julia Lesage (Havana: José Martí Publishing House, 1988), 47. See the analysis in the preceding chapter, esp. n101.

10. English-language scholarship addressing *La última cena* includes: Gilberto M. Blasini, "The Last Supper (1976): Cinema, History, and Decolonization," in *Film Analysis: A Norton Reader*, eds. Jeffrey Geiger and R. L. Rutsky (New York: Norton, 2005), 678-94; Michael Chanan, *Cuban Cinema* (Minneapolis: University of Minnesota Press, 2004), 329-31; Natalie Zemon Davis, "Ceremony and Revolt: *Burn!* and *The Last Supper*," in *Slaves on Screen* (Cambridge: Harvard University Press, 2000), 41-68; Marilyn G. Miller, "Truth, Lies and Telling Silences in Gutiérrez Alea's *The Last Supper* and Pontecorvo's *Burn!*," *Studies in Spanish & Latin American Cinemas* 10, no. 1 (2013): 59-74; Schroeder, "*The Last Supper*: Marxism Meets Christianity," in *Tomás Gutierrrez Alea: The Dialectics of a Filmmaker*, 78-91; and Dennis West, "Slavery and Cinema in Cuba: The Case of Gutiérrez Alea's *The Last Supper*," *Western Journal of Black Studies* 3, no. 2 (1979): 128-33.

11. Tomás Gutierrrez Alea, *Cumbite* ("Cooperative Labor") (Havana, Cuba: Instituto Cubano del Arte e Industria Cinematográficos, 1964); Jacques Roumain, *Les Gouverneurs de la Rosée* (1944), trans. as *Masters of the Dew* by Langston Hughes and John Mercer in 1947 (Oxford: Heinemann, 1978).

12. Schroeder, *Tomás Gutierrrez Alea*, 17.

13. Michael Chanan, "Enduring Memories," *New Statesman*, July 7, 2008, 40. Alea's standing in Cuban film and letters is conveyed in Dennis West, "In the Footsteps of Tomás Gutiérrez Alea," *Cinéaste* 35, no. 2 (2010): 18-25. West's essay

considers the feature-length documentary dedicated to Alea's life and work, *Titón: De la Habana a Guantanamera*, dir. Mirtha Ibarra (Spain: Brothers & Sisters, 2008), as well as the publication of a collection of Alea's correspondence from his studies in Rome in the early 1950s to the end of his life: Mirtha Ibarra, ed., *Titón: Tomás Gutiérrez Alea: Volver sobre mis pasos* (Habana: Ediciones Unión, 2008).

14. The classic statement of *littérature engagée* is Jean-Paul Sartre's 1947 essay, "What Is Literature?" Repr. in English translation in Jean-Paul Sartre, *What Is Literature?* trans. Bernard Frechtman (London, Routledge, 1993).

15. Buñuel's influence is strongest in Alea's most provocative, surreal, and black-comic works. These include 1966's *La muerte de un burócrata (Death of a Bureaucrat)* and 1979's *Los sobrevivientes (The Survivors)*. See n19 here for a capsule summary of *Los sobrevivientes*. Critics have also noted the intertextual connections between Luis Buñuel's *Viridiana* (1961) and *La última cena*. These are noted in the ensuing discussion.

16. Schroeder, *Tomás Gutiérrrez Alea: The Dialectics of a Filmmaker*, xii–xiii; Miller, "Truth," 62.

17. Alea's key theoretical text is *The Viewer's Dialectic*, trans. Julia Lesage (Havana: Editorial José Martí, 1988). The text is also available online, serialized in three issues of *Jump Cut: A Review of Contemporary Media*, nos. 29–32 (February 1984–April 1987), http://www.ejumpcut.org/home.html.

18. Schroeder, *Tomás Gutierrrez Alea*, 54.

19. Alea, qtd. in Zuzana Pick, "Towards a Renewal of Cuban Revolutionary Cinema: A Discussion of Cuban Cinema Today" [An interview with Tomás Gutiérrrez Alea, Jorge Fraga, Alina Sanchez, and Samuel Claxton by Zuzana Pick], *Ciné-Tracts* 2, nos. 3–4 (Summer/Fall 1979): 22.

20. Chanan, "Enduring Memories," *New Statesman*, 40.

21. In the course of his career, Alea directed twelve feature-length films. That Alea made documentary as well as fictional feature films was a product of the priority given to documentary filmmaking in the ICAIC, which considered the practice formative for its directors and an important didactic instrument. See Schroeder, *Tomás Gutiérrrez Alea*, 3.

22. Tomás Gutiérrez Alea, dir., *Memorias del subdesarrollo (Memories of Underdevelopment)* (Instituto Cubano del Arte e Industria Cinematográficos, 1968). The descriptor, "bourgeois misfit" appears in Chanan, "Enduring Memories," *New Statesman*, 40.

Alea's 1979, Buñuelesque black comedy, *Los sobrevivientes (The Survivors)*, employs a similar premise: a bourgeois family who elect to remain in Cuba after the revolution and articulates a critique of postrevolutionary bourgeois habits. *Los sobrevivientes* is however distinguished by its comedic savagery. In an ironic turning upside down of the materialist conception of history as defined by its relation to the mode of production, the family degenerates from capitalist social relations to a state of savagery and cannibalism, passing through feudalism, slavery, and primitivism along the way. Tomás Gutiérrez Alea, dir., *Los sobrevivientes* (1979). For analysis, see Michael Chanan, *Cuban Cinema*, 2nd ed. (Minneapolis: University of Minnesota Press, 2004), 368–69; and Schroeder, *Tomás Gutiérrez Alea*, 92–94.

23. Schroeder, *Tomás Gutierrrez Alea*, 54.

24. Schroeder, *Tomás Gutierrrez Alea*, 88.

25. Zuzana Pick, *The New Latin American Cinema: A Continental Project* (Austin: University of Texas Press, 1993), 130.

26. For an analysis of the retrenchment and intensification of slavery in Cuba as a consequence of the Haitian Revolution, see Ada Ferrer, *Freedom's Mirror: Cuba and Haiti in the Age of Revolution* (New York: Cambridge University Press, 2014).

27. The term "pseudo-republic" was coined by *Fidelista* historians. Richard Gott, *Cuba: A New History* (New Haven: Yale University Press, 2004), 113. That the historiography of the Cuban Republic founded in 1902 generally gave short shrift to the subject of Cuban slavery reflects the white supremacist foundations of the Republic. The African American historian Arthur Schomburg visited Cuba in 1905 and noted with dismay that Cuban Blacks had been better off and had "enjoyed a greater measure of freedom and happiness" under Spanish colonialism; qtd. in Gott, *Cuba*, 121. Natalie Zemon Davis considers the works of Fernando Ortiz Fernández, especially *Los negros esclavos* (Havana: Revista Bimestre Cubana, 1916), an important exception to the general tenor of Cuban slavery historiography in the years 1902–1952. Natalie Zemon Davis, *Slaves on Screen* (Cambridge, MA: Harvard University Press, 2000), 145–46, n. 13.

28. See, for example, Sara Gómez, *Y . . . temenos sabor* (ICAIC, 1968); and Juan Carlos Tabío, *Miriam Makeba* (ICAIC, 1973).

29. Pick, *The New Latin American Cinema*, 131. See also Davis, *Slaves on Screen*, 56.

30. Fidel Castro, *My Life*, ed. Ignacio Ramonet, trans. Andrew Hurley (London: Penguin, 2007), 320. In 1991, a monument in memory of Carlota was erected at the site of the rebellion. Carlota's resistance continues to inspire artistic commemorations, notably in the historical paintings of Lili Bernard, a Cuban-born, Los Angeles–based interdisciplinary artist. See Lili Bernard, "Carlota Leading the People (after Eugene Delacroix's Liberty Leading the People, 1830)," oil on Canvas, 60″ × 72″, 2011; and Lili Bernard, "Carlota Slaying the Slaver (after Artimesia Gentilesch's Judith Slaying Holofernes, 1612)," oil on Canvas, 60″ × 72″, 2016. Digital reproductions are available at: http://lilibernard.com/site/artwork/paintings/historical/.

31. Gott, *Cuba*, 250.

32. Gott, *Cuba*, 255. Also see Gabriel García Márquez, "Operation Carlota," trans. Patrick Camiller, *New Left Review*, nos. 101–2 (February–April 1977), 123–37.

33. Schroeder, *Tomás Gutierrrez Alea*, 136.

34. Alea's move here was neither unique nor without precedent. It can be profitably aligned with C. L. R. James's underanalyzed essay "From Toussaint

L'Ouverture to Fidel Castro," which appeared as an appendix to the second edition of his classic study of the Haitian Revolution, *The Black Jacobins*. C. L. R. James, *The Black Jacobins* [2nd ed. rev. 1963] (New York: Vintage, 1989), 391–418.

35. Manuel Moreno Fraginals, *The Sugar Mill: The Socioeconomic Complex of Sugar in Cuba, 1760*–1860, trans. Cedric Belfrage (New York: Monthly Review, 1976).

36. Moreno Fraginals, *The Sugar Mill*, 53.

37. Moreno Fraginals, *The Sugar Mill*, 53.

38. Aimé Césaire, *Discourse on Colonialism* [1955], trans. Joan Pinkham (New York: Monthly Review Press, 2000), 36.

39. Revelations, Chapter 7, Verse 9. Authorized King James Bible with Apocrypha.

40. Psalms, Psalm 92, Verse 12. Authorized King James Bible with Apocrypha.

41. The Gospel According to St. John, Chapter 12, Verse 13. Authorized King James Bible with Apocrypha.

42. Joseph Conrad, *Heart of Darkness* (1899; repr., 5th ed., New York: Norton, 2017), ed. Paul B. Armstrong.

43. Francis Ford Coppola, dir., *Apocalypse Now* (1979).

44. Patrick Hanks, Kate Hardcastle, and Flavia Hodges, *A Dictionary of First Names* (2nd ed., Oxford: Oxford University Press, 2006). Oxford Reference Online.

45. The history of Saint Sebastian's incorporation into representational forms is a vast subject. For a few important, illustrative examples executed in different mediums and from different historical periods, see Jacobus de Voraigne, *The Golden Legend* (c. 1260, repr., London: Penguin, 1998), 50–54; Francesco Botticini, "Saint Sebastian" (c. 1473–1474, tempera and oil on wood); Georges de La Tour, "Saint Sebastian Tended by Saint Irene" (1649, oil on canvas); poems, artworks, and letters by Salvador Dalí and Federico García Lorca (see n46 below); Damien Hirst, "Saint Sebastian, Exquisite Pain" (2007, glass, painted stainless steel, silicone, arrows, crossbow bolts, stainless steel cable and clamps, stainless steel carabiner, bullock and formaldehyde solution); and Gabriele D'Annunzio (libretto), Claude Debussy, comp., *Le Martyre de saint Sébastien* [a 5-act musical mystery play] (1911).

46. Federico García Lorca, *Poet in New York*, ed. Christopher Maurer, 2nd ed. (New York: Noonday Press, 1998), 186; Christopher Maurer, prologue to *Sebastian's Arrows: Letters and Mementos of Salvador Dalí and Federico García Lorca*, ed. and trans. Christopher Maurer (Chicago: Swan Isle Press, 2004), 20.

47. Italics in the original. Federico García Lorca, qtd. in *Sebastian's Arrows*, 78. Dalí and Lorca produced numerous artworks and writings on Saint Sebastian, many of which are collected in the Maurer volume. Lorca's view can be considered a response to the outlook of Gustav von Aschenbach, the aging writer in Thomas Mann's 1912 novella, *Death in Venice*. While Aschenbach finds Saint Sebastian's Apollonian beauty and his deportment despite the inflictions of cruelty both erotic

and aesthetic, he expresses doubts as to whether "the Sebastian figure is the most beautiful symbol . . . of art as a whole." Thomas Mann, *Death in Venice* (1912) trans. Michael Henry Heim (New York: Harper Collins, 2004), 17.

48. Charles Darwent, "Arrows of Desire: How Did St Sebastian Become an Enduring, Homo-Erotic Icon?" *Independent*, February 10, 2008, https://www.independent.co.uk/arts-entertainment/art/features/arrows-of-desire-how-did-st-sebastian-become-an-enduring-homoerotic-icon-779388.html.

49. Kurt Andersen, "Art and Advertising with George Lois," WNYC: New York Public Radio, August 28, 2004, https://www.wnyc.org/story/107063-art-and-advertising-with-george-lois/.

50. The US Supreme Court overturned Ali's conviction on June 28, 1971. See *Clay v. United States*, 403 U.S. 698 (1971).

51. French, "Crucified in Cuba," 14.

52. Susan Buck-Morss, "Hegel and Haiti," *Critical Inquiry* 26, no. 4 (2000): 865. For arguments for understanding the Haitian Revolution in the terms of radical universalism, see also Nick Nesbitt, *Universal Emancipation: The Haitian Revolution and the Radical Enlightenment* (Charlottesville: University of Virginia Press, 2008); and Philip Kaisary, *The Haitian Revolution in the Literary Imagination: Radical Horizons, Conservative Constraints* (Charlottesville: University of Virginia Press, 2014).

53. Césaire, *Discourse on Colonialism*, 33; italics in the original.

54. Césaire, *Discourse on Colonialism*, 32. Consider also the first chapter of Frantz Fanon's *The Wretched of the Earth*, "On Violence," which is replete with analysis of "Western values" as hypocritical in the colonial context. This leads Fanon at one particularly memorable point to liken Christianity not to civilization but to DDT, since both DDT and Christianity serve to destroy in the colonial environment. Frantz Fanon, *The Wretched of the Earth* [1961] trans. Richard Philcox (New York: Grove Press, 2004), 7.

55. Romans, Chapter 3, Verse 10; Genesis, Chapter 3, Verse 19. Authorized King James Bible with Apocrypha.

56. Michel-Rolf Trouillot famously argued that the Haitian Revolution was "unthinkable" in the late eighteenth and early nineteenth centuries. Going further, Sibylle Fischer has argued that the entire edifice of Western modernity was constructed on the disavowal of the Haitian Revolution and its political and philosophical ramifications. See Michel-Rolph Trouillot, *Silencing the Past: Power and the Production of History* (Boston: Beacon, 1995); and Sibylle Fischer, *Modernity Disavowed: Haiti and the Cultures of Slavery in the Age of Revolution* (Durham, NC: Duke University Press, 2004).

57. Here, too, Alea's analysis evokes C. L. R. James and his argument for linking Toussaint Louverture to Fidel Castro, Haiti to Cuba: "The History of the West Indies Is Governed by Two Factors, the Sugar Plantation and Negro Slavery." C. L. R. James, "Appendix: From Toussaint L'Ouverture to Fidel Castro," *The Black Jacobins*, 391.

58. Penelope Gilliat, "The Current Cinema: Last Supper in Havana," *New Yorker*, May 15, 1978, 120.

59. E. H. Gombrich, *The Story of Art* (1950), 16th ed. (London: Phaidon, 1997), 243, 411.

60. Gombrich, *The Story of Art*, 411. For examples of two traditions that, in contradistinction to Velázquez, stress fidelity to precision above all else, consider first the Eyckian tradition with its emphasis on "the most detailed rendering of objects" and second "the piercingly exact vision" of Ingres. See Peter and Linda Murray, *The Penguin Dictionary of Art and Artists*, 7th ed. (London: Penguin, 1997): entry on Eyck, van, 169–72; and entry on Ingres, Jean Auguste Dominique, 264–65. See also Gombrich, *The Story of Art*, 243 and 410–11 (for comparative analysis of van Eyck and Velázquez) and 504 (for discussion of the "cool clarity" and "smooth perfection" of Ingres's work).

61. Miller, "Truth," 63.

62. Julio García Espinosa, "Por un cine imperfecto" ("For an Imperfect Cinema"), first published in *Cine Cubano* (1967), trans. Julianne Burton, repr. *New Latin American Cinema: Volume 1: Theory, Practices and Transcontinental Articulations*, ed. Michael T. Martin (Detroit: Wayne State University Press, 1997), 71–82. For a précis of García Espinosa's essay and consideration of its impact on filmmaking in Cuba, see "Imperfect Cinema and the Seventies," chapter 13 of Chanan, *Cuban Cinema*, 305–31.

63. Chanan, *Cuban Cinema*, 329.

64. On the Haitian Revolution, silencing, and disavowal see Michel-Rolph Trouillot, "An Unthinkable History: The Haitian Revolution as a Non-Event," *Silencing the Past* (Boston: Beacon, 1995), 70–107; and Sibylle Fischer, *Modernity Disavowed: Haiti and the Cultures of Slavery* (Durham, NC: Duke University Press, 2004).

65. Stanley Aronowitz, *False Promises: The Shaping of American Working Class Consciousness* (New York: McGraw Hill, 1973), 116.

66. Fredric Jameson, "Reflections in Conclusion," in *Aesthetics and Politics*, ed. Theodor Adorno et al. (London: Verso, 2007), 211.

67. The existence of comparable factions, which could cross lines of race, color, and class, it should be recalled, are central to an understanding of the course of the Haitian Revolution.

68. Chanan, *Cuban Cinema*, 329; French, "Crucified in Cuba," 14; Schroeder, *Tomás Gutierrrez Alea*, 81–82; Dennis West, "Slavery and Cinema in Cuba: The Case of Gutiérrez Alea's *The Last Supper*," *Western Journal of Black Studies* 3, no. 2 (1979): 129–30.

69. Michael Wood, "*Viridiana*: The Human Comedy," *Criterion Collection: Essays*, May 22, 2006, available at: https://www.criterion.com/current/posts/423.

70. Wood, *The Horrible Gift of Freedom*, 22.

71. West, "Slavery and Cinema in Cuba," 132.

72. Natalie Zemon Davis has noted the depiction of spitting in three slavery films—*Spartacus, Burn!*, and *The Last Supper*—and poses the question of whether Pontecorvo and Alea are "quoting" Spartacus's act of spitting in Crassus's face in Kubrik's film. Davis, *Slaves on Screen*, 2.

73. Oscar Wilde, "The Soul of Man Under Socialism" (1891), available at: https://www.marxists.org/reference/archive/wilde-oscar/soul-man/. Slavoj Žižek is perhaps the most-recent high-profile commentator to repeat Wilde's claim. In his RSA lecture, "First as Tragedy, Then as Farce," Žižek asserted: "The worst slave owners were those who were kind to their slaves and so prevented the core of the system being realised by those who suffered from it, and understood by those who contemplated it." Slavoj Žižek, "First as Tragedy, Then as Farce," RSA Lecture, November 24, 2009, lecture transcript available at: https://www.thersa.org/globalassets/pdfs/blogs/rsa-lecture-slovoj-zizek-transcript.pdf.

74. Shaffer's play, a masterpiece of total theater, tells the story of Pizarro's conquest of Peru in the sixteenth century. Peter Shaffer, *The Royal Hunt of the Sun* (1964; repr., London: Penguin, 2007).

75. Alejo Carpentier, *El reino de este mundo* (1949; repr., Barcelona: Seix Barral, 2008).

76. Aimé Césaire, "An Interview with Aimé Césaire Conducted by René Depestre," in Césaire, *Discourse on Colonialism*, 90.

77. Carpentier, *El reino de este mundo* (*The Kingdom of This World*) (1949).

78. Tomás Gutiérrrez Alea, qtd. in Pick, "Towards a Renewal of Cuban Revolutionary Cinema," 29.

79. Three of the most-celebrated works in this burgeoning subfield are: Edward E. Baptist, *The Half Has Never Been Told: Slavery and the Making of American Capitalism* (New York: Basic Books, 2014); Sven Beckert, *Empire of Cotton: A Global History* (New York: Alfred A. Knopf, 2014); and Walter Johnson, *River of Dark Dreams: Slavery and Empire in the Cotton Kingdom* (Cambridge, MA: Harvard University Press, 2013).

80. Nick Nesbitt, *The Price of Slavery: Capitalism and Revolution in the Caribbean* (Charlottesville: University of Virginia Press, 2022), 31.

81. Peter James Hudson, "The Racist Dawn of Capitalism: Unearthing the Economy of Bondage," *Boston Review*, March 14, 2016, available at: http://bostonreview.net/books-ideas/peter-james-hudson-slavery-capitalism. For another compelling critique of NHC, but from a different angle (its lack of "theoretical clarity"), see Nesbitt, *The Price of* Slavery, 31–36.

Chapter 3

1. *El otro Francisco* (ICAIC, 1974), *Rancheador* (ICAIC, 1976), and *Maluala* (ICAIC, 1979), all dir. Sergio Giral. "Sergio Giral interviewed by María Caridad

Cumaná," in *The Cinema of Sara Gómez: Reframing Revolution*, eds. Susan Lord and María Caridad Cumaná (Bloomington: Indiana University Press, 2021), 83.

2. "Sergio Giral Interviewed by María Caridad Cumaná," 83. Unlike Giral, the scholar Aisha Z. Cort considers *"negrometraje"* a derogatory term. Aisha Z. Cort, "Rethinking Caliban: Shakespeare and Césaire in the *Negrometraje* of Sergio Giral," *Afro-Hispanic Review* 33, no. 2 (2014): 41.

3. Sara Gómez, dir., *De cierta manera* ("One Way or Another") (ICAIC, 1977).

4. The other Black filmmakers working in the ICAIC during this time were Sara Gómez and Nicolás Guillén Landrián, nephew of the Cuban poet Nicolás Guillén.

5. Susan Lord, "Introduction: New Women, Old Worlds," in *The Cinema of Sara Gómez: Reframing Revolution*, eds. Susan Lord and María Caridad Cumaná (Bloomington: Indiana University Press, 2021), 5.

6. Sergio Giral, "Filmmaking within and beyond Fidel's Cuba" [interview with David McIntosh], *Fuse Magazine* 22, no. 1 (1999): 41.

7. Noting that "it has been a commonplace of the scholarly literature on the New Latin American Cinema to point out the movement's stylistic indebtedness to both the Soviet cinematic avant-garde and Italian neorealism" (192), Salazkina's study of the ICAIC's theoretical investments in the 1960s and 1970s has led her to argue that a new and more expansive scholarly assessment of the theoretical basis of the entire New Latin American Cinema is required. See Masha Salazkina, "Transnational Genealogies of Institutional Film Culture of Cuba, 1960s–1970s," in *The Routledge Companion to Latin American Cinema*, eds. Marvin D'Lugo, Ana M. López, and Laura Podalsky (London: Routledge, 2017), 192–203. For a book-length study of the New Latin American Cinema, see Zuzana Pick, *The New Latin American Cinema* (Austin: University of Texas Press, 1993).

8. Cuban directors Héctor Veitia and Julio García Espinosa are also listed as collaborators. In addition, Giral cast many of the same actors that would appear the following year in Alea's *La última cena*. Giral spoke warmly of Alea in an interview conducted by María Caridad Cumaná: "I have a lot of respect for Tomás Gutierréz Alea—he was a good friend. I respect him as a filmmaker because I think he is the best Cuban filmmaker of that period." "Sergio Giral Interviewed by María Caridad Cumaná," 83. Rigoberto López, who worked with Sergio Giral on *El otro Francisco* as a first assistant director, remarked that Alea "was like a mentor" to Giral, "a magnet" to whom he was attracted. "Rigoberto López Interviewed by Víctor Fowler Calzada," in *The Cinema of Sara Gómez: Reframing Revolution*, eds. Susan Lord and María Caridad Cumaná (Bloomington: Indiana University Press, 2021), 264.

9. Ashley Clark, "Sergio Giral: A Giant of Cuban Cinema," *BFI: Features and Reviews*, February 7, 2014, https://www2.bfi.org.uk/news-opinnews-bfi/features/sergio-giral-giant-cuban-cinema.

10. Julianne Burton and Garry Crowdus, "Cuban Cinema and the Afro-Cuban Heritage: An Interview with Sergio Giral," *The Black Scholar* 8, nos. 8–10 (1977): 64.

11. Burton and Crowdus, "Cuban Cinema and the Afro-Cuban Heritage," 64.

12. Burton and Crowdus, "Cuban Cinema and the Afro-Cuban Heritage," 64.

13. Burton and Crowdus, "Cuban Cinema and the Afro-Cuban Heritage," 64.

14. Sergio Giral interview with Pablo Velez, "Close-Up on the Background: A Conversation with Sergio Giral, The Father of Afro-Cuban Cinema," *Abernathy Magazine*, https://abernathymagazine.com/sergio-giral/, accessed September 25, 2019.

15. Ana M. Lopez and Nicholas Peter Humy, "Sergio Giral on Filmmaking in Cuba" [interview], *Black Film Review* 3, no. 1 (1986): 4.

16. Giral, "Filmmaking within and beyond Fidel's Cuba," 39.

17. Lopez and Humy, "Sergio Giral on Filmmaking in Cuba," 4.

18. Lopez and Humy, "Sergio Giral on Filmmaking in Cuba," 4.

19. Lopez and Humy, "Sergio Giral on Filmmaking in Cuba," 4.

20. Lopez and Humy, "Sergio Giral on Filmmaking in Cuba," 4.

21. Giral, "Filmmaking within and beyond Fidel's Cuba," 38.

22. Giral, "Filmmaking within and beyond Fidel's Cuba," 38.

23. Néstor Almendros's credits as a cinematographer include *Days of Heaven* (dir. Terrence Malick, 1978), *Kramer vs. Kramer* (dir. Robert Benton, 1979), and *Sophie's Choice* (dir. Alan J. Pakula, 1982). He would also go on to direct *Mauvaise conduite* ("Improper Conduct"), a documentary film that exposed Cuba's state persecution of homosexuals and which was duly banned in Cuba. Néstor Almendros, *Mauvaise conduit* (France 2 / Les Films du Losange, 1984).

24. Lopez and Humy, "Sergio Giral on Filmmaking in Cuba," 4.

25. Sergio Giral, dir., *Cimarrón* ["Maroon"] (ICAIC, 1967).

26. Giral, "Filmmaking within and beyond Fidel's Cuba," 38.

27. Gott, *Cuba*, 64–67.

28. Sergio Giral, dir., *Plácido* (ICAIC, 1986). *La Escalera*, the name by which the rebellion became known, refers to a simple wooden ladder to which captured rebels were tied and then tortured. See Aisha K. Finch, *Rethinking Slave Rebellion in Cuba: La Escalera and the Insurgencies of 1841–1844* (Chapel Hill: University of North Carolina Press, 2015).

29. Aviva Chomsky, *A History of the Cuban Revolution*, 2nd ed. (Oxford: Wiley Blackwell, 2015), 98; Chanan, *Cuban Film*, 450.

30. Eugenio Hernández Espinosa, "María Antonia," in *Teatro Escogido/ Eugenio Hernández Espinosa*, ed. Inés María Martiatu Terry (Havana: Editorial Letras Cubanas, 2006), 261–368.

31. Sergio Giral, dir., *María Antonia* (ICAIC, 1991). For commentary, see Nadia Sophia Sanko, "Creolizing *Carmen*: Reading Performance in *María Antonia*, Cuba's Overlooked Carmen Adaptation," *Camera Obscura* 27, no. 1 (2012): 157–91;

Leo Cabranes-Grant, "Possession, Gender and Performance in Revolutionary Cuba: Eugenio Hernández Espinosa's *María Antonia*," *Theatre Research International* 35, no. 2 (2010): 126–38.

32. For contextualized English-language information on Sergio Giral and his work, see the index entry on "Giral, Sergio" in Chanan, *Cuban Cinema*. Also see Cort, "Rethinking Caliban," 41–58; Julia Lesage, "*The Other Francisco*: Creating History," *Jump Cut*, no. 30 (1985): 53–58, also available at: https://www.ejumpcut.org/archive/onlinessays/JC30folder/OtherFrancisco.html; and Andrea E. Morris, "Slave Rebellion and Cultural Resistance," *Afro-Cuban Identity in Post-Revolutionary Novel and Film: Inclusion, Loss, and Cultural Resistance* (Lewsiburg: Bucknell University Press, 2012), 39–60. Giral's work continues to attract the attention of Cuban film scholars; see, for example, Adriana Ramírez Gutiérrez, "Relectura cinematográfica de una novela antiesclavista decimonónica. De Francisco a El otro Francisco," *Esclavages & Post-esclavages*, no. 4 (May 2021), https://doi.org/10.4000/slaveries.3794.

33. Julianne Burton provides a concise overview of the shifting organizational context in the ICAIC that was the background to this effort. See Julianne Burton, "Film and Revolution in Cuba: The First Twenty-Five Years," in *Cuba: Twenty-Five Years of Revolution, 1959–1984*, eds. Sandor Halebsky and John M. Kirk (New York: Praegar, 1985), 134–53.

34. Chanan writes that the Congress "brought together about five hundred revolutionary and progressive artists and intellectuals from as many as seventy countries." Chanan, *Cuban Cinema*, 265.

35. I suggest that Giral's trilogy as a whole, and *Rancheador* in particular, endorses C. L. R. James's view: "The race question is subsidiary to the class question in politics, and to think of imperialism in terms of race is disastrous. But to neglect the racial factor as merely incidental is an error only less grave than to make it fundamental." James, *The Black Jacobins*, 283.

36. Anselmo Suárez y Romero, *Francisco: El ingenio o Las delcias del campo* (1839, 1880; repr., Havana: Instituto de Libro, 1970). For analysis, see Lorna Valerie Williams, *The Representation of Slavery in Cuban Fiction* (Columbia: University of Missouri Press, 1994), 52–83. Giral was not the first Cuban artist to critique Suárez's novel by way of retelling it: consider Antonio Zambrana's 1975 novel *El negro Francisco*; for analysis, see Williams, *The Representation of Slavery in Cuban Fiction*, 119–158.

37. Williams, *The Representation of Slavery in Cuban Fiction*, 2.

38. Dennis West, "In the Footsteps of Tomás Gutiérrez Alea," *Cineaste* 35, no. 2 (2010): 18.

39. Vince Canby, "A Cuban *Uncle Tom's Cabin*," *New York Times*, July 1, 1977, 47.

40. FIPRESCI: *Fédération Internationale de la Presse Cinématographique* [International Federation of Film Critics], see http://fipresci.org/awards/1975.

41. For a detailed examination of the cultural and political significance of death in the Black diasporic Atlantic World, see Vincent Brown, *The Reaper's Garden: Death and Power in the World of Atlantic Slavery* (Cambridge, MA: Harvard University Press, 2010).

42. Domingo Del Monte has been described as an "enlightened" slaveholder. Del Monte served as a patron for Suárez and other nineteenth-century Cuban writers, whom he directed to produce literary materials for use by European abolitionists. Williams, *The Representation of Slavery in Cuban Fiction*, 1–2, 57.

43. Chanan, *Cuban Cinema*, 59.

44. C. L. R. James, *The Black Jacobins*, 6–26.

45. Lesage, "The Other Francisco: Creating History."

46. Lesage, "The Other Francisco: Creating History."

47. Lesage, "The Other Francisco: Creating History."

48. Angela Davis, qtd. in Lesage, "The Other Francisco: Creating History."

49. Finch, *Rethinking Slave Rebellion in Cuba*, 40. Moreover, Finch notes that the sporadic available accounts, and the population imbalance along gender lines, also suggest that "Black women also had to be vigilant about sexual exploitation from Black men" (41).

50. Lesage, "The Other Francisco: Creating History."

51. Elise Andaya, *Conceiving Cuba: Reproduction, Women, and the State in the Post-Soviet Era* (New Brunswick: Rutgers University Press, 2014), 42–43, 70; Leila Hessini, "Global Progress in Abortion Advocacy and Policy: An Assessment of the Decade Since ICPD," *Reproductive Health Matters* 13, no. 25 (2005): 88–100; Dobbs v. Jackson Women's Health Organization, 597 U. S. 215 (2022), https://www.supremecourt.gov/opinions/21pdf/19-1392_6j37.pdf.

52. This glimpse of slavery as a thoroughly modern system that is here offered by Giral is elaborated in Manuel Moreno Fraginals, *The Sugar Mill: The Socioeconomic Complex of Sugar in Cuba, 1760–1860*, trans. Cedric Belfrage (New York: Monthly Review, 1976).

53. For an analysis of the retrenchment and intensification of slavery in Cuba as a consequence of the Haitian Revolution, see Ada Ferrer, *Freedom's Mirror: Cuba and Haiti in the Age of Revolution* (New York: Cambridge University Press, 2014). Also see Dolores González-Ripoll, Consuelo Naranjo, Ada Ferrer, Gloria García, and Josef Opatrný, *El rumor de Haití en Cuba: temor, raza y rebeldía, 1789–1844* (Madrid: Consejo Superior de Investigaciones Científicas, 2004).

54. For an account of the transnational networks that transmitted news of the Haitian Revolution and other insurrections and mutinies in this period, see Julius S. Scott, *The Common Wind: Afro-American Currents in the Age of the Haitian Revolution* (New York: Verso, 2018).

55. Gott, *Cuba*, 60–61. Madden's memoranda of his visit to Cuba was published as: Richard Madden, *The Island of Cuba: Its Resources, Progress, and*

Prospects, Considered in Relation Especially to the Influence of Its Prosperity on the Interests of the British West India Colonies (London: C. Gilpin, 1849).

56. Lesage, "The Other Francisco: Creating History."
57. Lesage, "The Other Francisco: Creating History."
58. Marc Silberman, "Brecht encounters 'the system,'" *Stanislavski Studies* 9, no. 1 (2021): 44, 45.
59. Silberman, "Brecht encounters 'the system,'" 46.
60. Georg Lukács, "Realism in the Balance," in *Aesthetics and Politics*, ed. Theodor Adorno et al. (London: Verso, 2007), 34.
61. Georg Lukács, "Realism in the Balance," 36.
62. Georg Lukács, "Realism in the Balance," 36, italics added.
63. Fredric Jameson, "Presentation II" in *Aesthetics and Politics*, ed. Theodor Adorno et al. (London: Verso, 2007), 62–63.
64. Bertolt Brecht, "Against Georg Lukács," in *Aesthetics and Politics*, ed. Theodor Adorno et al. (London: Verso, 2007), 85, 82.
65. Celli, *Gillo Pontecorvo*, 71.
66. Lesage, "The Other Francisco: Creating History."
67. For examination of suicide as a form of Cuban slave resistance, see Louis A. Pérez Jr., *To Die in Cuba: Suicide and Society* (Chapel Hill: University of North Carolina Press, 2012), 25–64.
68. Francisco Estévez, *Diario Del Rancheador* [1837–1842] (Havana: Letras cubanas, 1982).

For analysis, see Lorna V. Williams, "A Cuban Slave Hunter's Journal: Francisco Estévez's *Diario Del Rancheador* (1837–1842)," *Afro-Hispanic Review* 10, no. 3 (1991): 62–66.

69. Williams, "A Cuban Slave Hunter's Journal," 62–65.
70. For an elaboration of the classical mythological symbols of Hercules and the Hydra as analytic devices with which to understand Atlantic history in the age of slavery, see Peter Linebaugh and Marcus Rediker, *The Many-Headed Hydra: Sailors, Slaves, Commoners, and the Hidden History of the Revolutionary Atlantic* (Boston: Beacon, [2000] 2013).
71. Cort, "Rethinking Caliban," 49.
72. *Maluala* received prizes at the São Paulo International Film Festival (1980), the Karlovy Vary International Film Festival (1980), and the inaugural Havana International Festival of New Latin American Cinema (1979).
73. Ashley Clark, "Sergio Giral."
74. Sergio Vitier had worked in the ICAIC's Grupo de Experimentación Sonora from 1969, writing and performing scores for countless ICAIC productions. In 2014, Vitier was the receipient of a Cuban National Music Award. See Pedro de la Hoz, "Farewell to Sergio Vitier, a True, Essential Creator," May 4, 2016, *Granma*, available at: https://en.granma.cu/cultura/2016-05-04/farewell-to-sergio-vitier-a-true-essential-creator.

75. For a concise and rousing defense of the Enlightenment that concludes with an affirmation of its value in the context of the history of Black emancipation, see Terry Eagleton, "The Enlightenment is Dead! Long Live the Enlightenment!" *Harper's Magazine* (March 2005), 91–95.

76. Abbé Raynal, *Histoire des deux Indes (History of the East and West Indies)*, 6 vols. (1770–1779).

77. C. L. R. James, *The Black Jacobins*, 24–25.

78. For historical analysis of this conviction among Haiti's free Black population, see Carolyn Fick, "Emancipation in Haiti: From Plantation Labour to Peasant Proprietorship," *Slavery & Abolition* 21, no. 2 (2000): 11–40. See also Philip Kaisary, "Hercules, the Hydra, and the 1801 Constitution of Toussaint Louverture," *Atlantic Studies* 12, no. 4 (2015): 393–411.

79. Nikolai Bukharin, qtd. in John Quigley, *Soviet Legal Innovation and the Law of the Western World* (Cambridge: Cambridge University Press, 2007), 53.

80. For an account, see C. L. R. James, *The Black Jacobins*, 358–61.

81. Aimé Césaire, *La tragédie du roi Christoph* (Paris: Présence Africaine, 1963); and Aimé Césaire, *Une saison au Congo* [1967] (Paris: Seuil, 1973).

82. Edvard Munch, *The* Scream (1893), The National Museum of Art, Norway.

83. Fredric Jameson, *Postmodernism, or The Cultural Logic of Late Capitalism* (Durham, NC: Duke University Press, 1991), 11.

84. Gott, *Cuba*, 288.

85. Gott, *Cuba*, 288.

86. Giral, "Filmmaking within and beyond Fidel's Cuba," 38.

87. Giral, "Filmmaking within and beyond Fidel's Cuba," 40–41.

88. David Craven, *Art and Revolution in Latin America, 1910–1990* (New Haven: Yale University Press, 2006), 81.

89. Giral, qtd. in Chomsky, *A History of the Cuban Revolution*, 97.

90. Giral, qtd. in Chomsky, *A History of the Cuban Revolution*, 97. See also "Sergio Giral interviewed by María Caridad Cumaná," 84–85.

91. Lopez and Humy, "Sergio Giral on Filmmaking in Cuba," 4.

92. Giral, "Filmmaking within and beyond Fidel's Cuba," 43.

93. Giral, "Filmmaking within and beyond Fidel's Cuba," 41.

Chapter 4

1. For examples, see the discussion of *Amistad, Amazing Grace, Lincoln, Django Unchained,* and *Harriet* in the introduction to this book.

2. Steve McQueen, dir., *12 Years a Slave* (Fox Searchlight, 2013).

3. Solomon Northup, *Twelve Years a Slave* (1853; repr., London: Penguin, 2014).

4. David Denby, "Fighting to Survive: *12 Years a Slave* and *All is Lost*," *New Yorker*, October 14, 2013, https://www.newyorker.com/magazine/2013/10/21/

fighting-to-survive-2; Peter Bradshaw, "*12 Years a Slave*—Review," *Guardian*, January 9, 2014, https://www.theguardian.com/film/2014/jan/09/12-years-a-slave-review.

5. Steve McQueen, dir., *Small Axe* (Turbine Studios / EMU Films, 2020); Steve McQueen, dir., *Hunger* (Icon, 2008); Steve McQueen, dir., *Shame* (Momentum, 2011).

6. For examples, see, Cameron Bailey, "Survival, *Hunger* and *Shame*," in *Steve McQueen: Works 1993–2012*, eds. James Rondeau et al. (Heidelberg / Berlin: Kehrer Verlag, 2012), 184–90; and Jean Fisher, "McQueen's Dialogues with the Image of Precarious Life," essay commissioned by Espace Louis Vuitton Tokyo on the occasion of the exhibition "Steve McQueen," April 26–August 17, 2014, available at https://www.jeanfisher.com/steve-mcqueens-dialogues-with-the-image-of-precarious-life/.

7. In addition to the 2013 Academy Award for *12 Years a Slave* in the category of Best Picture, McQueen's numerous awards include the Turner Prize (1999), the Camera d'Or at Cannes (2008), a W. E. B. Du Bois medal (2014), and a British Film Institute Fellowship (2016).

8. "Power 100 List. No. 36: Steve McQueen," *Art Review* (November 2013): 116.

9. Stephanie Li, "*12 Years a Slave* as a Neo-Slave Narrative," *American Literary History* 26, no. 2 (2014): 336.

10. Sue Eakin and Joseph Lodgson, introduction to *Twelve Years a Slave*, Solomon Northup, eds. Sue Eatkin and Joseph Logsdon (1853; repr., Baton Rouge: Louisiana State University Press, 1968), xvi. It is also noteworthy that Solomon Northup dedicated his narrative to Harriet Beecher Stowe and that he offers his narrative as "another key to *Uncle Tom's Cabin*" (dedication page, xvii; Penguin 2014 ed.).

11. Li, "*12 Years a Slave* as a Neo-Slave Narrative," 336.

12. Daniel J. Sharfstein, *The Invisible Line: A Secret History of Race in America* (New York: Penguin, 2011), 57, 87. For further analysis of the Fugitive Slave Act of 1850, see Richard J. M. Blackett, *Making Freedom: The Underground Railroad and the Politics of Slavery* (Chapel Hill: University of North Carolina Press, 2013), 32–67.

13. Sharfstein, *The Invisible Line*, 58.

14. Sharfstein, *The Invisible Line*, 58.

15. Paul Gilroy, "*12 Years a Slave*: In Our 'Post-Racial' Age the Legacy of Slavery Lives On," *Guardian*, November 10, 2013, https://www.theguardian.com/commentisfree/2013/nov/10/12-years-a-slave-mcqueen-film-legacy-slavery.

16. Thomas Doherty, "Bringing the Slave Narrative to Screen: Steve McQueen and John Ridley's Searing Depiction of America's 'Peculiar Institution,'" *Cineaste* 39, no. 1 (2013): 4.

17. For examples of how McQueen sought to connect his *12 Years a Slave* project to contemporary politics and realities inherited from slavery, see Nelson George, "An Essentially American Narrative: A Discussion of Steve McQueen's Film *12 Years a Slave*," *New York Times*, October 11, 2013, https://www.nytimes.

com/2013/10/13/movies/a-discussion-of-steve-mcqueens-film-12-years-a-slave.html.

18. Ban Ki-Moon, "Remarks at Screening of *12 Years a Slave*," United Nations, New York, February 26, 2014, https://www.un.org/sg/en/content/sg/speeches/2014-02-26/remarks-screening-12-years-slave.

19. Steve McQueen, dir., *Caribs' Leap* [Two screens: (1) Film and sound installation; (2) Film, no sound], Tate Modern (2002); Steve McQueen, dir., *Western Deep* [Film and sound installation], Tate Modern (2002); Steve McQueen, dir., *Gravesend* [Film and sound installation], Museum of Modern Art (MoMA) (2007).

20. For additional stills from and analysis of these and other art films and video installations by McQueen, see the following exhibition catalogues: James Lingwood, ed., *Caribs' Leap/Western Deep: Steve McQueen*,(London: Artangel, 2002); and James Rondeau, et al., eds., *Steve McQueen: Works 1993–2012* (Heidelberg / Berlin: Kehrer Verlag, 2012).

21. James Rondeau, "Blues Before Sunrise," in *Steve McQueen: Works 1993–2012*, 182.

22. Interview with Hans Zimmer. DVD Special Feature: "The Score." Steve McQueen, dir., *12 Years a Slave*,(2013).

23. William L. Andrews, "Introduction to the Scholarly Bibliography of Slave and Ex-Slave Narratives," North American Slave Narratives, Documenting the American South, University Library, University of North Carolina, https://docsouth.unc.edu/neh/biblintro.html.

24. Frederick Douglass, *Narrative of the Life of Frederick Douglass, An American Slave* (1845; repr., New York: Penguin, 2014); Harriet Jacobs, *Incidents in the Life of a Slave Girl* (1861; repr., New York: Norton, 2001); Olaudah Equiano, *The Interesting Narrative and Other Writings* (1789; repr., New York: Penguin, 2003).

25. Eakin and Lodgson, introduction to *Twelve Years a Slave*, xi.

26. As Eakin and Lodgson also note, "the abduction of a free Negro adult from the North and his enslavement in the South . . . provides a sensational element which cannot be matched in any of the dozens of narratives written by former slaves." Eakin and Lodgson, introduction to *Twelve Years a Slave*, ix.

27. Steve McQueen and Henry Louis Gates Jr., "Steve McQueen and Henry Louis Gates Jr. Talk *12 Years a Slave*, Part 3," interview by Henry Louis Gates, Jr., *The Root*, December 26, 2013, www.theroot.com/steve-mcqueen-and-henry-louis-gates-jr-talk-12-years-a-1790899474.

28. Eakin and Lodgson, introduction to *Twelve Years a Slave*, xii–xiii.

29. Dan. P. Lee, "Where It Hurts: Steve McQueen on Why *12 Years a Slave* Isn't Just About Slavery," *Vulture*, December 8, 2013, https://www.vulture.com/2013/12/steve-mcqueen-talks-12-years-a-slave.html.

30. Wilson, editors preface to in Solomon Northup, *Twelve Years a Slave*, by Solomon Northup, eds. Sue Eakin and Joseph Logsdon (1853; repr., Baton Rouge: Louisiana State University Press, 1968), xxx–vii.

31. Northup, *Twelve Years a Slave*, 5.
32. Northup, *Twelve Years a Slave*, 5.
33. Northup, *Twelve Years a Slave*, 6, 6–7.
34. Northup, *Twelve Years a Slave*, 140.
35. Northup, *Twelve Years a Slave*, 142.
36. Doherty, "Bringing the Slave Narrative to Screen," 5.
37. Walter Johnson, *Soul by Soul: Life Inside the Antebellum Slave Market* (Cambridge, MA: Harvard University Press, 1999), 67.
38. Northup, *Twelve Years a Slave*, 11.
39. Northup, *Twelve Years a Slave*, 13.
40. Leon F. Litwack's *North of Slavery* remains the classic account of racism and oppression in the antebellum "free states." Leon F. Litwack, *North of Slavery: The Negro in the Free States, 1790–1860* (Chicago: University of Chicago Press, 1961).
41. Northup, *Twelve Years a Slave*, 135.
42. Northup, *Twelve Years a Slave*, 37–40, 107–13.
43. Eakin and Logsdon, introduction to *Twelve Years a Slave*, xvi.
44. Northup, *Twelve Years a Slave*, 138, 140.
45. Northup, *Twelve Years a Slave*, 57.
46. William Faulkner, *Absalom, Absalom!* [1936] (1935; repr, New York: Vintage, 1986).
47. Northup, *Twelve Years a Slave*, 135.
48. James, *The Black Jacobins*, 35.
49. Lee, "Where It Hurts."
50. Li, "*12 Years a Slave* as a Neo-Slave Narrative," 328.
51. Northup, *Twelve Years a Slave*, 163–64.
52. Northup, *Twelve Years a Slave*, 164–65.
53. "Danny Glover's Haiti Film Lacked 'White Heroes,' Producers Said," *Dominican Today*, July 26, 2008, https://web.archive.org/web/20160313065531/http://dominicantoday.com/dr/this-and-that/2008/7/26/28807/danny-glovers-haiti-film-lacked-white-heroes-producers-said.
54. Melissa Anderson, "Image Conscience," *Art Forum*, October 27, 2013, https://www.artforum.com/film/melissa-anderson-on-steve-mcqueen-s-12-years-a-slave-43508.
55. Ed Gonzalez, "*12 Years a Slave*: Review," *Slant Magazine*, September 14, 2013, https://www.slantmagazine.com/film/12-years-a-slave/.
56. Nick Nesbitt, *Voicing Memory: History and Subjectivity in French Caribbean Literature* (Charlottesville: University of Virginia Press, 2003), 207.
57. See, for example, McQueen and Henry Louis Gates Jr., "Steve McQueen and Henry Louis Gates Jr. Talk *12 Years a Slave*"; and Rob Nelson, "Steve McQueen: 'I Want to Be Useful,'" *Walker Magazine*, November 9, 2013, https://walkerart.org/magazine/steve-mcqueen-i-want-be-useful.

58. Paul Moakley, "Behind the Moving Image: The Cinematography of *12 Years a Slave*," *Time Magazine Lightbox*, February 27, 2014, https://time.com/3807491/behind-the-moving-image-the-cinematography-of-12-years-a-slave/.

59. Nelson, "Steve McQueen: 'I Want to Be Useful.'"

60. Northup, *Twelve Years a Slave*, 159.

61. Melvyn Stokes, "From *Uncle Tom* to Nat Turner: An Overview of Slavery in American Film, 1903–2016," *Transatlantica*, no. 1 (2018): 9, https://doi.org/10.4000/transatlantica.12814.

62. Thomas McEvilley, "Documenta 11," *Frieze*, no. 69 (2002), https://www.frieze.com/article/documenta-11.

63. On "slow" violence, see Rob Nixon, *Slow Violence and the Environmentalism of the Poor* (Cambridge, MA: Harvard University Press, 2013).

64. Joanne Laurier, "*12 Years a Slave* and Other Films," *World Socialist Web Site*, September 22, 2013, https://www.wsws.org/en/articles/2013/09/23/tff2-s23.html.

65. For a theorization of the relationship between slavery and modern capitalist modernity that moves beyond "the customary economic notion of slavery and capitalism as mere functional regimes of commercial production," Nesbitt, *The Price of Slavery*, 2–3.

66. Dana Stevens, "*12 Years a Slave*: A Beautiful Film about the Ugliest of Subjects," *Slate*, October 17, 2013, http://www.slate.com/articles/arts/movies/2013/10/_12_years_a_slave_directed_by_steve_mcqueen_reviewed.html.

67. Wood, *Blind Memory*, 38–40, 230–32.

68. McQueen and Henry Louis Gates Jr., "Steve McQueen and Henry Louis Gates Jr. Talk *12 Years a Slave*."

69. Laurier, "*12 Years a Slave*."

70. The film has attracted much praise for its alleged didacticism. See, for example, Richard Brody, "Should a Film Try to Depict Slavery?" *New Yorker*, October 21, 2013, https://www.newyorker.com/culture/richard-brody/should-a-film-try-to-depict-slavery.

71. Laurier, "*12 Years a Slave*"; Melvyn Stokes, "From Uncle Tom to Nat Turner: An Overview of Slavery in American Film, 1903–2016," *Transatlantica*, no. 1 (2019): 11, https://doi.org/10.4000/transatlantica.13801.

72. Jasmine Nichole Cobb, "Directed by Himself: Steve McQueen's *12 Years a Slave*," *American Literary History* 26, no. 2 (2014): 343.

73. Stokes, "From Uncle Tom to Nat Turner," 10.

74. Cobb, "Directed by Himself," 343.

75. Michael Wood, "At The Movies," *London Review of Books* 36, no. 3 (February 6, 2014): 23.

76. Julian Carrington, "12 Years a Slave," *Cinema Scope*, no. 57 (2014): 75.

77. Greg Grandin, "Capitalism and Slavery," *The Nation*, May 1, 2015, www.thenation.com/article/capitalism-and-slavery/.

78. David Simon and Eric Overmyer, dirs., *Tremé* (HBO, 2010–2013); Lars von Trier, dir., *Manderlay* (Zentropa, 2005).

79. Stephen Shapiro, "Realignment and Televisual Intellect: The Telepraxis of Class Alliances in Contemporary Subscription Television Drama," in *Class Divisions in Serial Television*, eds. Sieglinde Lemke and Wibke Schniedermann (London: Palgrave Macmillan, 2016), 187–89.

80. For analysis of forms of labor control and exploitation that developed in the wake of abolition (in the context of cotton cultivation, sharecropping was the dominant form), see Sven Beckert, "Emancipation and Empire: Reconstructing the Worldwide Web of Cotton Production in the Age of the American Civil War," *American Historical Review* 109, no. 5 (2004): 1405–38, esp. 1424.

81. Tate Taylor, dir., *The Help* (Walt Disney, 2011); Quentin Tarantino, dir., *Django Unchained* (Columbia Pictures, 2012); Amma Asante, dir., *Belle* (Fox Searchlight Pictures, 2013); Lee Daniels, dir., *The Butler* (Weinstein, 2013); Ava DuVernay, dir., *Selma* (Paramount Pictures, 2014).

Conclusion

1. Herbert Marcuse, *The Aesthetic Dimension: Toward a Critique of Marxist Aesthetics* (Boston: Beacon Press, 1978), 73.

2. C. L. R. James, *The Black Jacobins* (1938, 2nd ed. rev. 1963; New York: Vintage, 1989), xi.

Bibliography

Visual Materials

Film, Television, Documentary

Almendros, Néstor, dir. *Mauvaise conduit*. 1984. France. France 2 / Les Films du Losange.
Asante, Amma, dir. *Belle*. 2013. UK. DJ Films / Isle of Man Film / BFI / Metrol Technology / Pinewood Studios.
Benton, Robert, dir. *Kramer vs. Kramer*. 1979. USA. Columbia Pictures.
Biberman, Herbert, dir. *Slaves*. 1969. USA. Slaves Company / Theatre Guild.
Buñuel, Luis, dir. *Viridiana*. 1961. Spain / Mexico. Unión Industrial Cinematográfica / Producciones Gustavo Alatriste / Films 59.
Burnett, Charles, dir. *Nightjohn*. 1996. USA. RHI Entertainment / Disney Channel Productions.
———, dir. *Nat Turner: A Troublesome Property*. 2003 USA. Subpix / KQED Public Television / ITVS California Newsreel.
Bush, Gerard, and Christopher Renz, dirs. *Antebellum*. 2020. USA. Lionsgate / QC Entertainment.
Carver, Steve, dir. *Drum*. 1976. USA. United Artists.
Coppola, Francis Ford, dir. *Apocalypse Now*. 1979. USA. United Artists.
Craven, Wes, dir. *The Serpent and the Rainbow*. 1987. USA. MCA / Universal Pictures.
Daniels, Lee, dir. *The Butler*. 2013. USA. Follow Through Productions et al.
Deslauriers, Guy, dir. *Le passage du milieu*. 1999. France / Senegal / Martinique. Les Films du Raphia.
———, dir. *The Middle Passage*. 2003. USA. HBO Video.
Diegues, Carlos, dir. *Ganga Zumba*. 1963. Brazil. Copacabana Filmes / Tabajara Filmes.
———, dir. *Xica da Silva*. 1976. Brazil. Embrafilme / Terra Filmes.
———, dir. *Quilombo*. 1984. Brazil. CDK / Embrafilme / Gaumont.

DuVernay, Ava, dir. *Selma*. 2014. UK / France / USA. Pathé / Harpo / Plan B et al.
Fleischer, Richard, dir. *Mandingo*. 1975. USA. Paramount Pictures.
Fleming, Victor, dir. *Gone with the Wind*. 1939. USA. Selznick International Pictures / MGM.
Gerima, Haile, dir. *Sankofa*. 1993. USA / Ghana / Burkina Faso / UK / Germany / Ethiopia. Mypheduh Films.
Giral, Sergio, dir. *Cimarrón*. 1967. Cuba. Instituto Cubano del Arte e Industria Cinematográficos.
———, dir. *El otro Francisco*. 1974. Cuba. Instituto Cubano del Arte e Industria Cinematográficos.
———, dir. *Rancheador*. 1976. Cuba. Instituto Cubano del Arte e Industria Cinematográficos.
———, dir. *Maluala*. 1979. Cuba. Instituto Cubano del Arte e Industria Cinematográficos.
———, dir. *Plácido*. 1986. Cuba. Instituto Cubano del Arte e Industria Cinematográficos.
———, dir. *María Antonia*. 1991. Cuba. Instituto Cubano del Arte e Industria Cinematográficos.
———, dir. *La imagen rota*. 1995. USA. Global Image Group.
———, dir. *Chronicle of an Ordinance*. 2000. USA. Giral Films.
———, dir. *Al Bárbaro del Ritmo*. 2004. Re Gu Productions.
———, dir. *Dos Veces Ana*. 2010. Giral Media Production.
Gómez, Sara, dir. *Y . . . temenos sabor*. 1968. Cuba. Instituto Cubano del Arte e Industria Cinematográficos.
———, dir. *De cierta manera*. 1977. Cuba. Instituto Cubano del Arte e Industria Cinematográficos.
Griffith, D. W. dir. *The Birth of a Nation*. 1915. USA. David W. Griffith Corp.
Gutiérrez Alea, Tomás, dir. *Cumbite*, 1964. Cuba. Instituto Cubano del Arte e Industria Cinematográficos.
———, dir. *La muerte de un burócrata*. 1966. Cuba. Instituto Cubano del Arte e Industria Cinematográficos.
———, dir. *Memorias del subdesarrollo*. 1968. Cuba. Instituto Cubano del Arte e Industria Cinematográficos.
———, dir. *La última cena*. 1976. Cuba. Instituto Cubano del Arte e Industria Cinematográficos.
———, dir. *Los sobrevivientes*. 1979. Cuba. Instituto Cubano del Arte e Industria Cinematográficos.
Halperin, Victor, dir. *White Zombie*. 1932. USA. United Artists.
Ibarra, Mirtha, dir. *Titón: De la Habana a Guantanamera*. 2008. Spain. Brothers & Sisters.
Jenkins, Barry, dir. *The Underground Railroad*. 2021. USA. Amazon Studios.
Kubrik, Stanley, dir. *Spartacus*. 1960. USA. Bryna Productions.

Lemmons, Kasi, dir. *Harriet*. 2019. USA. Focus Features.
Malick, Terrence, dir. *Days of Heaven*. 1978. USA. Paramount Pictures.
Micheaux, Oscar, dir. *Within Our Gates*. 1920. USA. Micheaux Book & Film Company.
McQueen, Steve, dir. *Hunger*. 2008. UK / Ireland. Film4 / Channel 4 Film.
———, dir. *Shame*. 2011. UK / Canada / USA. Searchlight Pictures / Film4 / UK Film Council.
———, dir. *12 Years a Slave*. 2013. UK / USA. New Regency Productions / River Road / Plan B.
———, dir. *Small Axe*. 2020. Five-film TV miniseries. UK. BBC Films.
Pakula, Alan J., dir. *Sophie's Choice*. 1982. UK / USA. ITC Entertainment / Keith Barish Productions.
Pontecorvo, Gillo, dir. *The Battle of Algiers*. 1966. Italy / Algeria. Igor Film / Casbah Film.
———, dir. *Burn!*; aka *Queimada*. 1969. France / Italy. Produzioni Europee Associati / United Artists.
———, dir. *Kapò*. 1960. Italy / France / Yugoslavia. Cineriz / Vides Cinematografica / Zebra Films.
———, dir. *Ogro*. 1979. Italy / Spain. Vides Cinematografica / Sabre Films.
Porter, Edwin S., dir. *Uncle Tom's Cabin*. 1903. USA. Edison Manufacturing.
———, dir. *The Great Train Robbery*. 1903. USA. Edison Manufacturing.
Rock, Chris, dir. *Top Five*. 2014. USA. Paramount Pictures.
Sayles, John, dir. *Brother from Another Planet*. 1984. USA. Cinecom Pictures.
Simon, David, and Eric Overmyer, dirs. *Tremé*. 2010–2013. Four seasons. USA. HBO.
Solás, Humberto, dir. *El siglo de las luces / La siècle des lumières*. 1992. France / Cuba. Ekran / France 3 / Instituto Cubano del Arte e Industria Cinematográficos.
Spielberg, Steven, dir. *Amistad*. 1997. USA. DreamWorks.
———, dir. *Lincoln*. 2012. USA. DreamWorks.
Stahl, John M., dir. *The Foxes of Harrow*. USA. 20th Century Fox.
Tabío, Juan Carlos, dir. *Miriam Makeba*. 1973. Cuba. Instituto Cubano del Arte e Industria Cinematográficos.
Taylor, Tate, dir. *The Help*. 2011. USA. Walt Disney.
Tarantino, Quentin, dir. *Django Unchained*. 2012. USA. Columbia Pictures.
Trier, Lars von, dir. *Manderlay*. 2005. Denmark / Sweden / Netherlands / France / Germany / UK / Italy / USA. Zentropa.
Walsh, Raoul, dir. *Band of Angels*. 1957. USA. Warner Bros.

Artworks

Bernard, Lili. *Carlota Leading the People (after Eugene Delacroix's Liberty Leading the People, 1830)*. 2011. Oil on canvas.

———. *Carlota Slaying the Slaver (after Artimesia Gentilesch's Judith Slaying Holofernes, 1612)*. 2016. Oil on canvas.

Botticini, Francesco. *Saint Sebastian*. c. 1473–1474. Tempera and oil on wood. Metropolitan Museum of Art, New York.

Cartier-Bresson, Henri. *Martin Luther King. Atlanta*. 1961. Black-and-white photograph. Foundation Henri Cartier-Bresson.

Cauvin, François. *Toussaint Louverture*. 2009. Medium and location unknown.

Delpech, François Séraphin. Engraving of Nicolas-Eustache Maurin's *Toussaint L'Ouverture*. 1832. National Portrait Gallery, London.

Donkor, Kimathi. *Toussaint L'Ouverture at Bedourete*. 2004. Oil on linen. Collection of the artist.

Duval-Carrié, Edouard. *Memory #1*. 2017. Mixed media embedded in resin. Location unknown.

Fisher, Carl. *Muhammad Ali as Saint Sebastian*. Photograph 1967 (photographed), ca. 2004 (printed). Victoria and Albert Museum, London.

Girodet, Anne-Louis. *Portrait of Citizen Belley*. 1797. Oil on canvas. Châteaux de Versailles et de Trianon, Versailles.

Hirst, Damien. *Saint Sebastian, Exquisite Pain*. 2007. Glass, painted stainless steel, silicone, arrows, crossbow bolts, stainless steel cable and clamps, stainless steel carabiner, bullock, and formaldehyde solution. Private collection.

Lawrence, Jacob. "General Toussaint L'Ouverture." *The Life of Toussaint L'Ouverture, No. 20*. 1938. Tempera on paper. Aaron Douglas Collection, Amistad Research Center, Tulane University, New Orleans.

———. "Toussaint Captured." *The Life of Toussaint L'Ouverture, No. 17*. 1938. Tempera on paper. Aaron Douglas Collection, Amistad Research Center, Tulane University, New Orleans.

Light, Bob, and John Houston. *"Gone with the Wind" (Ronald Reagan; Margaret Thatcher)*. Printed by East End Offset Ltd, published by Socialist Workers Party, offset lithograph printed in blue and red, 1981 or after. 24.5" × 17.75" (617 mm x 452 mm). National Portrait Gallery, London.

McQueen, Steve. *Caribs' Leap*. Super 8mm color film video and sound installation, two screens. Tate Modern, London, 2002.

———. *Gravesend*. 35mm color film, transferred to HD digital format. Video and sound installation. Museum of Modern Art, New York, 2007.

———. *Western Deep*. Super 8mm color film video and sound installation. Tate Modern, London, 2002.

Munch, Edvard. *The Scream*. 1893. National Museum of Art, Norway.

Rodriguez Valdes, Elio. *Gone with the Macho*. Las Perlas de tu boca. 1995 Silkscreen on paper, 27.5" × 19.5", edition of 8. 1995. Elio Rodriguez and 532 Gallery Thomas Jaeckel, New York.

Tour, Georges de La. *Saint Sebastian Tended by Saint Irene*. 1649. Oil on canvas. Louvre, Paris.

Velázquez, Diego. *Portrait of Juan de Pareja.* c. 1650. Metropolitan Museum of Art, New York.

Primary Printed Materials

Case Law, Statute Law, Legal Documents

An Act for the Abolition of the Slave Trade. (UK). 1807. 47 George 3 session 1 c.36.
Clay v. United States, 403 U.S. 698 (1971).
Dobbs v. Jackson Women's Health Organization, 597 U.S. 215 (2022).
Plessy v. Ferguson 163 U.S. 537 (1896).
Report of the United Nations High Commissioner for Human Rights [Michelle Bachelet]. "Racism, Racial Discrimination, Xenophobia and Related Forms of Intolerance, Follow-Up to and Implementation of the Durban Declaration and Programme of Action." A/HRC/47/53, June 21–July 9, 2021.
Scott v. Sandford 60 U.S. 393 (1856).
United States v. The Amistad, 40 U.S. 15 Pet. 518 (1841).
U.S. Constitution amend. XIII. 1865.

Books, Essays, Speeches

Authorized King James Bible with Apocrypha. Oxford: Oxford University Press, 2008.
Carpentier, Alejo. *El reino de este mundo.* 1949. Barcelona: Seix Barral, 2008.
———. *Explosion in a Cathedral.* 1962. Translated by John Sturrock. Minneapolis: University of Minnesota Press, 2001.
Césaire, Aimé. *Notebook of a Return to My Native Land / Cahier d'un retour au pays natal.* 1939. Translated by Mireille Rosello with Annie Pritchard. Newcastle upon Tyne: Bloodaxe, 1995.
Césaire, Aimé. *La tragédie du roi Christophe.* Paris: Présence Africaine, 1963.
———. *Une saison au Congo.* 1967. Paris: Seuil, 1973.
Conrad, Joseph. *Heart of Darkness.* 1899. New York: Norton 5th ed., edited by Paul B. Armstrong, 2017.
Douglass, Frederick. *Narrative of the Life of Frederick Douglass, An American Slave.* 1845. New York: Penguin, 2014.
Dixon Jr., Thomas. *The Clansman: An Historical Romance of the Ku Klux Klan.* 1905. Lexington: University Press of Kentucky, 1970.
Du Bois, W. E. B. *The Suppression of the African Slave Trade to the United States of America.* 1896. New York: Oxford University Press, 2014.
Equiano, Olaudah. *The Interesting Narrative and Other Writings.* 1789. New York: Penguin, 2003.

Estévez, Francisco. *Diario Del Rancheador*. 1837–1842. Havana: Letras cubanas, 1982.
Fanon, Frantz. "Address to the First Congress of Negro Writers and Artists." 1956. Reprinted as "Racism and Culture" in *Toward the African Revolution* by Frantz Fanon. Translated by Haakon Chevalier. New York: Grove Press, 1967.
———, *Les damnés de la terre*. Paris: Présence Africaine, 1961.
———. *Peau noire, masques blancs*. Paris: Éditions du Seuil, 1952.
———. *The Wretched of the Earth*. 1961. Translated by Richard Philcox. New York: Grove Press, 2004.
Fast, Howard. *Spartacus*. 1951. London: Routledge, 1996.
Faulkner, William. *Absalom, Absalom!* 1936. New York: Vintage, 1986.
García Lorca, Federico. *Poet in New York*. Edited by Christopher Maurer, 2nd ed. New York: Noonday Press, 1998.
Jacobs, Harriet. *Incidents in the Life of a Slave Girl*. 1861. New York: Norton, 2001.
Hernández Espinosa, Eugenio. "María Antonia." 1967. In *Teatro Escogido / Eugenio Hernández Espinosa*, edited by Inés María Martiatu Terry. Havana: Editorial Letras Cubanas, 2006, 261–368.
Hughes, Langston. "Moscow and Me." July 1933. *The Collected Works of Langston Hughes: Vol. 9: Essays on Art, Race, Politics, and World Affairs*. Edited by Christopher C. De Santis. Columbia: University of Missouri Press, 2002, 56–64.
James, C. L. R. *The Black Jacobins*. 1938. 2nd ed. rev. 1963. New York: Vintage, 1989.
———. *A History of Negro Revolt*. London: Fact, 1938.
Ki-Moon, Ban, "Remarks at Screening of *12 Years a Slave*." United Nations. New York. February 26, 2014. https://www.un.org/sg/en/content/sg/speeches/2014-02-26/remarks-screening-12-years-slave.
Madden, Richard. *The Island of Cuba: Its Resources, Progress, and Prospects, Considered in Relation Especially to the Influence of Its Prosperity on the Interests of the British West India Colonies*. London: C. Gilpin, 1849.
Mann, Thomas. *Death in Venice*. 1912. Translated by Michael Henry Heim. New York: Harper Collins, 2004.
Northup, Solomon. *Twelve Years a Slave*. 1853. Edited by Sue Eakin and Joseph Logsdon. Baton Rouge: Louisiana State University Press, 1968.
Northup, Solomon. *Twelve Years a Slave*. 1853. London: Penguin, 2014.
Roumain, Jacques. *Masters of the Dew*. 1944. Translated by Langston Hughes and John Mercer 1947. Oxford: Heinemann, 1978.
Raynal, Guillaume Thomas François. *Histoire philosophique et politique des établissemens et du commerce des Européens dans les deux Indes*. 1770–1779. 8 vols. Genève: Pellet, 1780.
Seabrook, William. *The Magic Island*. 1929. London: George G. Harrap, 1931.
Shaffer, Peter. *The Royal Hunt of the Sun*. 1964. London: Penguin, 2007.

Solanas, Fernando, and Octavio Getino, "Towards a Third Cinema: Notes and Experiences for The Development of a Cinema of Liberation in the Third World." 1969. In *Twenty-Five Years of the New Latin American Cinema*, edited by Michael Chanan. London: BFI, 1983, 17–27.
Suárez y Romero, Anselmo. *Francisco: El ingenio o Las delcias del campo*. 1839, 1880. Havana: Instituto de Libro, 1970.
Voraigne, Jacobus de. *The Golden Legend*. c. 1260. London: Penguin, 1998.
Wilde, Oscar. "The Soul of Man Under Socialism." 1891. https://www.marxists.org/reference/archive/wilde-oscar/soul-man/.
Williams, Eric. *Capitalism and Slavery*. 1944. Chapel Hill: University of North Carolina Press, 1994.

Miscellaneous Secondary Materials

Andersen, Kurt. Radio interview with George Lois. "Art and Advertising with George Lois." WNYC: New York Public Radio, August 28, 2004. https://www.wnyc.org/story/107063-art-and-advertising-with-george-lois/.

Secondary Printed Materials

"The Birth of a Nation." *American Film Institute Catalog*. https://catalog.afi.com/Film/1826-THE-BIRTHOFANATION?sid=175416d2-788a-4066-b7fc-cca3c67c165d&sr=11.512245&cp=1&pos=0.
"Danny Glover's Haiti Film Lacked 'White Heroes,' Producers Said." *Dominican Today*, July 26, 2008. https://web.archive.org/web/20160313065531/http://dominicantoday.com/dr/this-and-that/2008/7/26/28807/danny-glovers-haiti-film-lacked-white-heroes-producers-said.
"Power 100 List. No. 36: Steve McQueen." *Art Review* (November 2013): 116.
Adorno, Theodor et al., *Aesthetics and Politics*. With an afterword by Fredric Jameson. London: Verso, 2007.
Andaya, Elise. *Conceiving Cuba: Reproduction, Women, and the State in the Post-Soviet Era*. New Brunswick: Rutgers University Press, 2014.
Anderson, Melissa. "Image Conscience." *Art Forum*, October 27, 2013. https://www.artforum.com/film/melissa-anderson-on-steve-mcqueen-s-12-years-a-slave-43508.
Anderson, Reynaldo, D. L. Stephenson, and Chante Anderson. " 'Crowdsourcing' 'The Bad-Ass Slave': A Critique of Quentin Tarantino's *Django Unchained*." In *Quentin Tarantino's Django Unchained: The Continuation of Metacinema*, edited by Oliver C. Speck. New York: Bloomsbury Academic, 2014, 227–42.

Andrew, Geoff. *"Queimada! (Burn!)."* In *Time Out Film Guide*, edited by John Pym. London: Time Out Guides, 2011, 865–66.
Andrews, William L. "Introduction to the Scholarly Bibliography of Slave and Ex-Slave Narratives." North American Slave Narratives, Documenting the American South. University Library, University of North Carolina. https://docsouth.unc.edu/neh/biblintro.html.
Aptheker, Herbert. *American Negro Slave Revolts*. New York: Columbia University Press, 1943.
Aptheker, Herbert. "American Negro Slave Revolts." *Science & Society* 1, no. 4 (1937): 512–38.
Aronowitz, Stanley. *False Promises: The Shaping of American Working Class Consciousness* New York: McGraw Hill, 1973.
Baptist, Edward E. *The Half Has Never Been Told: Slavery and the Making of American Capitalism*. New York: Basic Books, 2014.
Beckert, Sven. "Emancipation and Empire: Reconstructing the Worldwide Web of Cotton Production in the Age of the American Civil War." *American Historical Review* 109, no. 5 (2004): 1405–38.
———. *Empire of Cotton: A Global History*. New York: Alfred A. Knopf, 2014.
Berman, Marshall. *All That Is Solid Melts Into Air: The Experience of Modernity*. 1982. New York: Penguin, 1988.
Bettelheim, Judith. *AfroCuba: Works on Paper, 1968–2003*. San Francisco: San Francisco State University, 2005.
Blackett, Richard J. M. *Making Freedom: The Underground Railroad and the Politics of Slavery*. Chapel Hill: University of North Carolina Press, 2013.
Blasini, Gilberto M. "The Last Supper (1976): Cinema, History, and Decolonization." In *Film Analysis: A Norton Reader*, edited by Jeffrey Geiger and R. L. Rutsky. New York: Norton, 2005, 678–94.
Blight, David. *Race and Reunion: The Civil War in American Memory*. Cambridge, MA: Harvard University Press, 2001.
Bogle, Donald. *Toms, Coons, Mulattoes, Mammies, and Bucks: An Interpretative History of Blacks in America Films*. 1973. 5th edition, updated and expanded. New York: Bloomsbury, 2016.
Bradshaw, Peter. *"The Birth of a Nation* Review—Biblical Passion and Cheesy Emotion." December 8, 2016. https://www.theguardian.com/film/2016/dec/08/the-birth-of-a-nation-review-nat-turner-nate-parker.
———. "*Django Unchained: First Look Review*." *Guardian*, December 12, 2012. https://www.theguardian.com/film/2012/dec/12/django-unchained-first-look-review.
———. "*12 Years a Slave*—Review." *Guardian*, January 9, 2014. https://www.theguardian.com/film/2014/jan/09/12-years-a-slave-review.
Brando, Marlon, with Robert Lindsey. *Brando: Songs My Mother Taught Me*. New York: Random House, 1994.

Brecht, Bertolt. "Against Georg Lukács." Translated by Stuart Hood. In *Aesthetics and Politics*, eds. Theodor Adorno et al. London: Verso, 2007, 68–85.
Brennan, Timothy. *Places of Mind: A Life of Edward Said*. New York: Farrar, Straus, and Giroux, 2021.
Brody, Richard. "The Cinematic Merits and Flaws of Nate Parker's *The Birth of a Nation*." *New Yorker*, October 9, 2016. https://www.newyorker.com/culture/richard-brody/the-cinematic-merits-and-flaws-of-nate-parkers-the-birth-of-a-nation.
———. "Should a Film Try to Depict Slavery?" *New Yorker*, October 21, 2013. https://www.newyorker.com/culture/richard-brody/should-a-film-try-to-depict-slavery.
Brown, Vincent. *The Reaper's Garden: Death and Power in the World of Atlantic Slavery*. Cambridge: Harvard University Press, 2010.
Buck-Morss, Susan. "Hegel and Haiti." *Critical Inquiry* 26, no. 4 (2000): 821–65.
Burton, Julianne. "Film and Revolution in Cuba: The First Twenty-Five Years." In *Cuba: Twenty-Five Years of Revolution, 1959–1984*, edited by Sandor Halebsky and John M. Kirk. New York: Praegar, 1985, 134–153.
———. "Part I: Revolutionary Cuban Cinema." *Jump Cut*, no. 19 (December 1978): 17–20.
Burton, Vernon, et al., "*The Birth of a Nation*: A Roundtable." *Civil War History* 64, no. 1 (2018): 56–91.
Cabranes-Grant, Leo. "Possession, Gender and Performance in Revolutionary Cuba: Eugenio Hernández Espinosa's *María Antonia*." *Theatre Research International* 35, no. 2 (2010): 126–38.
———. "*The Last Supper*, A Parable from Cuba." *New York Times,* May 5, 1978, C6.
———. "The Screen: Marlon Brando and Black Revolution." *New York Times*, October 22, 1970, 62.
Canby, Vincent. "A Cuban *Uncle Tom's Cabin*." *New York Times*, July 1, 1977, 47.
Carrington, Julian. "12 Years a Slave." *Cinema Scope*, no. 57 (2014): 74–75.
Castro, Fidel. *My Life*. Edited by Ignacio Ramonet. Translated by Andrew Hurley. London: Penguin, 2007.
Celli, Carlo. *Gillo Pontecorvo: From Resistance to Terrorism*. Lanham, MD: Scarecrow Press, 2005.
Césaire, Aimé. *Discourse on Colonialism*. 1955. Translated by Joan Pinkham. New York: Monthly Review, 2000.
———. Interview by René Depestre. 1967. In *Discourse on Colonialism*, by Aimé Césaire. Translated by Joan Pinkham. New York: Monthly Review, 2000, 79–94.
Chanan, Michael. *Cuban Cinema*. Minneapolis: University of Minnesota Press, 2004.
———. "Enduring Memories." *New Statesman*. July 7, 2008, 40–42.

Chomsky, Aviva. *A History of the Cuban Revolution*. 2nd ed. Oxford: Wiley Blackwell, 2015.

Clark, Ashley. "Sergio Giral: A Giant of Cuban Cinema." *BFI: Features and Reviews*, February 7, 2014. https://www2.bfi.org.uk/news-opinnews-bfi/features/sergio-giral-giant-cuban-cinema.

Coates, Ta-Nehisi. "The Case for Reparations." *The Atlantic*, June 2014. https://www.theatlantic.com/magazine/archive/2014/06/the-case-for-reparations/361631/.

Cobb, Jasmine Nichole. "Directed by Himself: Steve McQueen's *12 Years a Slave*." *American Literary History* 26, no. 2 (2014): 339–46.

Connelly, Thomas L., and Barbara L. Bellows. *God and General Longstreet: The Lost Cause and the Southern Mind*. Baton Rouge: Louisiana State University Press, 1982.

Cort, Aisha Z. "Rethinking Caliban: Shakespeare and Césaire in the *Negrometraje* of Sergio Giral." *Afro-Hispanic Review* 33, no. 2 (2014): 41–58.

Craven, David. *Art and Revolution in Latin America, 1910–1990*. New Haven: Yale University Press, 2006.

Darwent, Charles. "Arrows of Desire: How Did St Sebastian Become an Enduring, Homo-Erotic Icon?" *Independent*, February 10, 2008. https://www.independent.co.uk/arts-entertainment/art/features/arrows-of-desire-how-did-st-sebastian-become-an-enduring-homoerotic-icon-779388.html.

Davies, Natalie Zemon. *Slaves on Screen: Films and Historical Vision*. Cambridge, MA: Harvard University Press, 2000.

Davis, Wade. *The Serpent and the Rainbow: A Harvard Scientist's Astonishing Journey into the Secret Societies of Haitian Voodoo, Zombis, and Magic*. 1985. New York: Simon & Schuster, 2010.

Denby, David. "Fighting to Survive: *12 Years a Slave* and *All is Lost*." *New Yorker*, October 14, 2013. https://www.newyorker.com/magazine/2013/10/21/fighting-to-survive-2.

Dobie, Madeleine. "*The Battle of Algiers* at 50: From 1960s Radicalism to the Classrooms of West Point." *Los Angeles Review of Books*, September 25, 2016. https://www.lareviewofbooks.org/article/battle-algiers-50-1960s-radicalism-classrooms-west-point/.

Doherty, Thomas. "Bringing the Slave Narrative to Screen: Steve McQueen and John Ridley's Searing Depiction of America's 'Peculiar Institution.'" *Cineaste* 39, no. 1 (2013): 4–8.

Eagleton, Terry. "The Enlightenment is Dead! Long Live the Enlightenment!" *Harper's Magazine*, March 2005, 91–95.

———. *The Gospels: Jesus Christ*. Texts selected and annotated by Giles Fraser. London: Verso, 2007.

Ebert, Roger. "Pontecorvo: 'We Trust the Face of Brando.'" *New York Times*, April 13, 1960, D11.

Ferrer, Ada. *Freedom's Mirror: Cuba and Haiti in the Age of Revolution.* New York: Cambridge University Press, 2014.
Fick, Carolyn. "Emancipation in Haiti: From Plantation Labour to Peasant Proprietorship." *Slavery & Abolition* 21, no. 2 (2000): 11–40.
Foreman, P. Gabrielle, et al. "Writing About Slavery/Teaching About Slavery: This Might Help." Community-sourced document. August 10, 2023. https://naacpculpeper.org/resources/writing-about-slavery-this-might-help/
García Espinosa, Julio. "Por un cine imperfecto." 1967. In *New Latin American Cinema: Volume 1: Theory, Practices and Transcontinental Articulations*, translated by Julianne Burton, edited by Michael T. Martin. Detroit: Wayne State University Press, 1997, 71–82.
Gutiérrez Alea, Tomás. *The Viewer's Dialectic.* 1982. Translated by Julia Lesage. La Habana: José Martí Publishing House, 1988.
Gutiérrez Alea, Tomás, Jorge Fraga, Alina Sanchez, and Samuel Claxton. "Towards a Renewal of Cuban Revolutionary Cinema: A Discussion of Cuban Cinema Today." Interview by Zuzana Pick. *Ciné-Tracts* 2, nos. 3–4 (Summer/Fall 1979): 22.
Finch, Aisha K. *Rethinking Slave Rebellion in Cuba: La Escalera and the Insurgencies of 1841–1844.* Chapel Hill: University of North Carolina Press, 2015.
Fischer, Sibylle. *Modernity Disavowed: Haiti and the Cultures of Slavery in the Age of Revolution.* Durham, NC: Duke University Press, 2004.
Fisher, Jean. "McQueen's Dialogues with the Image of Precarious Life." Essay commissioned by Espace Louis Vuitton Tokyo on the occasion of the exhibition "Steve McQueen," April 26–August 17, 2014. https://www.jeanfisher.com/steve-mcqueens-dialogues-with-the-image-of-precarious-life/.
Forbes, Remeike. "The Black Jacobin: Our Visual Identity." *Jacobin*, March 3, 2021. https://jacobinmag.com/2012/03/the-Black-jacobin-2.
Foreman, Amanda. *A World on Fire: An Epic History of Two Nations Divided.* London: Allen Lane, 2010.
Forsdick, Charles. "Interpreting 2004: Politics, Memory, Scholarship." *Small Axe*, no. 27 (October 2008): 1–13.
Forsdick, Charles, and Christian Høgsbjerg. "Sergei Eisenstein and the Haitian Revolution: 'The Confrontation Between Black and White Explodes Into Red'." *History Workshop Journal* 78, no. 1 (2014): 157–85.
French, Philip. "Crucified in Cuba," *The Observer*, March 11, 1979, 14.
Gabriel, Teshome H. *Third Cinema in the Third World: The Aesthetics of Liberation.* Ann Arbor: UMI Research Press, 1982.
García Márquez, Gabriel. "Operation Carlota." Translated by Patrick Camiller. *New Left Review*, nos. 101–2 (February–April 1977): 123–37.
Genovese, Eugene. *Roll, Jordan, Roll: The World the Slaves Made.* 1974. New York: Vintage, 2008.

George, Nelson. "An Essentially American Narrative: A Discussion of Steve McQueen's Film *12 Years a Slave*." *New York Times*, October 11, 2013. AR18.

Ghirelli, Massimo. *Gillo Pontecorvo*. Firenze, Italy: La Nuova Italia, 1978.

Gilliatt, Penelope. "Last Supper in Havana." *New Yorker*, May 15, 1978, 120–124.

Gilroy, Paul. *The Black Atlantic: Modernity and Double Consciousness*. London: Verso, 1993.

———. "*12 Years a Slave*: In Our 'Post-Racial' Age the Legacy of Slavery Lives On." *Guardian*, November 10, 2013. https://www.theguardian.com/commentisfree/2013/nov/10/12-years-a-slave-mcqueen-film-legacy-slavery.

Giral, Sergio. "Cuban Cinema and the Afro-Cuban Heritage." Interview by Julianne Burton and Garry Crowdus. *The Black Scholar* 8, nos. 8–10 (1977): 62–72.

Giral, Sergio. "Close-Up on the Background: A Conversation with Sergio Giral, The Father of Afro-Cuban Cinema." Interview with Pablo Velez. *Abernathy Magazine*, November 30, 2016. https://abernathymagazine.com/sergio-giral/.

———. "Filmmaking within and beyond Fidel's Cuba." Interview by David McIntosh. *Fuse Magazine* 22, no. 1 (1999): 36–43.

———. Interview by María Caridad Cumaná. *The Cinema of Sara Gómez: Reframing Revolution*. Edited by Susan Lord and María Caridad Cumaná. Bloomington: Indiana University Press, 2021, 80–86.

———. "Sergio Giral on Filmmaking in Cuba." Interview by Ana M. Lopez and Nicholas Peter Humy. *Black Film Review* 3, no. 1 (1986): 4–6.

Gombrich, E. H. *The Story of Art*. 1950. 16th edition. London: Phaidon, 1997.

Gonzalez, Ed. "*12 Years a Slave*: Review." *Slant Magazine*, September 14, 2013. https://www.slantmagazine.com/film/12-years-a-slave/.

Gott, Richard. *Cuba: A New History*. New Haven and London: Yale University Press, 2004.

González-Ripoll, et al. *El rumor de Haití en Cuba: temor, raza y rebeldía, 1789–1844*. Madrid: Consejo Superior de Investigaciones Científicas, 2004.

Grandin, Greg. "Capitalism and Slavery." *The Nation*, May 1, 2015. www.thenation.com/article/capitalism-and-slavery/.

Green, J. Ronald. *Straight Lick: The Cinema of Oscar Micheaux*. Bloomington: Indiana University Press, 2000.

Gros, Emmeline, et al. "*Gone with the Wind* after *Gone With the Wind*." *Transatlantica*, no. 1 (2019). https://doi.org/10.4000/transatlantica.13801.

Hanks, Patrick, Kate Hardcastle, and Flavia Hodges. *A Dictionary of First Names*. 2nd ed. Oxford: Oxford University Press, 2006.

Harvey, David. *A Brief History of Neoliberalism*. Oxford: Oxford University Press, 2005.

Hessini, Leila. "Global Progress in Abortion Advocacy and Policy: An Assessment of the Decade Since ICPD." *Reproductive Health Matters* 13, no. 25 (2005): 88–100.

Hill, John, and Pamela Church Gibson, eds. *The Oxford Guide to Film Studies*. Oxford: Oxford University Press, 1998.

Hoz, Pedro de la. "Farewell to Sergio Vitier, a True, Essential Creator." *Granma*, May 4, 2016. https://en.granma.cu/cultura/2016-05-04/farewell-to-sergio-vitier-a-true-essential-creator

Hudson, Peter James. "The Racist Dawn of Capitalism: Unearthing the Economy of Bondage." *Boston Review*, March 14, 2016. http://bostonreview.net/books-ideas/peter-james-hudson-slavery-capitalism.

Hunter, Stephen. "*Queimada*: Revolution in Perpetual Motion." *The Washington Post*, October 15, 2004, C4.

Ibarra, Mirtha, ed. *Titón: Tomás Gutiérrez Alea: Volver sobre mis pasos*. Habana: Ediciones Unión, 2008.

Ide, Wendy. "The Birth of a Nation Review—Hardly Revolutionary." *Guardian*, December 11, 2016. https://www.theguardian.com/film/2016/dec/11/the-birth-of-a-nation-review-ridden-cliches-nate-parker-nat-turner.

Jack, Ian. "All That Bloody Mayhem and We're Still Supposed to Take *Django Unchained* seriously?" *Guardian*, January 25, 2013. https://www.theguardian.com/commentisfree/2013/jan/25/bloody-mayhem-tarantino-django-seriously.

Jameson, Fredric. "The Future City." *New Left Review* no. 21 (2003): 65–79.

———. *The Geopolitical Aesthetic: Cinema and Space in the World-System*. 1992. Bloomington: Indiana University Press, 1995.

———. *The Political Unconscious: Narrative as a Socially Symbolic Act*. Ithaca: Cornell University Press, 1981.

———. *Postmodernism, or The Cultural Logic of Late Capitalism*. Durham, NC: Duke University Press, 1991.

———. "Reification and Utopia in Mass Culture." 1979. In *Signatures of the Visible*. London: Routledge, 1992, 11–46.

———. "Third-World Literature in the Era of Multinational Capitalism." *Social Text*, no. 15 (1986): 65–88.

Johnson, Amy Marie. "Slave Resistance in the Atlantic World." *Oxford Bibliographies*, January 15, 2019.https://doi.org/10.1093/OBO/9780199730414-0310.

Johnson, Walter. *River of Dark Dreams: Slavery and Empire in the Cotton Kingdom*. Cambridge, MA: Harvard University Press, 2013.

———. *Soul by Soul: Life Inside the Antebellum Slave Market*. Cambridge, MA: Harvard University Press, 1999.

Kaisary, Philip. *The Haitian Revolution in the Literary Imagination: Radical Horizons, Conservative Constraints*. Charlottesville: University of Virginia Press, 2014.

———. "Hercules, the Hydra, and the 1801 Constitution of Toussaint Louverture." *Atlantic Studies* 12, no. 4 (2015): 393–411.

———. "'To Break Our Chains and Form a Free People': Race, Nation, and Haiti's Imperial Constitution of 1805." In *Race and Nation in the Age of*

Emancipations, edited by Whitney Stewart and John Garrison Marks. Athens: University of Georgia Press, 2018, 71–88.

———. "Socioeconomic Rights and the Haitian Revolution." In *Social Rights and the Politics of Obligation in History*, edited by Charles Walton and Steven Jenson. Cambridge: Cambridge University Press, 2022, 82–98.

Lee, Dan. P. "Where It Hurts: Steve McQueen on Why *12 Years a Slave* Isn't Just About Slavery." *Vulture*, December 8, 2013. https://www.vulture.com/2013/12/steve-mcqueen-talks-12-years-a-slave.html.

Laurier, Joanne. "Barry Jenkins' *The Underground Railroad*: 'Freed' from Important Realities of History." *World Socialist Web Site*, May 31, 2021. https://www.wsws.org/en/articles/2021/06/01/unde-j01.html.

———. "*12 Years a Slave* and Other Films." *World Socialist Web Site*, September 22, 2013. https://www.wsws.org/en/articles/2013/09/23/tff2-s23.html.

Lazarus, Neil. *The Postcolonial Unconscious*. Cambridge: Cambridge University Press, 2011.

Lesage, Julia. "*The Other Francisco*: Creating History." *Jump Cut*, No. 30, 1985, 53–58.

Linebaugh, Peter. "Amazing Disgrace." *Counterpunch*, February 28, 2007. http://www.counterpunch.org/2007/02/28/an-amazing-disgrace/.

Linebaugh, Peter, and Marcus Rediker. *The Many-Headed Hydra: Sailors, Slaves, Commoners, and the Hidden History of the Revolutionary Atlantic*. 2000. Boston: Beacon Press, 2013.

Lingwood, James, ed. *Caribs' Leap / Western Deep: Steve McQueen*. London: Artangel, 2002.

Li, Stephanie. "*12 Years a Slave* as a Neo-Slave Narrative." *American Literary History* 26, no. 2 (2014): 326–31.

Litwack, Leon F. *North of Slavery: The Negro in the Free States, 1790–1860*. Chicago: University of Chicago Press, 1961.

Lord, Susan, and María Caridad Cumaná, eds. *The Cinema of Sara Gómez: Reframing Revolution*. Bloomington: Indiana University Press, 2021.

Lukács, Georg. "Realism in the Balance." Translated by Rodney Livingstone. In, *Aesthetics and Politics* by Theodor Adorno et al. London: Verso, 2007, 28–59.

Marcuse, Herbert. *The Aesthetic Dimension*. Boston: Beacon, 1978.

Martin, Michael T. "Podium for the Truth? Reading Slavery and the Neocolonial Project in the Historical Film: *Queimada! (Burn!)* and *Sankofa* in Counterpoint." *Third Text* 23, no. 6 (2009): 717–31.

Martin, Michael T., and David C. Wall. "The Politics of Cine-Memory: Signifying Slavery in the Historical Film." In *A Companion to the Historical Film*, edited by Robert A. Rosenstone and Constantin Parvulescu. Oxford: Wiley-Blackwell, 2013, 445–67.

Marx, Karl. *Capital: Vol. 3: The Process of Capitalist Production as a Whole*. 1894. Edited by Frederick Engels. New York: International Publishers, 1977.

Maurer, Christopher. *Sebastian's Arrows: Letters and Mementos of Salvador Dalí and Federico García Lorca*. Edited and translated by Christopher Maurer. Chicago: Swan Isle Press, 2004.

McEvilley, Thomas. "Documenta 11." *Frieze*, 69, 2002. https://www.frieze.com/article/documenta-11.

McQueen, Steve. "Steve McQueen and Henry Louis Gates Jr. Talk *12 Years a Slave*, Part 3." Interview by Henry Louis Gates Jr. *The Root*, December 26, 2013. www.theroot.com/steve-mcqueen-and-henry-louis-gates-jr-talk-12-years-a-1790899474.

Mellen, Joan. "A Reassessment of Gillo Pontecorvo's *Burn!*" *Cinema*, no. 32 (1972): 38–47.

Michalczyk, John J. *The Italian Political Filmmakers*. London: Associated University Presses, 1986.

Miller, Marilyn G. "Truth, Lies and Telling Silences in Gutiérez Alea's *The Last Supper* and Pontecorvo's *Burn!*" *Studies in Spanish & Latin American Cinemas* 10, no. 1 (2013): 59–74.

Moakley, Paul. "Behind the Moving Image: The Cinematography of *12 Years a Slave*." *Time Magazine Lightbox*, February 27, 2014. https://time.com/3807491/behind-the-moving-image-the-cinematography-of-12-years-a-slave/.

Mohammed, Kenneth. "Sorrow and Regret Are Not Enough. Britain Must Finally Pay Reparations for Slavery." *Guardian*, March 29, 2022. https://www.theguardian.com/global-development/2022/mar/29/sorrow-and-regret-are-not-enough-britain-must-finally-pay-reparations-for-slavery.

Moreno Fraginals, Manuel. *The Sugar Mill: The Socioeconomic Complex of Sugar in Cuba, 1760–1860*. Translated by Cedric Belfrage. New York: Monthly Review, 1976.

Morris, Andrea E. "Slave Rebellion and Cultural Resistance." In *Afro-Cuban Identity in Post-Revolutionary Novel and Film: Inclusion, Loss, and Cultural Resistance*. Lewisburg: Bucknell University Press, 2012, 39–60.

Murray, Peter, and Linda Murray. *The Penguin Dictionary of Art and Artists*. 7th ed. London: Penguin, 1997.

Nelson, Rob. "Steve McQueen: 'I Want to Be Useful.'" *Walker Magazine*, November 9, 2013. https://walkerart.org/magazine/steve-mcqueen-i-want-be-useful.

Nesbitt, Nick. "Négritude." In *Africana: The Encyclopedia of the African American Experience*, 2nd ed., vol. 4, edited by Kwame Anthony Appiah and Henry Louis Gates Jr. Oxford: Oxford University Press 2005, 193–99.

———. *The Price of Slavery: Capitalism and Revolution in the Caribbean*. Charlottesville: University of Virginia Press, 2022.

———. *Universal Emancipation: The Haitian Revolution and the Radical Enlightenment*. Charlottesville: University of Virginia Press, 2008.

———. *Voicing Memory: History and Subjectivity in French Caribbean Literature*. Charlottesville: University of Virginia Press, 2003.

Nixon, Rob. *Slow Violence and the Environmentalism of the Poor*. Cambridge, MA: Harvard University Press, 2013.

Orr, Christopher. "Grappling With *The Birth of a Nation*." *The Atlantic*, October 6, 2016. https://www.theatlantic.com/entertainment/archive/2016/10/grappling-with-the-birth-of-a-nation/503246/.

Paradis, Michel. "The Lost Cause's Long Legacy." *The Atlantic*, June 26, 2020. https://www.theatlantic.com/ideas/archive/2020/06/the-lost-causes-long-legacy/613288/.

Parry, Benita. *Conrad and Imperialism: Ideological Boundaries and Visionary Frontiers*. London: Macmillan, 1983.

Peary, Danny. *Cult Movies: The Classics, the Sleepers, the Weird, and the Wonderful*. New York: Delta, 1981.

Peary, Danny. "*Burn!*" *Criterion Collection*. December 10, 1991. https://www.criterion.com/current/posts/947-burn.

Pérez Jr., Louis A. *To Die in Cuba: Suicide and Society*. Chapel Hill: University of North Carolina Press, 2012.

Pick, Zuzana. *The New Latin American Cinema: A Continental Project*. Austin: University of Texas Press, 1993.

Pontecorvo, Gillo. "An Interview with Gillo Pontecorvo by Joan Mellen." *Film Quarterly* 26, no. 1 (1972): 2–10.

———. "Interview with the Italian Film Director Gillo Pontecorvo, Rome, Italy, July 1, 2003." Interview by Neelem Srivastava. *Interventions: International Journal of Postcolonial Studies* 7, no. 1 (2005): 107–17.

———. "Using the Contradictions of the System." Interview by Harold Kalishman and Gabriel Landau. *Cinéaste* 6, no. 2 (1974): 2–6.

Quigley, John. *Soviet Legal Innovation and the Law of the Western World*. Cambridge: Cambridge University Press, 2007.

Railton, Stephen. "Readapting *Uncle Tom's Cabin*." In *Nineteenth Century American Fiction on Screen*, edited by R. Barton Palmer. Cambridge: Cambridge University Press, 2007, 62–76.

Railton, Stephen. *Uncle Tom's Cabin and American Culture: A Multi-Media Archive*. Institute for Advanced Technology in the Humanities. http://utc.iath.virginia.edu/onstage/films/fihp.html.

Ramírez Gutiérrez, Adriana. "Relectura cinematográfica de una novela antiesclavista Decimonónica. De *Francisco* a *El otro Francisco*." *Esclavages & Post-esclavages*, no. 4 (2021). https://doi.org/10.4000/slaveries.3794.

Rondeau, James et al., eds. *Steve McQueen: Works 1993–2012*. Heidelberg / Berlin: Kehrer Verlag, 2012.

Rosenbaum, Jonathan. "Chains of Ignorance: Charles Burnett's *Nightjohn*." In *Essential Cinema: On the Necessity of Film Canons*. Baltimore: Johns Hopkins University Press, 2004, 285–90.

Rowley, Hazel. *Richard Wright: The Life and Times*. New York: Henry Holt and Company, 2001.

Said, Edward W. *Culture and Imperialism.* New York: Alfred A. Knopf, 1993.
———. *Orientalism: Western Conceptions of the Orient.* 1978. London: Penguin, 1995.
———. "Politics of Knowledge." 1991. In *Reflections on Exile and Other Literary and Cultural Essays.* London: Granta, 2001, 372–85.
———. "Through Gringo Eyes: With Conrad in Latin America." 1988. In *Reflections on Exile and Other Literary and Cultural Essays.* London: Granta, 2001, 276–81.
———. "The Quest for Gillo Pontecorvo." 1988. In *Reflections on Exile and Other Literary and Cultural Essays.* London: Granta, 2001, 282–92.
———. *The World, the Text, and the Critic.* Cambridge: Harvard University Press, 1983.
Saint-Just, Sophie. "Creolization on screen: Guy Deslauriers's *The Middle Passage* as Afro-Diasporic Discourse [*Le passage du milieu*]." *African and Black Diaspora: An International Journal* 12, no. 3 (2019): 287–303.
Salazkina, Masha. "Transnational Genealogies of Institutional Film Culture of Cuba, 1960s–1970s." In *The Routledge Companion to Latin American Cinema*, edited by Marvin D'Lugo, Ana M. López, and Laura Podalsky. London: Routledge, 2017, 192–203.
Sanko, Nadia Sophia. "Creolizing *Carmen*: Reading Performance in *María Antonia*, Cuba's Overlooked Carmen Adaptation." *Camera Obscura* 27, no. 1 (2012): 157–91.
Sartre, Jean-Paul. *What is Literature?* 1948. Translated by Bernard Frechtman. London: Routledge, 1993.
Scott, David. *Conscripts of Modernity: The Tragedy of Colonial Enlightenment.* Durham, NC: Duke University Press, 2004.
Scott, Julius S. *The Common Wind: Afro-American Currents in the Age of the Haitian Revolution* London: Verso, 2018.
Schroeder, Paul A. *Tomás Gutiérrez Alea: The Dialectics of a Filmmaker.* New York: Routledge, 2002.
Sepinwall, Alyssa Goldstein. *Slave Revolt on Screen: The Haitian Revolution in Film and Video Games.* Jackson: University Press of Mississippi, 2021.
Shapiro, Stephen. "Realignment and Televisual Intellect: The Telepraxis of Class Alliances in Contemporary Subscription Television Drama." In *Class Divisions in Serial Television*, edited by Sieglinde Lemke and Wibke Schniedermann. London: Palgrave Macmillan, 2016, 177–205.
Sharfstein, Daniel J. *The Invisible Line: A Secret History of Race in America.* New York: Penguin, 2011.
Shohat, Ella, and Robert Stam. *Unthinking Eurocentrism: Multiculturalism and the Media.* New York: Routledge, 2014.
Shumway, David R. *John Sayles.* Urbana: University of Illinois Press, 2012.
Silberman, Marc. "Brecht Encounters 'the System.'" *Stanislavski Studies* 9, no. 1 (2021): 41–49.

Slaughter, Joseph R. *Human Rights, Inc.: The World Novel, Narrative Form, and International Law.* New York: Fordham University Press, 2007.

Stam, Robert. *Tropical Multiculturalism: A Comparative History of Race in Brazilian Cinema and Culture.* Durham, NC: Duke University Press, 1997.

Stevens, Dana. "*12 Years a Slave*: A Beautiful Film about the Ugliest of Subjects." *Slate*, October 17, 2013. http://www.slate.com/articles/arts/movies/2013/10/_12_years_a_slave_directed_by_steve_mcqueen_reviewed.html.

Stevenson, Brenda. "Filming Black Voices and Stories: Slavery on Americas Screens." *Journal of the Civil War Era* 8, no. 3 (2018): 488–520.

Stokes, Melvyn. *D.W. Griffith's the Birth of a Nation: A History of the Most Controversial Motion Picture of All Time.* Oxford: Oxford University Press, 2007.

Stokes, Melvyn. *American History through Hollywood Film: From the Revolution to the 1960s.* London: Bloomsbury, 2013.

Stokes, Melvyn. "From Uncle Tom to Nat Turner: An Overview of Slavery in American Film, 1903–2016." *Transatlantica*, no. 1 (2018). https://doi.org/10.4000/transatlantica.12814.

Stone, Alan. "Last Battle: Gillo Pontecorvo's *Burn!*" *Boston Review* 29, no. 2 (April/May 2004). https://bostonreview.net/articles/alan-stone-last-battle/.

Taubin, Amy. "Art and Industry." *Film Comment* (July/August 2007). http://filmlinccom.siteprotect.net/fcm/artandindustry/burn.htm.

Tomba, Massimiliano. *Insurgent Universality: An Alternative Legacy of Modernity.* New York: Oxford University Press, 2019.

Trouillot, Michel-Rolph. *Silencing the Past: Power and the Production of History.* Boston: Beacon, 1995.

Turner, Michael J. *Stonewall Jackson, Beresford Hope, and the Meaning of the American Civil War in Britain.* Baton Rouge: Louisiana State University Press, 2020.

Vos, Andrew de. "'Expect the Truth': Exploiting History with *Mandingo*." *American Studies* 52, no. 2 (2013): 5–21.

Walvin, James. "Introduction." *The Black Jacobins* by C. L. R James. 1938. 2nd ed. rev. 1963. 2nd ed. London: Penguin, 2001, vii–xiv.

Waterton, Emma, Laurajane Smith, Ross Wilson, and Kalliopi Fouseki. "Forgetting to Heal: Remembering the Abolition Act of 1807." *European Journal of English Studies* 14, no. 1 (2010): 23–36.

Wayne, Mike. *Political Film: The Dialectics of Third Cinema.* London: Pluto Press, 2001.

West, Dennis. "In the Footsteps of Tomás Gutiérrez Alea," *Cineaste* 35, no. 2 (2010): 18–25.

———. "Slavery and Cinema in Cuba: The Case of Gutiérrez Alea's *The Last Supper*." *Western Journal of Black Studies* 3, no. 2 (1979): 128–33.

Wilkinson, Alissa. "Why 'the Whole Environment in Hollywood Had to Change' for *Harriet* to Get Made," *Vox*, November 4, 2019. https://www.vox.com/culture/2019/11/4/20940561/harriet-interview-gregory-allen-howard.

Williams, Linda. "Skin Flicks on the Racial Border: Pornography, Exploitation, and Interracial Lust." In *Porn Studies*, edited by Linda Williams. Durham, NC: Duke University Press, 2004, 271–308.

Williams, Lorna V. "A Cuban Slave Hunter's Journal: Francisco Estévez's *Diario Del Rancheador* (1837–1842)." *Afro-Hispanic Review* 10, no. 3 (1991): 62–66.

———. *The Representation of Slavery in Cuban Fiction*. Columbia: University of Missouri Press, 1994.

Williams, Raymond. "Base and Superstructure in Marxist Cultural Theory." *New Left Review*, no. 82 (1973): 3–16.

Wood, Marcus. *Blind Memory: Visual Representations of Slavery in England and America 1780–1865*. Manchester: Manchester University Press, 2000.

Wood, Marcus. *The Horrible Gift of Freedom: Atlantic Slavery and the Representation of Emancipation*. Athens: University of Georgia Press, 2010.

———. *Slavery, Empathy, Pornography*. Oxford: Oxford University Press, 2002.

Wood, Michael. "*Viridiana*: The Human Comedy." *Criterion Collection: Essays*. May 22, 2006. https://www.criterion.com/current/posts/423.

Wood, Michael. "At The Movies: *12 Years a Slave*," *London Review of Books* 36, no. 3 (February 6, 2014): 23.

Wood, Robin. *Sexual Politics and Narrative Film: Hollywood and Beyond*. New York: Columbia University Press, 1998.

WReC: Warwick Research Collective. *Combined and Uneven Development: Towards a New Theory of World-Literature*. Liverpool: Liverpool University Press, 2015.

Zimmer, Hans. "The Score." Interview. DVD Special Feature. Steve McQueen, dir., *12 Years a Slave*. Fox Searchlight, 2013.

Žižek, Slavoj. "First As Tragedy, Then As Farce." RSA Lecture, November 24, 2009. Lecture transcript available at https://www.thersa.org/globalassets/pdfs/blogs/rsa-lecture-slovoj-zizek-transcript.pdf.

Index

abolition, 3–4, 9, 18, 22–25, 42–43, 71, 77, 111–12, 120–22, 125, 128, 157, 172–73. *See also* freedom
Abolition of the Slave Trade Act of 1807, 23–24
abortion, 119–20. *See also* women
Absalom, Absalom! (Faulkner), 162
absolute spirit, 85
Al Bárbaro del Ritmo, 147
Alessandro Alessandroni choristers, 58
Ali, Muhammad, 83–84
Almendros, Néstor, 109, 200n23
Amazing Grace, 2–3, 23–24
Amerindian resistance, 44
Amistad, 22–23
Anderson, Kurt, 83
Anderson, Melissa, 165
Angola, 78–79, 111
Antebellum, 185n129
anticolonialism, 7–8, 35, 41–43, 52, 55, 67–68, 85–86, 104. *See also* anti-imperialism; colonialism; decolonization; imperialism
anti-imperialism, 6, 8, 40–42, 44, 60, 67–68, 71. *See also* anticolonialism; colonialism; decolonization; imperialism
Antonio Aponte, Jose, 128

Apocalypse Now, 81
Apted, Michael, 2–3
Aristotle, 76–77
Aronowitz, Stanley, 95–96
Austen, Jane, 5

Bach, Johann Sebastian, 56, 58, 69, 85
Balzac, Honoré de, 126–27
Batista, Fulgencio, 108
The Battle of Algiers, 35, 39–43, 49, 51, 53, 60, 71, 185n3
Behold a Pale Horse, 55
Belle, 173
Bellows, Barbara L., 14
Berman, Marshall, 21
Biberman, Herbert, 19–20
The Birth of a Nation (1915), 13–15, 26, 156, 167
The Birth of a Nation (2016), 25–26
Bizet, Georges, 110
Black agency, 3; and Hollywood, 11–19, 22, 24, 28, 108, 147, 164, 171, 175; and scholarship, 10, 43; and Third Cinema, 32–33, 39–40, 44–45, 50–51, 70–71, 96, 104, 112, 124, 129–30, 133, 140, 149, 176; and transnationality, 115; and women, 118, 122–24, 131. *See also* Black resistance; Black Revolution

231

Black autonomy, 130–31, 140, 144
Black Cuban history, 77–80, 96, 107–8, 111–12
Black culture, 11, 13, 46, 62–63, 144
Black diaspora, 57, 59, 62, 78–79, 114–15, 140, 150, 171, 173
Black dignity, 59
The Black Jacobins (James), 116, 162, 176, 194n34
Black liberty, 68–70, 134–35, 138–39, 142–43
Black Lives Matter, 25–26
Black Power, 41, 70, 172
Black pride, 61
Black rebels, 18, 59, 66, 82–83, 127–29, 141
Black resistance: and abolition, 23–24; and Angola, 78; and Cuban folklore, 110; everyday forms of, 116; and Hollywood, 3, 19–20, 23, 27, 149–50, 158, 163–64, 173; and independent films, 28–33, 172; and literature, 2, 162–63, 173; and the Lost Cause, 15, 18; and magical realism, 103–4, 135; and plantation life, 88; and scholarship, 7, 10–11, 40, 43, 48; and suicide, 128; and Third Cinema, 3–4, 9, 36–38, 41–46, 59, 73–75, 77–78, 82–83, 88–89, 101–2, 111, 123–27, 129, 136, 144–48, 175–76; and transnationality, 115; and women, 118, 130, 132, 143. *See also* Black Revolution
Black Revolution, 7, 36–41, 45–46, 52, 55, 59–60, 66–70, 98. *See also* Black agency; Black resistance; Haitian Revolution
Black Spartacus, 2, 141
Black Studies, 6, 157
Black subjectivity, 111–12, 130, 147
Blaxpoitation films, 20, 140

Bloch, Ernst, 126
Bobbitt, Sean, 151, 165, 167
Bogle, Donald, 9–10, 16
Botticini, Francesco, 83
Bradshaw, Peter, 25, 149
Brando, Marlon, 4, 32, 37, 41, 47–49, 51–54, 69–70, 125–26, 191n105
Brecht, Bertolt, 76–77, 114–15, 122, 125–27
Brecht-Lukács debate, 126–27
Brennan, Timothy, 5–6, 185n2
The Brother from Another Planet, 28–29
Brown, Michael, 26
brutality, 44, 82, 84–85, 88, 93, 116, 122, 127–29, 133, 137, 167–70
Buck-Morss, Susan, 85
Buñuel, Luis, 97, 193n15
Burn!, 3–4, 10, 32, 35–74, 121, 125–27, 130, 147, 173, 175, 187nn20–21, 191n105
Burnett, Charles, 28–30
The Butler, 173

Cahier d'un retour au pays natal ("Notebook of a Return to My Native Land") (Césaire), 66
Canby, Vincent, 113
capitalism, 9, 36, 39–43, 47–49, 70–72, 75, 103–5, 112, 120–23, 140, 150–56, 161–62, 175
Capitalism and Slavery (Williams), 40
capitalist world-system, 36, 97, 112, 120, 153–56
Caribs' Leap, 153–54, 156, 171
Carmen, 110
Carpentier, Alejo, 10, 101, 103, 180n45
Carrié, Edouard Duval, 61
Carrington, Julian, 171
Cartier-Bresson, Henri, 62, 65
"The Case for Reparations" (Coates), 26

Castro, Fidel, 78–79, 108–9
Catholicism, 75, 81–86, 90, 100, 141
Cauvin, François, 61
Celli, Carlo, 40–41, 48–49, 52, 60, 185n3
censorship, 112, 128, 146–47
Césaire, Aimé, 40, 45, 59–63, 66, 70, 85–86, 102, 143
Chamoiseau, Patrick, 30–31
Chanan, Michael, 76, 201n34
Chapman, Maria, 23
Cheney, Lew, 164
Chomsky, Aviva, 146
Chonville, Claude, 31–32
Christianity. *See* Catholicism; Jesus Christ
Chronicle of an Ordinance, 147
Cimarrón ("Maroon"), 110
cinematography, 91–96, 151, 158–59, 165–67. *See also* ethics; photography
Cine Rebelde, 191n4
Civil Rights Movement, 18
Clark, Ashly, 140
Clarkson, Thomas, 23
Claxton, Samuel, 123, 134
Coates, Ta-Nehisi, 26
Cobb, Jasmine Nichole, 170
colonialism, 43, 48–52, 55, 67, 70, 81, 89, 127, 150, 167. *See also* anticolonialism; anti-imperialism; decolonization; imperialism
communism, 8, 19, 51–52, 146
comparative cultural criticism, 5–7
Connelly, Thomas L., 14
Conrad, Joseph, 40, 48–50, 70, 81, 127, 173
"The Conspiracy of the Ladder" ("La Conspiración de La Escalara"), 110, 200n28
conspiracy theories, 43
contemplative insert shots, 168

controtipare, 185n3
"Cooperative Labor" *(Cumbite)*, 74–76
Coppola, Francis Ford, 81
Cort, Aisha Z., 133
Craven, Wes, 27
Cuban Revolution, 109–10, 130. *See also* Haitian Revolution
Culture and Imperialism (Said), 5–6
Cumberbatch, Benedict, 162
Cumbite ("Cooperative Labor"), 74–76

Dalí, Salvador, 82, 195n47
Danticat, Edwidge, 165
da Vinci, Leonardo, 97
Davis, Angela, 118
Davis, Natalie Zemon, 10, 39, 41, 45, 48, 60, 66, 70, 198n72
Davis, Wade, 27
Death in Venice (Mann), 195n47
De cierta manera, 107
decolonization, 41–43, 60, 186n14. *See also* anticolonialism; anti-imperialism; colonialism; imperialism
Del Monte, Domingo, 114–15, 124–25, 202n42
Delpech, François Séraphin, 190n92
Denby, David, 149
Depestre, René, 59, 75
Deslauriers, Guy, 30–31
Dessalines, Jean-Jacques, 67
dialectics of core and periphery, 11, 180n46
Diegues, Carlos, 31–32
Diocletian, 82–83, 85
Discourse on Colonialism (Césaire), 86
Dixon, Jr. Thomas, 13
Django Unchained, 25, 167, 173
docudrama, 112
Doherty, Thomas, 152
Donkor, Kimathi, 61–62, 64
Dos Veces Ana ("Two Times Ana"), 147

Douglas, Kirk, 2
Douglass, Frederick, 23, 157
dramatic irony, 88–89, 97, 105
Dred Scott v. Sandford, 22
Du Bois, W. E. B., 2, 104

Eagleton, Terry, 68–69
Eakin, Sue, 157, 206n26
Edison, Thomas, 12
Eisenstein, Sergei, 27, 50, 56, 70, 188n45
El Ingenio (The Sugar Mill) (Fraginals), 79–80
El otro Francisco (The Other Francisco), 3–4, 33, 107–8, 111–30
El reino de este mundo (The Kingdom of This World) (Carpentier), 101, 103
El siglo de las luces (Explosion in a Cathedral) (Carpentier), 10
Equiano, Olaudah, 23
Estévez, Francisco, 130–38
ethics, 151, 165–67, 170
eugenics, 13
Explosion in a Cathedral (El siglo de las luces) (Carpentier), 10

Fanon, Frantz, 38, 40, 42, 45, 50, 59–60, 66–70, 73, 76, 85, 98, 144, 196n54
Fassbender, Michael, 162, 170
Fast, Howard, 2
Faulkner, William, 162
feminism, 6. *See also* women
film scores. *See* music
Finch, Aisha K., 202n49
First Cinema, 7, 32, 40, 55, 59, 70, 171, 186n14. *See also* Second Cinema; Third Cinema
Fischer, Carl, 83–84
Fischer, Sibylle, 196n56
Fleischer, Richard, 20–21

Fleming, Victor, 16, 167
"For an Imperfect Cinema" ("Por un cine imperfecto") (García Espinosa), 93
Forbes, Remeike, 61, *63*
Forsdick, Charles, 3, 41
Foxx, Jamie, 25
Francisco (Suárez y Romero), 112, 114–15, 120–25, 128
Franco, Francisco, 55
freedom, 57, 60, 66, 71, 75, 85, 89, 96–98, 101–5, 112, 161. *See also* abolition
French, Philip, 85
French realism, 109
Freud, Sigmund, 50–51
"From Toussaint L'Ouverture to Fidel Castro" (James), 194n34
Fugitive Slave Act of 1850, 152
fusion films, 48, 50, 52–53, 59, 70, 171

Ganga Zumba, 31–32
García Espinosa, Julio, 93, 199n8
Garner, Eric, 25–26
Garrison, William Lloyd, 23
Gaye, Marvin, 140
genocide, 102, 155
Genovese, Eugene, 2
Gerima, Haile, 32
Getino, Octavio, 186n14
Ghirelli, Massimo, 60
Gilliat, Penelope, 90
Gilroy, Paul, 32, 152
Ginsberg, Allen, 108
Giral, Sergio, 3–4, 7, 16, 39, 77–78, 107–21, 123–49, 175–76, 199n8. *See also specific films*
Girodet, Anne-Louis, 61, *64*
"Glass Ceiling" *(Techo de vidrio)*, 145–47
Glover, Danny, 27, 147, 164

Gómez, Sara, 107
"Gone with the Macho" (Rodriguez Valdes), 16–17, 182n73
Gone with the Wind, 16, 18, 167, 181n72
Gott, Richard, 78–79, 146
Goya, Francisco, 165
Grandin, Greg, 171
Gravesend, 153, 155–56, 171–73
The Great Train Robbery, 180n49
Griffith, D. W., 13–15, 26, 156, 167
Grimaldi, Alberto, 52
Grimké, Angelina, 23
Grimké, Sarah, 23
guerilla movements, 44
Guevara, Che, 44
Gutiérrez Alea, Tomás, 3–4, 7, 39, 59, 70, 73–105, 107–8, 149, 175–76, 191n105, 199n8. *See also specific films*

Haitian Revolution: and Hollywood, 3, 18–19, 26–27, 32; lessons from the, 37–38; and literature, 2, 101, 162; paintings of the, 60–61; and scholarship, 10–11, 196n56, 197n67; and Third Cinema, 41, 43, 67, 70–72, 74–75, 79–80, 85, 89, 94–96, 98, 102–5, 115–16, 122, 124, 141–43, 147, 180n45. *See also* Cuban Revolution
Haley, Alex, 21–22
Halperin, Victor, 27
Harper, Frances, 23
Harriet, 27–28
Havana Cultural Congress of 1968, 111
Hazlitt, William, 31
Heart of Darkness (Conrad), 49, 81, 173
Hegel, Georg, 85, 98
The Help, 173

Hernández Espinosa, Eugenio, 110
Hirst, Damien, 82
Histoire des deux Indes (Raynal), 141
A History of Negro Revolt (James), 2
Høgsbjerg, Christian, 41
Hollywood Ten, 19
homoeroticism, 51
Houston, John, 181n72
Howard, Gregory Allen, 28
Hudson, Peter James, 104
Hughes, Langston, 1
humanism, 67–68, 70–71, 85, 89, 105

iconography, 60–61, 81–85, 117
imperfect cinema, 93
imperialism, 6, 36–49, 60–61, 66–67, 153, 175. *See also* anticolonialism; anti-imperialism; colonialism; decolonization
Incidents in the Life of a Slave Girl (Jacobs), 157
Instituto Cubano del Arte e Industria Cinematográficos (ICAIC), 74, 76–79, 107–12, 146–47, 191n4, 193n21, 199n7
Instituto Nacional de Reforma Agraria (INRA), 109
insurgent universalism, 3
The Interesting Narrative of the Life of Olaudah Equiano, 157

Jacobin magazine, 61, 63
Jacobs, Harriet, 157
James, C. L. R., 2, 104, 116, 141, 162, 176, 194n34, 201n35
Jameson, Fredric, 8–9, 40, 42, 48, 50, 57–58, 72, 96, 127
Jean-Claude, Martha, 115
Jesus Christ, 58–59, 68–69, 85, 93, 99–100, 102
Johnson, Lyndon B., 84
Johnson, Walter, 160

Kael, Pauline, 41
Kansas-Nebraska Act of 1854, 152
Kapò, 35, 51
Kerouac, Jack, 108
Ki-Moon, Ban, 152–53
King, Jr. Martin Luther, 62, *65*, 83
The Kingdom of This World (El reino de este mundo) (Carpentier), 101, 103
Kubrik, Stanley, 2

"La Conspiración de La Escalara" ("The Conspiracy of the Ladder"), 110, 200n28
La imagen rota, 147
La siècle des lumières, 180n45
La Sortie des ouvriers de l'usine Lumière ("Workers Leaving the Lumière Factory"), 12
The Last Supper (da Vinci), 97
The Last Supper (La última cena). See *La última cena (The Last Supper)*
La última cena (The Last Supper), 3, 10, 33, 59, 74–82, 85–105, 107, 121, 123, 147, 175
Laurier, Joanne, 28, 168–70
law, 22–24. *See also* reparations
Lawrence, Jacob, 60–61, 63, 190n92
Lazarus, Neil, 5, 7
Leclerc, Charles, 38
Leibowitz, René, 55–56
Lemmon, Kasi, 27
Leone, Sergio, 52, 140
Le passage du milieu, 30–31
Lesage, Julia, 117–19, 125–26
Les damnés de la terre (Fanon), 45, 196n54
Les Governeurs de la Rosée (Roumain), 74
Li, Stephanie, 151, 163
The Life of Toussaint Louverture (Lawrence), 60–63

Light, Bob, 181n72
Lincoln, 2–3, 24
Lincoln, Abraham, 23
Lindbergh, Peter, 117
littérature engagée, 76
Litwack, Leon F., 207n40
Lodgson, Joseph, 157, 206n26
Lois, George, 83–84
Lorca, Federico García, 82, 84, 195n47
Lord, Susan, 74
Lord Jim (Conrad), 40, 48
Los sobrevivientes (The Survivors), 193n22
Lost Cause, 13, 15, 18. *See also* myth
Louverture, Toussaint, 19, 37–38, 60–62, *64*, 102, 141, 164, 185n5, 190n92
Lucimí, Carlota, 78, 194n30
Lukács, György, 5, 126–27
Lukács-Brecht debate, 126–27
Lydia Bailey, 18–19, 26
lynching, 169

Madden, Richard, 125–27
magical realism, 103–4, 112, 135, 138
The Magic Island (Seabrook), 27
The Magic Mountain (Mann), 126–27
Malcolm X, 59
Malualua, 3–4, 33, 107–8, 111–12, 118, 123, 138–45
Manderlay, 172–73
Mandingo, 20–21
Mann, Thomas, 126–27, 195n47
Mansfield Park (Austen), 5
Marcuse, Herbert, 95, 176
María Antonia, 110, 146
"Maroon" *(Cimarrón)*, 110
Márquez, Evaristo, 38, 47, 53
Martin, Trayvon, 25
Marxism, 31, 52, 57, 70–71, 76, 127, 180n46

Maurin, Nicolas-Eustache, 190n92
Mayfield, Curtis, 140
McDaniel, Hattie, 16, 18
McEvilley, Thomas, 167
McNamara, Robert, 84
McQueen, Steve (actor), 53
McQueen, Steve (director), 2–4, 7, 39, 49–50, 140, 149–73, 175–76
Mellen, Joan, 41, 54
Memorias del subdesarrollo (Memories of Underdevelopment), 76–77, 146
Micheaux, Oscar, 15
The Middle Passage, 31
modernity, 11, 31, 44, 89, 103, 112, 135, 145, 156
Mohammed, Kenneth, 3
Monáe, Janelle, 185n129
Montejo, Esteban, 110
Moreno Fraginals, Manuel, 78–80, 104
Morricone, Ennio, 39, 56, 58
Mosley, Walter, 31
Movimento Popular de Libertaçao de Angola (MPLA), 78–79
Munch, Edvard, 144–45
music, 15–16, 55–59, 69–70, 85–86, 102–3, 140, 156–57
myth, 3–4, 11, 13–15, 18, 101, 156, 167. See also Lost Cause

Napoleon Bonaparte, 67
Naremore, James, 30
National Front for the Liberation of Angola (FNLA), 78
Nat Turner (movie), 30
négritude, 45, 50, 59–63, 66, 75
negrometrajes, 107, 147, 175
Negulesco, Jean, 18–19
neocolonialism, 3, 37, 40, 42–43, 50, 54
neoliberalism, 8–9, 155

neorealism, 35, 50, 52–53, 59, 73, 75–76, 81, 109, 199n7. See also realism
Nesbitt, Nick, 165
Neto, Agostinho, 78
New History of Capitalism (NHC), 104
New Latin American Cinema, 199n7
Nightjohn, 30
North of Slavery (Litwack), 207n40
Northup, Solomon, 4, 149, 151–52, 156–64, 166, 169–71, 205n10
Norton, Ken, 20
Norton, Marc, 163
Nostromo (Conrad), 40, 48
"Notebook of a Return to My Native Land" *(Cahier d'un retour au pays natal)* (Césaire), 66

Ogro, 188n50
O'Keefe, Georgia, 168
Orientalism (Said), 11
"Osanna" (Morricone), 39
Ostoot, Kyle, 20–21
The Other Francisco. See *El otro Francisco* (The Other Francisco)
Overmyer, Eric, 172

palenque, 112, 124, 130–31, 133, 135, 137, 140–43
Paradis, Michel, 13
Parker, Nate, 25–26, 183n111
Paulsen, Gary, 30
Peary, Danny, 47
Peau noire, masques blancs (Fanon), 45, 73
photography, 56–59, 69. See also cinematography
Pick, Zuzana, 77
Pitt, Brad, 24–25
Plácido, 110, 146
plantation life, 16–21, 25, 88–90, 112, 116, 162, 167–70

plantation pornography, 20
Plessy v. Ferguson, 22
Poitier, Sidney, 53
The Political Unconscious (Jameson), 40
"The Politics of Knowledge" (Said), 5–7
Pontecorvo, Gillo, 3, 7, 35, 40–41, 45–57, 60–62, 68–70, 73, 85, 126–27, 149, 175–76, 188n50. See also *specific films*
Porter, Edwin S., 12
Portrait of Citizen Belley (Girodet), 61, 64
"Portrait of Juan de Pareja" (Velázquez), 91–93
Portrait of Teresa, 146
"Por un cine imperfecto" ("For an Imperfect Cinema") (García Espinosa), 93
postcolonialism, 50
prostitution, 46–47
Proust, Marcel, 50

Queimada. See *Burn!*
"The Quest for Gillo Pontecorvo" (Said), 35
Quilombo, 31–32

racism, 3, 13–15, 26, 32, 46, 110, 145–46, 150, 152, 161, 170
Radical Enlightenment, 85, 141
Railton, Stephen, 12
Rancheador (The Slave Hunter), 3–4, 33, 107–8, 111–12, 118, 123, 130–39, 201n35
Raynal, Abbé, 141
Reagan, Ronald, 181n72
realism, 126–27. See also neorealism
reparations, 3, 26
Ridley, John, 171
Rock, Chris, 27
Rodney, Walter, 104

Rodriguez Valdes, Elio, 16–17
Roe v. Wade, 120
Roll, Jordan, Roll (Genovese), 2
Rondeau, James, 156
Roots, 21–22
Rosenbaum, Jonathan, 30
Rossellini, Roberto, 50, 70, 188n45
Roumain, Jacques, 74
The Royal Hunt of the Sun, 100

Said, Edward, 4–7, 11, 35–36, 176, 185n2
Saint Francis, 100
Saint-Just, Sophie, 32
Saint Sebastian, 82–85, 94, 100–101, 195n45
Salazkina, Masha, 199n7
Salvatori, Renato, 54
Sands, Bobby, 150
Sankofa, 31
santéria, 110
Sarny (Paulsen), 30
Sartre, Jean-Paul, 76, 108
Sayles, John, 28–29
Schindler's List, 22
Schoenberg, Arnold, 55–56
Schomburg, Arthur, 194n27
Schroeder, Paul, 77
scientific racism, 13
Scott, David, 8
Scott, Walter, 126
The Scream, 144–45
Seabrook, William, 27
Sebastian's Arrows, 195n47
Second Cinema, 7, 32, 40, 55, 59, 70, 171, 186n14. See also First Cinema; Third Cinema
Selma, 173
Sepinwall, Alyssa Goldstein, 10–11, 19, 46
The Serpent and the Rainbow, 27
sex tourism, 181n72

sexual abuse, 21, 114, 118–20, 122, 137, 169–70. See also women
Shaffer, Peter, 100
Shame, 170
Shapiro, Stephen, 172
Sharfstein, Daniel, 152
Shelton, Richard, 54
Shohat, Ella, 47
Shumway, David, 29
Simon, David, 172
The Slave Hunter. See *Rancheador (The Slave Hunter)*
slave narratives (discussion of), 10–33, 152, 156–60, 164. See also ethics
Slave Revolt on Screen (Sepinwall), 10
slavery. See abolition; Black agency; Black resistance; Black Revolution; brutality; capitalism; freedom; Haitian Revolution; plantation life; reparations; sexual abuse; systemic comprehension (of slavery); technology
Slaves, 19–20
Slaves on Screen (Davis), 10
Small Axe, 150
social division, 135–36
socialism, 8
Solanas, Fernando, 186n14
Solinas, Franco, 48–49, 53
Spartacus (Fast), 2
special period (in Cuba), 146
Spielberg, Steven, 2–3, 22–24
Stam, Robert, 32, 47
Stanislavsky, Konstantin, 126–27
Stevens, Dana, 168
Stevenson, Brenda, 12–13, 16, 43, 45
Stevenson, Robert Louis, 50
Stokes, Melvyn, 13, 15, 20, 170
Stone, Alan, 43, 45, 54, 56
Stowe, Harriet Beecher, 12, 151–52, 205n10

strategic formation, 11
strategic location, 11
Suárez y Romero, Anselmo, 112, 114–15, 120–25, 128, 201n36
subaltern studies, 6
The Sugar Mill (El Ingenio) (Fraginals), 79–80
The Suppression of the African Slave Trade (Du Bois), 2
Supreme Court, 22–23
The Survivors (Los sobrevivientes), 193n22
systemic comprehension (of slavery), 1–2, 30, 49, 87, 90, 105, 120, 151, 153, 161–63, 168–73

Tarantino, Quentin, 25, 167
technology, 89–90, 121, 156, 172–73
Techo de vidrio ("Glass Ceiling"), 145–47
Thatcher, Margaret, 181n72
Third Cinema, 7–11, 32, 40–41, 45, 48, 52, 55, 59–60, 70, 93, 171, 176, 179n35, 186n14. See also First Cinema; Second Cinema
Third World, 7–9, 32, 41, 45, 47, 52, 55, 60, 70, 144
Thirteenth Amendment, 24
Thompson, E. P., 95
Tolstoy, Leo, 126–27
Tomba, Massimiliano, 3
Toms, Coons, Mulattoes, Mammies, and Bucks (Bogle), 9–10
Top Five, 27
totality (Leninist ideal of), 127
Toussaint Louverture at Bedourette (Donkor), 61–62, 64
Tremé, 172
Trier, Lars von, 172
Trouillot, Michel-Rolf, 196n56
Truth, Sojourner, 23
Tubman, Harriet, 23

Turner, Tina, 140
12 Year's A Slave, 2–4, 7, 24–25, 28, 33, 39, 49–50, 59, 86, 140, 149–76
Twelve Years a Slave (Northup), 4, 149, 151–52, 156–64, 166, 169–71
"Two Times Ana" *(Dos Veces Ana),* 147

Un arc-en-ciel pour l'occident chrétien (Depestre), 59
Uncle Tom's Cabin (Stowe), 12, 151–52
The Underground Railroad, 28
United Artists, 41, 52–55, 60, 71
universalism, 3, 28, 85
utopianism, 9, 32, 46, 70–72

Vega, Pastor, 146
Veitia, Héctor, 199n8
Velázquez, Diego, 90–93, 197n60
verfremdungseffekt, 127
video games, 10
violence. *See* brutality; sexual abuse
Viridiana, 97
Vitier, Sergio, 140, 203n74
vodou ("voodoo"), 19, 27, 75, 101, 103

Walvin, James, 2
Washington, Kerry, 25
Wayne, Mike, 42, 48, 54
West, Dennis, 98, 112
Western Deep, 153–54, 156, 167, 171
Westmoreland, William, 84
white supremacy, 14, 194n27
White Zombie, 27

Wilberforce, William, 3, 23
Wilde, Oscar, 99, 198n73
Williams, Eric, 40, 104
Williams, Raymond, 2
Wilson, David, 151, 157–58
Wilson, Woodrow, 13
Within Our Gates, 15
Wollstonecraft, Mary, 23
women, 16, 19, 23, 27–28, 43, 46–47, 70–71, 116–20, 131–34, 143. *See also* abortion; feminism; sexual abuse
Wood, Marcus, 20, 24, 69, 98, 169
Wood, Michael, 170–71
Wood, Robin, 21
"Workers Leaving the Lumière Factory" *(La Sortie des ouvriers de l'usine Lumière),* 12
The World, the Text, and the Critic (Said), 5
World Cinema, 4, 8, 179n35
worldliness, 4–7, 9, 18, 176
WReC (Warwick Research Collective), 180n46
The Wretched of the Earth (Fanon), 45, 196n54
Wright, Richard, 27

Xica da Silva, 31–32

Zimmer, Hans, 140, 156–57
Zimmerman, George, 25
Zinnemann, Fred, 55
Žižek, Slavoj, 198n73
Zurbarán, Francisco de, 90

www.ingramcontent.com/pod-product-compliance
Lightning Source LLC
Chambersburg PA
CBHW062021020325
22763CB00004B/139